PRO/CON VOLUME 21

U.S. JUDICIARY

Published 2005 by Grolier,
an imprint of Scholastic Library Publishing
Old Sherman Turnpike
Danbury, Connecticut 06816

© 2005 The Brown Reference Group plc

Library of Congress Cataloging-in-Publication Data

Pro/con
   p. cm
   Includes bibliographical references and index.
   Contents: v. 19. World Politics – v. 20 Religion and Morality – v. 21. U.S.
Judiciary – v. 22. International Law – v. 23. Poverty and Wealth – v. 24. Work and
the Workplace.
   ISBN 0-7172-5950-1 (set : alk. paper) – ISBN 0-7172-5951-X (vol. 19 : alk. paper) –
ISBN 0-7172-5952-8 (vol. 20 : alk. paper) – ISBN 0-7172-5953-6 (vol. 21 : alk. paper)
– ISBN 0-7172-5954-4 (vol. 22 : alk. paper) – ISBN 0-7172-5955-2 (vol. 23 : alk.
paper) – ISBN 0-7172-5956-0 (vol. 24 : alk. paper)
   1. Social problems. I. Scholastic Publishing Ltd Grolier (Firm)

HN17.5 P756 2002
361.1–dc22

                                                                    2001053234

Printed and bound in Singapore

SET ISBN 0-7172-5950-1
VOLUME ISBN 0-7172-5953-6

For The Brown Reference Group plc
Project Editor: Aruna Vasudevan, Claire Chandler
Editors: Mark Fletcher, Fiona Plowman, Chris Marshall
Consultant Editor: Susan Bandes, Distinguished Professor of Law, DePaul
University College of Law, Chicago, IL
Designer: Sarah Williams
Picture Research and Permissions: Clare Newman, Susy Forbes
Set Index: Kay Ollerenshaw

Senior Managing Editor: Tim Cooke
Art Director: Dave Goodman
Production Director: Alastair Gourlay

GENERAL PREFACE

"All that is necessary for evil to triumph is for good men to do nothing."
—Edmund Burke, 18th-century English political philosopher

Decisions

Life is full of choices and decisions. Some are more important than others. Some affect only your daily life—the route you take to school, for example, or what you prefer to eat for supper—while others are more abstract and concern questions of right and wrong rather than practicality. That does not mean that your choice of presidential candidate or your views on abortion are necessarily more important than your answers to purely personal questions. But it is likely that those wider questions are more complex and subtle and that you therefore will need to know more information about the subject before you can try to answer them. They are also likely to be questions about which you might have to justify your views to other people. In order to do that, you need to be able to make informed decisions, be able to analyze every fact at your disposal, and evaluate them in an unbiased manner.

What Is *Pro/Con*?

Pro/Con is a collection of debates that presents conflicting views on some of the more complex and general issues facing Americans today. By bringing together extracts from a wide range of sources—mainstream newspapers and magazines, books, famous speeches, legal judgments, religious tracts, government surveys—the set reflects current informed attitudes toward dilemmas that range from the best way to feed the world's growing population to gay rights, from the connection between political freedom and capitalism to the fate of Napster.

The people whose arguments make up the set are for the most part acknowledged experts in their fields, making the vast differences in their points of view even more remarkable. The arguments are presented in the form of debates for and against various propositions, such as "Do extradition treaties violate human rights?" or "Should companies be allowed to relocate abroad?" This question format reflects the way in which ideas often occur in daily life: in the classroom, on TV shows, in business meetings, or even in state or federal politics.

The contents

The subjects of the six volumes of *Pro/Con 4—World Politics, Religion and Morality, U.S. Judiciary, International Law, Poverty and Wealth,* and *Work and the Workplace—* are issues on which it is preferable that people's opinions be based on information rather than personal bias.

Special boxes throughout *Pro/Con* comment on the debates as you are reading them, pointing out facts, explaining terms, or analyzing arguments to help you think about what is being said.

Introductions and summaries also provide background information that might help you reach your own conclusions. There are also tips about how to structure an argument that you can apply on an everyday basis to any debate or conversation, learning how to present your point of view as effectively and persuasively as possible.

VOLUME PREFACE
U.S. Judiciary

James Madison, one of the Framers of the Constitution, once said that "The accumulation of all powers, legislative, executive, and judiciary, in the same hands, whether of one, a few, or many, and whether hereditary, self-appointed, or elective, may justly be pronounced the very definition of tyranny."

The founding fathers of the United States were very careful to make sure that their citizens were protected from unfair or discriminatory treatment through the formulation of the Constitution and the creation of an independent federal judiciary. Article III of the Constitution establishes the judicial branch as one of the three separate and distinct branches of federal government, along with the legislative and executive branches.

Guardians of the Constitution
For many experts the federal courts are the guardians of the Constitution since they act to protect, in theory at least, the rights and liberties afforded to U.S. citizens. While Congress makes the law, the federal courts interpret and apply them.

In recent years, however, several high-profile cases, including that of African American celebrity and former sports star O.J. Simpson's trial for the murder of his wife, and more recently lifestyle guru Martha Stewart's trial for insider trading, have focused public attention on whether the judiciary is as independent or impartial as the Framers intended, and whether citizens in fact receive equal and unbiased treatment by judges and juries.

Blurring of boundaries
The increasing influence and blurring of boundaries between politics and the law have also come into question. One of the ways in which the federal judiciary is meant to be independent is that judges are appointed for life. The Constitution also protects the salaries of judges, therefore allowing them independence. Fear of impeachment for improper behavior also serves to assure that the judiciary is held accountable for any misdemeanors.

Among the other issues that concern law commentators is discrimination. Critics believe that it occurs both against people from minority groups accused of crimes and also among people working in the judiciary. Although affirmative action policies have helped more women and people from ethnic groups, among others, to study law and enter the judiciary, recent studies show that there is still a long way to go before minority groups achieve equality. The numbers of people from ethnic minorities on death row or who have received harsher sentencing than whites tried for similar crimes also call into question how the judiciary works.

As many celebrated verdicts show, the law is open to interpretation. It is also, like anything else, affected by biases. It is therefore important to have the critical skills to be able to make informed and rational decisions. This book should help the reader do so.

HOW TO USE THIS BOOK

Each volume of *Pro/Con* is divided into sections, each of which has an introduction that examines its theme. Within each section are a series of debates that present arguments for and against a proposition, such as whether or not the death penalty should be abolished. An introduction to each debate puts it into its wider context, and a summary and key map (see below) highlight the main points of the debate clearly and concisely. Each debate has marginal boxes that focus on particular points, give tips on how to present an argument, or help question the writer's case. The summary page to the debates contains supplementary material to help you do further research.

Boxes and other materials provide additional background information. There are also special spreads on how to improve your debating and writing skills. At the end of each book is a glossary and an index. The glossary provides explanations of key words in the volume. The index covers all 24 books; it will help you find topics throughout this set and previous ones.

background information
Frequent text boxes provide background information on important concepts and key individuals or events.

summary boxes
Summary boxes are useful reminders of both sides of the argument.

further information
Further Reading lists for each debate direct you to related books, articles, and websites so you can do your own research.

other articles in the *Pro/Con* series
This box lists related debates throughout the *Pro/Con* series.

marginal boxes
Margin boxes highlight key points of the argument, give extra information, or help you question the author's meaning.

key map
Key maps provide a graphic representation of the central points of the debate.

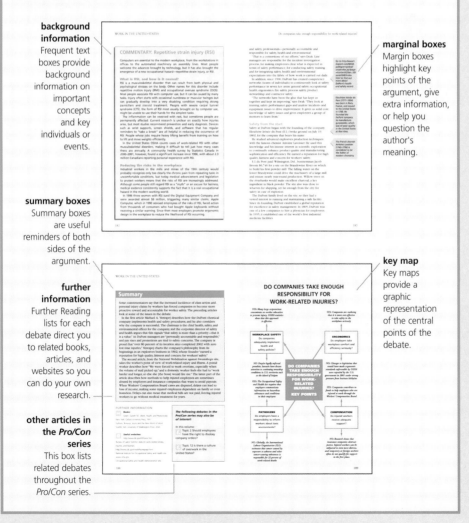

CONTENTS

PART 1
THE FEDERAL JUDICIARY: CHECKS AND BALANCES

INTRODUCTION

Article III of the U.S. Constitution creates the federal judicial power. In conjunction with Article I, which defines the legislative (congressional) power, and Article II, which delimits the executive (presidential) power, it establishes a complex division of power among the three branches of the federal government. This separation ensures a system of checks and balances among the three branches, which enables each to fulfill its obligations while guarding against the undue aggregation of power by any single branch.

Purpose

Article III creates the sole nonelected branch of federal government: Federal judges are given life tenure "during good behavior." This provides independence to the federal judiciary and enables it to act as an effective check on the political (elected) branches—Congress and the executive. Federal judges exercise the power of judicial review, which enables them to check abuse of power by the political branches by declaring laws or executive acts unconstitutional or otherwise unlawful. One argument for life tenure is that it enables judges to act without fear of political reprisal. However, it also creates a judiciary that is less accountable than state courts (whose judges are elected or else appointed for

limited terms) or the courts of other nations. The federal judges' unelected status and relative insulation from political pressure, coupled with their power to strike down the acts of the elected branches, have from the beginning been a source of controversy. The Supreme Court is sometimes viewed as a bulwark against unchecked political power, at others as an out of touch and undemocratic institution. The viewpoint one takes may depend on whether the court's decisions comport with one's idea of what is a good judgment.

The federal judiciary, although unelected, is subject to a number of checks on its power by the political branches. Article III provides for the establishment of the Supreme Court and gives Congress the power to establish lower federal (district and appellate) courts. This congressional power to "ordain and establish" the lower federal courts grows from the Madisonian compromise, in which Framers James Madison and James Wilson agreed to give the elected Congress power to control the creation of lower federal courts. The political branches also play an important role in the appointment of federal judges: Judges are appointed by the executive with the "advice and consent" of the Senate. Moreover, the Senate has the power to impeach judges who do not maintain the constitutional mandate of good behavior. The scope of the role of the political branches is also a source of continuing controversy.

Analysis

The topics in this section explore a number of the tensions that arise from the separation of powers. Topic 1 looks

a Supreme Court that is often ideologically polarized between a five-person majority and a four-person minority, it seems that judicial philosophy has substantial influence on the outcome of many high court cases.

Topics 3 and 4 explore the delicate balance between judicial independence and judicial accountability. Life tenure is designed to protect judges from

---

"The Senate's role in the judicial confirmation process is not to rubber-stamp the president's nominees."

—RALPH NEAS, PEOPLE FOR THE AMERICAN WAY (2002)

---

at whether the Supreme Court is too activist. This question goes to the heart of the nature of the Court's power. As an unelected branch, the judiciary is simply supposed to interpret the law, not make law. However, the question of what sorts of decisions are within the proper bounds of interpretation is not an easy one.

The 2003–2004 term provided a dramatic reminder of how controversial the court's role can be. The court considered the president's claims of broad and in some respects unreviewable power to wage the War on Terrorism. In three landmark decisions the court articulated limits on executive power. Whether these decisions were insufficiently deferential to the executive and therefore activist, or were needed to curb an excess of presidential power and safeguard the Constitution, is a topic much debated.

The question of activism also underlies the second topic, which asks whether politics are too influential in the selection of federal judges. With

political pressure, but this protection carries the danger of creating judges who are not accountable to anyone. Some people believe that a limited term, if long enough, would ensure sufficient independence. Topic 4 asks whether it ought to be easier to impeach federal judges who exceed their authority. In doing so it also considers the proper role of Congress in defining judicial authority.

The role of Congress

The Constitution explicitly gives Congress a role in the judicial confirmation process, and there is continuing debate over how aggressively it should pursue that role. Topic 5 asks whether Congress has the right to question candidates about their views, and Topic 6 asks whether there ought to be a set of requirements judicial candidates must meet. Finally, Topic 7 ask whether Congress should be able to limit the power of federal judges to sentence criminals. It focuses on the federal sentencing guidelines.

THE STATE AND FEDERAL JUDICIAL SYSTEMS

UNITED STATES

STATE SUPREME COURTS

STATE INTERMEDIATE COURTS

STATE TRIAL COURTS

GENERAL STATE JURISDICTION

Examples of the subject matter jurisdiction of the states:

- State constitution
- State statute
- Property
- Contract
- Tort
- Crime
- Domestic relations
- Nonexclusive grants of federal jurisdiction

SUPREME COURT

FEDERAL APPELLATE COURTS

U.S. COURTS OF APPEALS
- 12 Regional Circuit Courts of Appeals
  - 1 U.S. Court of Appeals for the Federal Circuit

FEDERAL TRIAL COURTS

U.S. DISTRICT COURTS
- 94 judicial districts
  - U.S. Bankruptcy Courts

U.S. COURT OF
INTERNATIONAL TRADE
U.S. COURT OF
FEDERAL CLAIMS

LIMITED FEDERAL JURISDICTION

1. Subject matter:
- U.S. Constitution
- Federal statute
- Treaty
- Admiralty

2. Party:
- United States
- Ambassador, public minister, consul
- States
- Citizens of different states
- Foreign states
  - amounts in excess of $75,000

Topic 1

IS THE SUPREME COURT TOO ACTIVIST?

YES

FROM "A HAND IN THE MATTER"
LEGAL AFFAIRS, MARCH/APRIL 2003
CASS R. SUNSTEIN

NO

FROM "UPHOLDING THE LAW"
LEGAL AFFAIRS, MARCH/APRIL 2003
ORIN S. KERR

INTRODUCTION

Article III, section 1, of the Constitution entrusts the federal judicial power to the Supreme Court of the United States and such inferior courts as Congress chooses to establish. The Supreme Court is thus the highest court in the United States. Most of its work consists of appellate review of cases from lower federal courts or state supreme courts relating to the Constitution. That the Supreme Court has the final authority to interpret the Constitution gives it a great deal of influence over public policy. Throughout its history, however, critics have accused the Supreme Court of exceeding this authority and even of usurping the power to make law rather than interpret it. This controversial issue is known as judicial activism.

Some commentators argue that the Framers did not anticipate the Supreme Court would become as influential as it is today. Writing in *The Federalist No. 78*, Alexander Hamilton (1755–1804) called the judiciary the "least dangerous" of the branches of federal government since it possessed neither

the power of "the purse" (the legislative) nor that of "the sword" (the executive). The Framers designed a system of checks and balances to ensure that no single branch dominated the government. The chief weapon that the court has against legislative or executive abuses of power is judicial review. This is the authority of the federal judiciary to review and declare null and void any federal or state law or executive act that it deems to be in conflict with the Constitution. Chief Justice John Marshall (1755–1835) established this doctrine in *Marbury v. Madison* (1803) when he asserted that the Supreme Court had the power to invalidate legislation enacted by Congress.

Not all commentators agree on what constitutes judicial activism. Some describe any Supreme Court decision that rejects its own precedent (a ruling on a prior case) as activist. For example, *Brown v. Board of Education* (1954) declared racial segregation in schools unconstitutional, thus rejecting *Plessy v.*

Ferguson (1896), which decided that separate facilities for blacks and whites were constitutional as long as they were "equal." Frequently, however, critics use the term "judicial activism" to refer to the Supreme Court using judicial review to strike down acts of Congress and state governments. For example, in the mid-1930s the court struck down legislation that Congress had passed to alleviate the Great Depression. President Franklin D. Roosevelt (1933-1945) tried to increase the size of the court so that he could appoint justices who would validate his New Deal programs. Critics accuse the Rehnquist Court—named for William Rehnquist, chief justice since 1986—of being equally committed to activism. They cite the fact that the court has invalidated almost 30 federal laws in the past decade. Critics say the court has acted illegitimately because it has often struck down legislation when they claim the Constitution is unclear.

"Liberty can have nothing to fear from the judiciary alone...."
—ALEXANDER HAMILTON,
THE FEDERALIST NO. 78 (1788)

Commentators often contend that the Supreme Court under Chief Justice Earl Warren (1891-1974) was the most activist in U.S. history. Critics attacked its activism in expanding the protection given to individuals accused of crimes. For example, in deciding *Miranda v. Arizona* (1966) the Warren Court imposed a new procedure for interrogating suspects in custody. This type of activism is sometimes known as "legislating from the bench"—that is, creating new law. A further example is *Roe v. Wade* (1973), the controversial decision of the court under Chief Justice Warren Burger (1907-1995), which ruled that the Fourteenth Amendment implies a right to privacy that includes a woman's right to an abortion. Critics say such activism is dangerous because it makes the least democratic branch of government also the most powerful. When justices overstep their constitutional duty and formulate new policies, they become in effect unelected legislators.

Some experts stress that ideology usually lies behind charges of judicial activism. They say that people tend to label as activist any decision conflicting with their own political views. Thus conservatives, who traditionally favor a narrow interpretation of the law, have accused liberal courts—such as the Warren Court—of rampant activism. In contrast, liberals have historically been more open to the idea of using the court to enact change. But they too have criticized today's conservative court for lacking restraint, in particular for taking an unprecedented role in determining the outcome of the 2000 presidential election in *Bush v. Gore.*

Others point out, however, that judicial activism is not necessarily a bad thing: It is in everyone's interest that the Supreme Court overturns outdated precedents and strikes down laws that are clearly unconstitutional. Some claim that if the court had not invalidated racial segregation in *Brown v. Board of Education* in 1954, for example, it might still be legal today.

The following articles examine judicial activism in Rehnquist's Court.

A HAND IN THE MATTER
Cass R. Sunstein

Cass R. Sunstein is a professor of jurisprudence at the University of Chicago. He wrote this piece for the magazine Legal Affairs in 2003.

YES

What is judicial activism? Would it be activist for courts to attempt to restore the Constitution as it was understood in the decades before the New Deal, when the founding document was read to embody laissez-faire economics? Does *Brown v. Board of Education*, invalidating racial segregation, count as an activist decision? Does *Roe v. Wade*, because it extended the right to privacy to include a woman's right to an abortion? Would it be activist for the current court to overrule *Roe*?

More than one meaning

The principle of precedent derives from English common law, which relies on similar decided cases or points of law to reach a judgment. Common law contrasts with the European system of civil law, in which law is laid down as a complete, codified system by means of legislation.

There are, broadly speaking, two accounts of judicial activism. Some people label a decision "activist" when they think that the court has departed from the correct approach to the Constitution. On this view, the word "activist" isn't merely a description; it is also and always an insult....

On a different account, the word "activist" is purely descriptive, and a decision that is activist is not necessarily wrong. A court that rejects its own precedents might be thought to be activist. Of course some courts should reject some precedents because they are ludicrously mistaken or hopelessly outdated. A court that is activist, in this sense, might be entirely right. Or a court might be described as activist if it strikes down the actions of other branches of government. No one thinks that a court should uphold all actions of the other branches, and so a court that is activist, in this sense, might be something to celebrate....

I suggest that it is helpful to measure judicial activism in the way just mentioned—by seeing how often a court strikes down the actions of other parts of government, especially the actions of Congress....

Go to http://usinfo.state.gov/usa/infousa/facts/democrac/33.htm for an overview of the history of and court opinion on Plessy v. Ferguson.

On this definition, *Roe v. Wade* is an activist decision, whereas the much-despised *Plessy v. Ferguson*, upholding racial segregation, is not.... We might agree that a court that frequently invalidates statutes is activist, while a court that rarely does so is restrained....

A court that wrongly invalidates statutes might be said to show *unjustified activism*; a court that wrongly upholds statutes might be said to show *unjustified restraint*. We could go further. A court that fails to root its decisions in the Constitution, that does so on numerous occasions, that decides in accordance with its own political predilections, and that frequently invalidates the decisions of others is guilty of *illegitimate activism*. A court that fails to invalidate the decisions of other branches, even those other branches that have conspicuously violated the Constitution, and that embarks on this path on numerous occasions is guilty of *illegitimate restraint*....

Evidence of illegitimate activism

These distinctions are useful because they give us clearer tools for analyzing what courts do and prevent the word "activism" from becoming a kind of all-purpose term of unhelpful abuse. Consider the Rehnquist Court. As a result of its performance over the past decade it has now joined the Lochner Court (so-called for its 1905 *Lochner v. New York* decision) and the Warren Court of the 1950s and '60s as one of the few courts in the nation's history that have engaged in illegitimate judicial activism. Such activism blocks voters from enacting the laws they choose and does so without a sufficient constitutional basis....

Here is some evidence that the Rehnquist Court can be fairly charged with illegitimate activism:

1. The Rehnquist Court has ruled that Congress lacks the power to give citizens the right to sue the federal government for unlawful action under environmental statutes. In so doing, the court invalidated, in effect, dozens of Congressional enactments, which purport to give citizens that very right. Constitutional history strongly suggests that Congress has the power that the court denied it. But in invalidating the citizens' suit, the court ventured not a word about the history or about the framers' original understanding. Indeed the court made no effort to connect its unprecedented decision to the text, structure, or history of the Constitution....

2. The court has struck down a number of affirmative action programs adopted at both the state and federal levels. Does the Constitution clearly forbid such programs? It does not. Justices Scalia and Thomas have expressed the greatest willingness to strike down affirmative action programs, but the history of the equal protection clause strongly suggests that such programs were not thought to be unconstitutional....

Joseph Lochner was convicted under a New York law prohibiting bakery employees from working more than 10 hours a day. The Supreme Court invalidated the law, maintaining that it interfered with the Fourteenth Amendment's right to liberty afforded to both employer and employee.

"Original understanding" is the notion that the Constitution should mean what it was understood to mean when it was written. Advocates insist that applying original understanding to a decision is the only way for judges to remain politically neutral. Do you think it is always still possible to determine the Framers' original intentions?

Antonin Scalia (1936–) has been an associate justice of the Supreme Court since 1986; Clarence Thomas (1948–) has been an associate justice since 1991. Both are considered to be very conservative judges.

State sovereign immunity is a doctrine that, under some circumstances, protects state governments from lawsuits that would cause them to pay out money, real estate, or goods.

3. The court has struck down a number of state and federal efforts to regulate commercial advertising. Justice Thomas has gone so far as to suggest that commercial advertising should receive the same level of constitutional protection as political dissent … [T]he court has made no effort to show that the idea is compelled by the original understanding, or any plausible understanding, of the Constitution.

4. The court has used the idea of state sovereign immunity to strike down a number of congressional enactments, including parts of the Age Discrimination in Employment Act and the Americans With Disabilities Act. In doing so, the court acknowledged that its decisions are not based on the text of the Constitution.

The Fourteenth Amendment prohibits states from denying or abridging the privileges or immunities of citizens of the United States, depriving any person of his life, liberty, or property without due process of law, or denying to any person within their jurisdiction the equal protection of the laws.

5. Section 5 of the Fourteenth Amendment gives Congress the power to "enforce, by appropriate legislation," the provisions of that amendment. In a remarkable, precedent-busting series of decisions … the Rehnquist Court has dramatically reduced Congress's power under Section 5. It has effectively concluded that Congress is limited to preventing conduct that, in the court's own view, would violate the Fourteenth Amendment—and has thus forbidden Congress from legislating on the basis of its own views about what that amendment means.…

This clause refers to Article I, section 8, paragraph 3 of the Constitution, which gives Congress authority "To regulate Commerce with Foreign Nations, and among the several States, and with the Indian Tribes."

6. For the first time in 50 years, the Rehnquist Court has struck down federal legislation as beyond congressional power under the Commerce Clause.… [T]he court struck down a key provision of the Violence Against Women Act, notwithstanding extensive testimony before Congress, and extensive findings by Congress, that sex-related violence has a significant effect on interstate commerce.

In these six areas (and more), the Rehnquist Court has been highly activist in my understanding of that term.… The tendency toward activism is important because it denies other parts of government the power to act. If the court concludes that the Constitution does not protect the right to choose abortion, the electoral process can be used to protect that right. But if the court rules that the Constitution forbids affirmative action programs, or campaign finance reform, those issues are closed.

Earl Warren served as chief justice between 1953 and 1969.

In one respect, the activism of the Rehnquist Court represents a curious replay of history. The Warren Court … emphasized … that it would not impose limitations on federal and state government that could not be found in the Constitution itself. Hence the court upheld a great deal of legislation that would have been struck down in the Lochner era, when the court was extremely aggressive....

In a way, the Rehnquist Court has the same relationship to the Warren Court as that court had to the Lochner Court.... But there is something genuinely new about the Rehnquist Court: its cavalier attitude toward Congress....

> *"Cavalier" means "disdainful" or "dismissive."*

The last point is noteworthy, because Congress is a coordinate branch of government, one that usually enacts laws with the president's approval (or by a supermajority over his veto) and that therefore deserves a large measure of respect from the court. For most of the nation's history, the Supreme Court has been reluctant to invalidate congressional enactments precisely on the ground that such invalidations raise serious questions about the judicial role in a democracy. Of course the court should strike down acts of Congress when they are plainly unconstitutional. The problem with the Rehnquist Court is that it has done so when the Constitution is unclear and when many reasonable people have concluded that Congress has the power to enact the law under review.

> *Commentators point out that on an annual basis, the Rehnquist Court has struck down more federal laws than any other Supreme Court in the last half-century.*

Political preferences

Of course many of the Rehnquist Court's decisions are defensible. But too much of the time, the court has invalidated legislative enactments without anchoring its judgments in a plausible understanding of the Constitution. Consider two important clues. First, a number of the justices on the Rehnquist Court have insisted on the relevance of the "original understanding" to constitutional interpretation; but many of their invalidations have occurred without the slightest consideration of history. Second, many of the invalidations fit uncomfortably well with the political preferences of the extreme right. When the court is invalidating legislation without looking at the ordinary sources of law, and when its decisions match its own political predilections, we are entitled to suspect that its activism is illegitimate....

> *For more on Sunstein's views regarding the political preferences of the Rehnquist Court go to http://www. prospect.org/print/ V14/3/sunstein-c.html to read his article "The Right-Wing Assault."*

None of this means that the sky has fallen in. For the most part, the Rehnquist Court's decisions have been incremental, and the court has not imposed huge new impediments to democratic government in the United States. But if the current tendencies are not monitored and exposed for what they are, they will turn out to be the start of a major transformation in American law....

UPHOLDING THE LAW
Orin S. Kerr

Orin S. Kerr is an associate professor of law at George Washington University, Washington, D.C. This piece appeared in the same 2003 edition of Legal Affairs as the article by Cass R. Sunstein.

NO

A decade ago, the public debate over the proper role of the courts had settled into a familiar pattern. Liberals extolled using the courts as agents of social change. Conservatives objected, insisting that courts should interpret the law, not make it. To conservatives, using the courts for political change was "judicial activism."…

Times have changed, it seems. Today charges of judicial activism come as often from liberals targeting conservatives as vice versa.… I … believe that judges from both sides of the political spectrum have been guilty of activism, but accusations against the Rehnquist Court often overstate the case considerably.

Let's start with a definition. What is judicial activism? It begins with an attitude: a confidence in judicial solutions to legal problems and relative scorn toward the handiwork of the executive and legislative branches.…

How do you think Kerr's idea of "separation-of-powers activism" differs from Sunstein's preferred definition of activism as judicial invalidation on page 14?

Two types of activism

The activist attitude manifests itself in two major ways. Perhaps the most powerful form of judicial activism is what you might call separation-of-powers activism: judicial decision making that takes away the power to create governing rules from the executive or legislative branches and gives that power to the courts. Critics sometimes describe this as "legislating from the bench." …

A second manifestation of the activist impulse could be called precedent activism: judicial decision making that changes a prior judicial rule or announces a creative interpretation of a statute, usually rejecting a rule that the judges dislike as a policy matter in favor of one they prefer.…

What's the harm of judicial activism? Why does any of this matter? It matters because we live in a democracy, and our democracy generally functions best if the political branches have the power to create the rules we want.…

Learned Hand (1872–1961) served as a federal judge for a record 52 years. Although he never sat on the Supreme Court, he was widely acknowledged as a "first among American judges."

The more the courts roam, the less power the elected branches retain. And the less power the elected branches retain, the less ability we have to control the rules through what Learned Hand called the "common venture" of voting at the polls.

Now let's turn to politics, or at least the political spectrum. Who are the activists? Are they liberals or conservatives?

The historical answer is both. In the *Lochner v. New York* era a century ago, conservative justices regularly struck down newly-enacted progressive legislation.… In the Warren Court era of the 1950s and '60s, the sides switched.… [L]iberal justices voted to invalidate a wide range of longstanding laws and practices in fields such as criminal procedure, voting rights, and the relationship between church and state. Judicial activism gained favor among liberals, and judicial restraint shifted from a liberal position to a conservative one.…

Clearly the politics of the judiciary explains a great deal. A century ago, the federal judiciary was on average more conservative than the voting public; 35 years ago, it was on average more liberal. When the politics of the judges differs significantly from the politics of the public, judges can be tempted to exercise their powers broadly.…

Read the interview with constitutional scholar Jamin Raskin at http://www.tompaine.com/feature2.cfm/ID/7632, in which he discusses both the Lochner and Warren courts. Raskin describes the Warren Court as "progressive" but accuses the Lochner Court of being "reactionary." Do you think someone with different political views would agree with his analysis?

Considering the Rehnquist Court

I think it is fairly clear that under my definition of activism, the current court is not activist on the scale of either the Lochner Court or the Warren Court.… In both periods, the Supreme Court played a major role in several of the most significant political debates of the day. The court created new rules that often eclipsed legislative and executive action, engaging in both separation-of-powers activism and precedent activism.

In contrast, the current court generally has carved out a narrower role for itself. The court accepts only about 80 cases a year, roughly half the caseload of the Warren Court. Most of those cases involve narrow questions of law. Today's court usually considers how to interpret and apply existing precedents, rather than whether to reject existing law and start afresh. The court still plays an important role, of course, but that role is defined largely by established precedents. Plus … the court's decisions have tended to involve fairly arcane legal questions more than major political disputes. Of course, you can agree or disagree with individual decisions. But on the whole, the current Supreme Court has engaged in less precedent activism and separation-of-powers activism than the Warren Court or the Lochner Court.

Consider *United States v. Lopez*, the 1995 Commerce Clause decision invalidating a federal law that made it a crime to possess a gun in a school zone.… The five justices in the majority concluded that the law banning possession of a gun near a school was not a regulation of "Commerce … among

Go to http://supct.law.cornell.edu/supct/html/93-1260.ZO.html to read the Supreme Court decision on United States v. Lopez.

the several states," and therefore exceeded Congress's power. Notably, the decision did not demonstrate precedent activism: It did not overrule any prior cases.... The decision hardly revealed separation-of-powers activism, either: It did not block all legislative regulation of guns in school zones and did not interfere with a political movement seeking the regulation of guns in school zones.

In fact, *Lopez* resulted in very little change in substantive law. In addition to leaving state legislatures free to regulate guns in school zones, the decision indicated that Congress could do the same, as long as its regulations were restricted to guns that have traveled in or otherwise affected interstate commerce. Congress did exactly that: It re-passed the statute with the added interstate commerce element shortly after the *Lopez* decision. Lower courts have upheld the amended statute. Because nearly every gun has traveled in or affected interstate commerce, the law of possessing guns in school zones is essentially the same today as it was pre-*Lopez*. Of course, this doesn't necessarily mean that *Lopez* was correctly decided. But it does make the decision a weak target for complaints about judicial activism.

Nonetheless, accusations that today's conservative justices are as activist as the Warren Court's liberals remain common. Proponents of this view often note that the Supreme Court has invalidated at least parts of over 26 acts of Congress in the last few years, a much higher rate than in the past....

Judicial invalidation

While I agree that the conservative justices have not consistently embraced judicial restraint, this argument strikes me as weak. First, using judicial invalidation as a proxy for activism suffers from an obvious flaw: If a legislature passes a plainly unconstitutional law, striking down the statute by applying established precedents reflects neither separation-of-powers activism nor precedent activism....

[T]he focus on decisions striking down federal laws unfairly stacks the deck against the Rehnquist Court. The Warren Court's reform efforts focused primarily on invalidating state and local laws, rather than federal laws.... Perhaps the more relevant quantitative measure would compare how often the Rehnquist Court and Warren Court have struck down legislative acts as a whole, or, better yet, how often they have overruled precedents....

It's also a mistake to assume that every Rehnquist Court decision striking down a legislative act features the conservative justices acting over the dissents of more liberal

Use the Internet to research some of the acts of Congress invalidated by the Rehnquist Court. Do you think the court generally made valid decisions in accordance with the Constitution, or was it acting illegitimately?

Kerr argues that judicial invalidation is not an accurate measure of activism. This contradicts Sunstein's thoughts. Which author do you think presents the better argument?

colleagues. Based on my review of the last Supreme Court term, it's more often the other way around. I recently examined last year's Supreme Court cases looking for decisions in which the more conservative and more liberal justices disagreed about the constitutionality of existing laws or administrative acts. In cases that split the justices into relatively predictable ideological camps, I asked, which group voted to invalidate the other branches more often?…

Roughly a dozen of the court's 83 cases involved fairly clear ideological splits on the scope of constitutional rights…. [T]he more liberal justices favored striking down the other branch of government almost twice as often as the conservatives did….

[A]t the very least, the pattern suggests a certain myopia among those who rely on the number of laws the Supreme Court invalidates as a sign of its conservative activism….

Judicial inconsistencies

A response to my argument might go something like this: Even if the Rehnquist Court's conservatives are not outright activists, they still deserve criticism for failing to consistently embrace judicial restraint. After four decades of attacking judicial activism, surely conservatives have a special duty to embrace restraint even though they now have the votes to push the courts in an activist rightward direction.

I largely agree with this critique. It is easy for a dissenting judge to charge activism; it is far harder for a majority of judges to exercise restraint. I think the current court has a decent record on this front, but plainly not a perfect one. *Bush v. Gore* provides one example of the court's conservatives straying from the principles of restraint…. [T]he court constitutionalized a question that should have been left to state law and state courts…. At the same time, such inconsistency extends beyond the more conservative justices of the current court…. If the charge is occasional inconsistency, perhaps everyone should plead guilty.

In the end, the fact that both sides of the political spectrum now make charges of judicial activism against the other isn't a bad thing. It shows that on a rhetorical level, at least, judicial restraint has won favor…. Perhaps this reflects that the politics of the judges and the public roughly match; both sides can appreciate the risks of losing in the courts. Or perhaps each side's ox has been gored often enough that they're beginning to see the institutional benefits of a less activist judiciary. Either way, I hope that our judges are listening. Our democracy will be the better for it.

Visit http://usgovinfo.about.com/library/weekly/aa081400a.htm for an analysis of the political ideology of the nine Supreme Court justices.

This eye condition makes sufferers shortsighted; they have problems focusing on long-distance objects.

Supreme Court justices take a vote to reach a decision on a case. The chief justice, when voting with the majority, may write the majority opinion or ask another justice to do this. Justices who vote in the minority write what is known as a dissenting opinion.

Go to www.google.com to research reaction to the Supreme Court's Bush v. Gore decision. Do you think the court exceeded its authority in this case?

Summary

Cass R. Sunstein and Orin S. Kerr present opposing views on whether the Rehnquist Court is guilty of judicial activism. In the first article Sunstein explains that there are different accounts of activism. While he agrees that a court that rejects its own precedents might be considered activist, he suggests that the most helpful way to measure activism is to see how often a court strikes down the acts of other parts of government, particularly Congress. He defines a court as being guilty of illegitimate activism if it makes its decisions according to political preferences rather than basing them on the Constitution, and if it frequently invalidates the decisions of others. Sunstein contends that the Rehnquist Court can be charged with illegitimate activism, and he examines six pieces of evidence. He criticizes the court's "cavalier attitude toward Congress," which, he says, is shown in its invalidation of acts according to its right-wing views rather than historical consideration.

Kerr begins the second article by claiming that both right-wing and left-wing judges have been guilty of judicial activism. He makes a distinction between what he calls "separation-of-powers activism" and "precedent activism." Compared to previous courts, he maintains that the Rehnquist Court has engaged in less of both types of activism. As evidence, he considers the 1995 case *United States v. Lopez*. In contrast to Sunstein, Kerr argues that judicial invalidation is a poor measure of activism. While he admits that the court has been activist on occasions, he concludes that judicial restraint has found favor among both conservatives and liberals.

FURTHER INFORMATION:

Books:

Langran, Robert W., *The Supreme Court: A Concise History*. New York: Peter Lang, 2004.

Schwartz, Herman (ed.), *The Rehnquist Court: Judicial Activism on the Right*. New York: Hill and Wang, 2002.

Useful websites:

http://www-hoover.stanford.edu/publications/digest/974/meese.html
"How Congress Can Rein in the Courts" by Edwin L. Meese III.

http://www.weeklydig.com/dig/content/5458.aspx
"Who You Callin' a Judicial Activist?" by Seth McM. Donlin.

http://writ.news.findlaw.com/lazarus/20001212.html
"The Supreme Court's Monday Oral Argument in *Gore v. Bush*, and the Meaning of Judicial Activism" by Edward Lazarus.

The following debates in the Pro/Con series may also be of interest:

In this volume:
Topic 2 Are politics too influential in the selection of federal judges?

Topic 5 Should Supreme Court judges be asked their views on legal issues during confirmation proceedings?

In *The Constitution*:
Topic 2 Is the Supreme Court too powerful?

IS THE SUPREME COURT TOO ACTIVIST?

YES: There are examples of the Supreme Court striking down laws that experts suggest Congress had the power to enact

YES: Both conservative and liberal justices have been guilty of judicial activism. They overstep their authority in order to impose their own political preferences.

JUDICIAL REVIEW
Does judicial review give too much power to the Supreme Court?

IDEOLOGY
Is judicial activism more than a term of insult thrown at political opponents?

NO: On the contrary, judicial review prevents the legislative and executive branches of federal government from abusing their authority

NO: People usually denounce as activist any decision that is not in keeping with their own political views

IS THE SUPREME COURT TOO ACTIVIST?
KEY POINTS

YES: Justices should not stray from a narrow interpretation of the Constitution. Their duty is to try to divine its original meaning at all times.

YES: Supreme Court justices are unelected; they have no right to usurp the power to make laws from the elected branches of government

A BAD THING?
Is judicial activism inherently wrong?

NO: A strict reading of the Constitution is absurd. Justices should interpret the text to serve the needs of contemporary society.

NO: It is in everyone's interest that the Supreme Court overturns outdated precedents and invalidates unconstitutional laws

Topic 2

ARE POLITICS TOO INFLUENTIAL IN THE SELECTION OF FEDERAL JUDGES?

YES

FROM "SELECTING FEDERAL JUDGES: THE NEW, LESS PARTISAN CALIFORNIA PLAN"
WWW.FINDLAW.COM, JUNE 8, 2001
JOHN DEAN

NO

FROM "REJECTION SUSTAINED"
THE ATLANTIC MONTHLY, SEPTEMBER 2002
RANDALL KENNEDY

INTRODUCTION

The question of whether it is possible for the president with the advice of the Senate to disregard politics and choose federal judges solely on their qualifications has been debated since the ratification of the Constitution.

The president—the chief executive—is invested with the power to appoint federal judges with the advice and consent of the Senate under Article II of the Constitution, which defines the powers of the executive branch. This succinct provision creates a complex separation of federal power among the three branches of national government. It divides the power of judicial confirmation between the executive and legislative branches, known as the "political branches" since they are both chosen by popular election rather than appointment. Therefore, while Article III safeguards judicial independence by granting federal judges life tenure and salary protection, Article II places certain limits on that independence

by putting the decision for the appointment of these judges in the hands of elected officials. The Constitution gives no other criteria or guidelines for their selection.

Since the founding fathers framed the Constitution, people have questioned whether it is possible to keep politics out of the federal judicial selection process. Many believe that it is inevitable that the president and the Senate will support judicial candidates who are sympathetic to their own political and philosophical ideologies. But some scholars counter that there is no reason to assume that a judge, once appointed for life, will make a decision on a case based on his or her party affiliation or any particular ideology. They assert that elected officials should rise above politics and choose federal judges who they believe will decide cases intelligently and fairly.

Other commentators have asked whether it would, in fact, be wrong to exclude politics from the process. Since federal judicial appointments are for life and the appointed person has the power to influence every aspect of an individual's life—from whether a woman can have an abortion to whether an ethnic minority should be able to practice his or her religion—it is crucial, they argue, that the nominees be questioned rigorously about their political and philosophical ideologies.

"Justice delayed is justice denied."

—WILLIAM GLADSTONE

(1809–1898),

BRITISH POLITICIAN

Sometimes the term "political" is used in a narrow sense, as in the phrase "partisan politics," connoting support or opposition toward a candidate solely based on his or her party affiliation. Some scholars argue that in recent years the process of confirming judicial candidates has become increasingly partisan. But others believe that this is far from new and that judicial nominees have been rejected on the basis of their political beliefs since George Washington's presidency (1789-1797).

Possibly the most cited example of politics influencing the selection of a nominee is the case of Robert Bork (see pages 72-73), who was rejected on the basis of what opponents believed were his extreme views on the federal courts' proper role in interpreting the Constitution. Certain interested parties, such as civil rights groups and opposition politicians, also used the media to an unprecedented degree to vilify Bork, opening the doors for this to happen to future candidates. Since then some commentators argue that the process has become far less cooperative and courteous. During Democrat Bill Clinton's presidency (1993-2001), for example, very few of Clinton's nominees were confirmed by the Republican-controlled Senate. This led to numerous unfilled vacancies, a backlog of cases, and much bad feeling between Democrats and Republicans.

Some critics believe that the Bush administration (2001-) has suffered a backlash to this time. Bush's supporters called for him to nominate conservative candidates. Many argue that the Democrats have prevented several Bush nominees from advancing past the Judiciary Committee stage. In some cases Democrats have claimed that these candidates hold politically extreme views. They have used the power to filibuster—or continue debating in order to prevent a matter from coming to a vote—in order to prevent a vote on candidates they viewed as unacceptable.

Some people also believe that Bush exacerbated existing problems by stopping the nonpartisan American Bar Association (ABA) from rating the qualifications of federal judicial candidates. For many years the ABA assessed candidates on the basis of prior judicial experience, temperament, and ethics, for example, but Bush claimed that he was concerned that the ABA had a preferential role in the selection process. Conservative groups praised this decision—they thought that the ABA was far too liberal—but others believe that it has led to even greater politicization.

Pages 26-33 look at this debate.

SELECTING FEDERAL JUDGES: THE NEW, LESS PARTISAN CALIFORNIA PLAN
John Dean

John Dean is a former White House counsel who has written extensively on legal and government matters. This article was published on www.findlaw.com in 2001.

YES

The judicial branch of the federal government has grown tremendously in the last 50 years, largely because Congress has continually added new federal crimes and civil causes of action.

Today, some 600 judges sit on the federal district trial courts, and another 200 on the appellate courts. The Judicial Conference of the United States predicts that 2,350 federal judges will be needed by 2010, and 4,110 by 2020.

Unfortunately, the federal judiciary is becoming as partisan as the other two branches of government. And given the combination of the projected growth, and the fact that a significant number of sitting judges retire or leave the bench during the term of most presidencies, the politicization of the judiciary is only likely to get worse.

Federal courts are the arbiters not only of disputes between citizens, but also of disputes between citizens and their government, as well as disputes between the branches of government. Should either Republicans or Democrats manage to stack the courts to lean in their direction, we are all in deep trouble. Yet that has become the game.

The American Judicature Society issued a statement in 2004 stating that "Judging is not a political process, and the judiciary should not be politicized by either the executive branch or the Senate." Do you agree with this statement? Why?

Why federal judges are political

Presidential candidates of both parties pledge to appoint federal judges, from the lowest to highest courts, whose views reflect the candidates' own political philosophy. When elected, the candidates must do their best to deliver. Judicial independence starts fading with the highly partisan selection process.

Presidents select judges who will conspicuously represent their philosophy. Often the chosen jurist is a candidate more noted for his political activism than legal skills, resulting in political hacks from both parties finding seats on the bench.

The Constitution, while setting some guidelines in federal judicial nominations, does not comment on the qualifications of a candidate. Do you think the establishment of criteria that nominees would have to meet would make the process more fair?

Moreover, notwithstanding life tenure, by the time a man or woman is appointed to the bench they are typically set in their ways. While there are exceptions, the political affiliation of a judge often determines how he or she will rule from the bench.

Federal judgeships have changed

A federal judgeship is not what it used to be, despite pretenses to the contrary. Today, it is a relatively low-paying job, from the point of view of a man or woman qualified for the job. A lawyer in private practice—particularly those most qualified for the bench—can earn three to ten times or more what he or she might as a federal judge.

Granted, no one goes to the federal bench for the money. But many refuse judicial appointments because the money is so bad, compared to their earning power in private practice.

Also, the best and brightest of the legal profession often turn down judgeships because they have no interest in going through the selection process. To become a federal judge, one must be politically active—not as a good citizen, but rather as a partisan. More people are disgusted with partisan politics than desirous of participating.

The judicial selection process is onerous. A prospective judicial candidate must fill out complex and lengthy questionnaires for the Justice Department, the White House, the American Bar Association, and the Senate. There is no guarantee that the confidential information provided will remain confidential. Indeed, more than a few nominees have been utterly humiliated when such information has been leaked for political reasons.

The confirmation process of the United States Senate, as many candidates have discovered, is an invitation for abuse. This is particularly true when there is a divided government—that is, when the political party controlling the Congress (particularly the Senate) and the White House are different.

Senate selection prerogatives ...

There is no mystery why the federal courts—and the judicial selection process—have become more political. A review of the past five decades shows that the federal courts and judges have become a part of presidential politics.

In addition, during the past five decades, we have increasingly had a divided federal government. Confirmations have become pitched political battles. While the most visible are Supreme Court appointments, lower federal courts often produce similar but less media-attracting confrontations. Once again, with Senator Jeffords (I-VT) moving his desk across the isle in the Senate, we have a divided government....

As of March 2004 a chief justice receives $203,000. Some commentators believe that this is far too low and that salaries have an effect on the quality of people who agree to stand for nomination since financially independent candidates are more likely to stand for nomination. Similarly some people claim that federal judges are retiring early because of poor salaries.

Should the information supplied by judicial nominees be confidential? Do you think people who break confidentiality agreements should be imprisoned?

Senator James Jeffords of Vermont left the Republican Party in May 2001 to run as an independent. This threw control of the Senate to the Democrats for the first time since 1994. There were 50 Democrats, 49 Republicans, and one independent in the Senate.

President John F. Kennedy (1961–1963) appointed his brother Robert F. Kennedy attorney general in 1961. Robert F. Kennedy proved an effective attorney general. He tackled the problem of organized crime and fought hard to end segregation, particularly in schools and colleges.

Does "Senatorial patronage" seem outdated in this day and age? Is it fairer to share judicial appointments in these circumstances?

In 1998 Supreme Court Chief Justice William Rehnquist criticized the Senate for stonewalling President Bill Clinton's judicial nominees. Go to http://slate.msn.com/default.aspx?id=1846 to read about this.

Is this fair? Do you think there should be a time limit on hearings?

[T]he Senate has long forced all Presidents to confer with Senators about judicial appointments in their state. Attorney General Robert Kennedy—who had believed his brother, as President, would appoint judges with advice and consent of the Senate, as the Constitution mandates—said he quickly learned that in truth, Senators appoint federal judges with the advice and consent of the President.

With Democrats now controlling the Senate, the Republican President cannot appoint federal judges in the 18 states where both Senators are Democrats, without obtaining the blessings of those Senators. Obviously this fact is going to temper the Bush selections, for right-wing zealots are not going to be approved by the Democrats.

When government is divided, it is the tradition that if a state has both a Republican and a Democratic Senator, then the Senator of the same party as the President gets to exercise the "Senatorial patronage."

However, occasionally (but not very often) in states that are politically divided, the tradition is broken and two Senators work out an allotment system between themselves whereby they share the judicial appointments.

The long and short of a divided government is that it can create either logjams or forced compromise—when vacancies jeopardize the operations of a local federal court. The "forced compromise" scenario usually results in finding the best candidate, rather than the politically or philosophically chosen candidate. In contrast, logjams, the product of political hardball, hurt everyone.…

Republican refusal to confirm Clinton judges

During the Clinton presidency, Republicans aggressively sought to block his judicial nominations. The problem became so serious, with a backlog of federal judgeships that needed to be filled, that Chief Justice Rehnquist (a Republican) publicly chided and prodded the Republican-controlled Senate for failing to act on nominations. The prodding didn't help.

Republicans sat on judicial nominations, refusing to act on them for years. Some nominees were never given hearings, and in one case, Republicans ignored a nominee for over four years and then rejected him.

Clearly, Republicans are now concerned that they not be treated as they did Democrats. In fact, this is the last matter being resolved in the transfer of leadership power. But Democrats have not indicated that they are going to play it as Republicans did.

When President Bush assumed office on January 20, there were 100 federal judgeships to be filled. Many of the judgeships were those that the Republicans had refused to fill during the Clinton years. Just before the Senate slipped from Republican control, President Bush sent 11 names to the Senate for judicial nominations, which are now pending.

The California plan—a partial solution

California's two Democratic Senators, Dianne Feinstein and Barbara Boxer, have adopted a bipartisan plan for judicial selection that the White House has accepted. The plan recognizes the political realities of judicial appointments. It will remove political extremists from serious consideration.

The California Senators have created a Judicial Advisory Committee to recommend nominations to fill vacancies in the four federal district courts of California. It will be comprised of four six-member subcommittees—one subcommittee for each judicial district.

Each subcommittee will have one member selected by Senator Boxer, one selected by Senator Feinstein, and one selected jointly by both Senators along with three members named by President Bush's California chairman for judicial appointments.

Each subcommittee will name three to five possible candidates for each vacancy in that subcommittee's jurisdiction. For a candidate to go forward requires a majority vote of the subcommittee. Once the selections have been made, the White House's designated chairman will review them and forward them to the Washington for final selection.

On paper this system looks good. The 24 lawyers who have been named to the four panels are distinguished and knowledgeable about the bar, and prospective candidates, in their respective parts of the state.

Moreover, given the requirement of a majority vote within each panel, candidates on the far right or left are not going to pass muster. Thus, the arrangement should produce highly qualified but moderate candidates. This is excellent....

I have only broadly highlighted the basics of a subject that needs serious attention and study. The new California plan is a small step in the right direction. Judges, practicing attorneys, those involved in the selection of judges, and persons having business with federal courts know there are serious problems with the judicial selection process and the partisan nature of that process....

In 2001 California's Democrat Senators and the White House agreed to create a bipartisan commission to recommend California federal judicial nominees. The commission was intended "by its nature, [to] value qualified moderates." Furthermore, the commission was intended to partially counteract the removal of the American Bar Association (ABA) from the process of vetting nominees. Does this sound more fair than the system used in other states?

Is there a danger that moderate candidates will never challenge the status quo?

REJECTION SUSTAINED
Randall Kennedy

Randall Kennedy is professor of law at Harvard Law School. This article was published in The Atlantic Monthly in September 2002.

NO

Is it inevitable that a president will nominate candidates of a similar political persuasion?

Few aspects of American political life generate more fatuous obfuscation than the selection of judges to sit on the federal bench. President George W. Bush decries opposition to his nominees by Democratic senators, charging that their resistance derives, shamefully, from "politics." Yet he almost always nominates Republicans for judgeships. Conservatives denounce liberals who openly admit that for them ideology is a major basis for assessing the President's nominees. Yet simultaneously the President makes clear that ideology matters greatly to him in choosing them; after all, he has declared publicly that he is looking to appoint "conservatives." Senate Republicans accuse Senate Democrats of creating a "vacancy crisis" by delaying hearings for judicial nominees, but during the years when Bill Clinton was President, Orrin Hatch, Trent Lott, and their Republican allies conspicuously slowed the confirmation process to a crawl.

Go to pages 72–73 to read The Bork nomination.

After the Senate blocked Robert Bork's confirmation, in 1987, bitter supporters complained that Democrats had prejudged Bork negatively, which was largely true. His champions, of course, had also prejudged him, but positively. Republicans charge that Democrats have a litmus test for assessing a nominee—namely, the jurist's views on the legal status of abortion rights. But Republican Presidents have the same litmus test; they just want the opposite result.

Playing politics

Since the appointments are for life, is it understandable that opposition senators will want to choose federal judicial candidates sympathetic to their viewpoints?

In the face of these charges and countercharges, many Americans are inclined to chastise the ideologues on the left and the right. They would contend that our heated and protracted disputes over judgeships are dangerous, that those on both sides of the fighting are wrong, that the left and the right should stop "playing politics" with judicial selection, that considerable deference should be given to any President's choice, and that in deciding whether or not to confirm the President's pick, senators ought to confine themselves to evaluating the nominee's integrity and competence. Proponents of this view evoke with warmth memories of a time when nominees, even for the Supreme Court, were confirmed by acclamation, and when "law" was thought to occupy a plane altogether different from and higher than "politics." This school of thought—call it the deference school—ought to be rejected. To some extent the past it evokes is imaginary, the product of yearning for a consensus that has frequently been absent. The Senate rejected George Washington's nomination of John Rutledge to be Chief Justice even though Rutledge had been confirmed as an associate justice and was already serving as Chief Justice thanks to a recess appointment. Why did the Senate rebuff the nominee of the Father of His Country? Because Rutledge had harshly criticized the Jay Treaty with Great Britain, prompting a majority in the Senate to doubt the political soundness of his judgment. Since then senators have often voted against nominees on substantive political grounds, openly stating their concern that such candidates would be likely to rule the wrong way on matters of high public importance.

Sometimes, as in the case of Rutledge, ideological opposition has prevailed.… But contrary to the claims of the deference school, senatorial opposition based on publicly aired ideological disagreement is by no means new.

Right or wrong?

Senators ought not to accord to any nominee a presumptive entitlement to confirmation. The Constitution declares no such presumption. It vests the President alone with the power to nominate federal judges, but it also directs the President to obtain "the Advice and Consent" of the Senate. As a functional matter, the Constitution thus gives the Senate a veto over the President's judicial selections. Expecting senators to ignore politics when exercising this responsibility is silly. Judges, after all, are policymakers who, like legislators and other officeholders, exercise discretion, express values, and weigh consequences in reaching conclusions. Whether one thinks a given nominee would be likely to carry out these tasks well—or even tolerably—depends on one's own political preferences and tenets. Of course, we (through our senators) need to evaluate the basic honesty and competence of nominees. But we need equally to assess their philosophy, ideology, politics (in this context I see these words as synonyms). Jurists may be perfectly competent, honest, and honorable—and yet may also be properly regarded as wholly unfit to wield judicial power.

One of the worst features of the current regime is the incentive it gives for scandal-mongering. People who are nervous about opposing a nominee straightforwardly on ideological grounds search for any sort of peccadillo to serve

On December 15, 1795, the Senate rejected by 10 to 14 President George Washington's nomination of South Carolina's John Rutledge to be chief justice of the United States following the retirement of Chief Justice John Jay. Rutledge, however, objected to the Jay Treaty on the grounds that it was far too pro-British, even though the president had supported it. In turning down his nomination the Senate made it clear that political ideology as well as qualifications mattered in the selection process.

A "peccadillo" is a petty sin or trifling fault.

Should a potential
Supreme Court
judge be treated
differently though?
Do you think his or
her peccadilloes
might be of
relevance to future
court decisions?

In 1993 Bill Clinton
chose Ruth Bader
Ginsberg (1933–) as
his first Supreme
Court candidate.

The cases referred
to here are
landmark cases. For
more information
on the 1803 case
Marbury v. Madison
see http://usinfo.
state.gov/usa/
infousa/facts/
democrac/9.htm;
similarly, go to
http://www.
landmarkcases.
org/dredscott/
home.html to read
about the 1857
court case Dred
Scott v. Sandford.

Quoting the
opinion of an
authoritative or
well-known figure
of the opposition
and disproving his
or her statement is
a good way to
enforce your
arguments.

as a nonideological pretext for opposition. We would be far better off if senators openly opposed nominees for substantive reasons, rather than ones that would probably have been overlooked in the absence of substantive disagreement.

Since senators ought to take into account the likely voting pattern of a nominee, they ought also to have access to information that helps them predict that pattern. Yet nominees (often on instruction from White House handlers) thwart information-gathering by declining to answer certain questions during confirmation hearings. They do not mind, of course, questions that will generate entirely uncontroversial answers. For example, during her Supreme Court confirmation hearing, in 1993, Ruth Bader Ginsburg eagerly declared her belief that *Marbury v. Madison* (the case establishing the authority of the Supreme Court to invalidate congressional statutes) was rightly decided and that *Dred Scott v. Sandford* (the case holding that blacks could not be citizens of the United States) was wrongly decided. However, nominees seek to avoid articulating beliefs about controversial subjects. For example, Ginsburg declined to answer Senator Strom Thurmond's rather general query about the constitutionality of vouchers in public schooling. Explaining at the outset of her hearing why she would refuse to answer certain questions, Ginsburg declared,

Judges in our system are bound to decide concrete cases, not abstract issues. Each case comes to the Court based on particular facts, and its decision should turn on those facts and the governing law, stated and explained in light of the particular arguments the parties or their representatives present. A judge sworn to decide impartially can offer no forecasts, no hints, for that would show not only disregard for the specifics of the particular case, it would display disdain for the entire judicial process.

That explanation is unpersuasive. Since, in Ginsburg's view, justices ought to decide only specific, concrete cases, she should not worry about sharing with the public her general views about disputes that are likely to come before the Court in some form. When those disputes arrive, they will necessarily be garbed in the particularities of a given controversy and thus will be subject to considerations different from (though related to) those posed by a question at a hearing.

Besides, many nominees have already served on lower courts, and have thus displayed more than a hint of their considered opinions; they may have made several pertinent and revealing rulings on a given subject. Such judgments offer a very clear forecast of how these jurists are likely to rule in the future. But presumably Ginsburg (herself an appellate judge before her advancement to the Supreme Court) would agree that having issued a ruling on a subject in the past does not, and should not, preclude a jurist from adjudicating future cases in which that same subject emerges.

Those who have not left a paper trail sometimes simply plead ignorance—claiming that they have thought little about a vexing subject, and attempting to make a virtue out of emptiness. When confronting this line, senators ought to say that a nominee is either disqualified for dishonesty or—if he or she truly lacks well-developed ideas about privacy, or federalism, or equal protection—insufficiently learned or thoughtful to be placed on the bench. The savvy conservatives at *The Weekly Standard* were absolutely right when, in 1997, they asserted,

> … *The Senate should demand [that nominees] thoroughly explain their understanding of constitutional principle and jurisprudential practice—whether they want to or not. And any judicial nominee who refuses this invitation to public debate about the law, we think, should be rejected.*

Although they may have changed their minds after the Republican take-over of the White House, their demand for searching scrutiny of nominees remains correct today.

A realistic understanding of what judges do, and of how and why they are selected, makes clear that all interested segments of the polity should, without embarrassment, support or oppose candidates on the basis of educated perceptions of what those candidates are likely to do if confirmed. Trying to banish politics from the process is futile; after all, it is inconceivable that the President's influence could be depoliticized. And even if it were possible … doing so would be wrongheaded. Judges are endowed with tenure for life and with the authority to strike down legislation. The active role of dissident senators in examining and confirming them is a vital hedge against political error—especially when the White House and the judiciary are dominated by the same party.

Many people believe that Robert Bork's nomination was struck down because of his extremely right-wing views on subjects such as abortion. If nominees can justify their viewpoints from a constitutional perspective, should they be penalized because some people think their opinions are old-fashioned or contentious?

Should federal judicial appointments be time specific? Do you think elderly judges may be out of touch with what should be permissible in modern society?

Summary

Article II of the Constitution gives the president the right to nominate federal judges with the approval of the Senate. Many people believe that this process has over time become overly politicized and that the system is inefficient and works against the best interests of both the judiciary and society at large.

In the first article John Dean argues that the judicial branch is becoming too partisan. He believes the increasingly contentious nature of the confirmation process, coupled with the fact that judgeships are no longer well paid compared to salaries in private practice, has discouraged many good judicial candidates. This problem has become worse as the number of judgeships has increased, and as many vacancies go unfilled. In his view the practice of choosing judges based on their political philosophy threatens judicial integrity and independence. He suggests taking a careful look at California's promising bipartisan plan for judicial selection, which would encourage compromise and avoid the logjams that have been plaguing the process.

Randall Kennedy, in the second article, rejects the idea that politics is irrelevant or harmful to the confirmation process. He refutes the notion that the politicization is of recent origin, suggesting that judges have been rejected on political grounds since the time of President George Washington, and that is as it should be, in his view. The Constitution specifically gives the Senate a role in the process, and neither the Senate nor the president can be expected to act nonpolitically. They should take competence into account, but an essential part of their job is to evaluate the candidate's constitutional philosophy.

FURTHER INFORMATION:

Books:

Goldman, Sheldon, *Picking Federal Judges: Lower Court Selection from Roosevelt through Reagan.* New Haven, CT: Yale University Press, 1997.

Useful websites:

http://www.ajs.org/selection/sel_fedselect.aspt American Judicature Society page on federal judicial selection. Contains articles and links to useful sites.
http://www.pfaw.org/pfaw/general/default.aspx?oid=629 People for the American Way focus on George W. Bush and the federal judiciary. Provides background, history, and analysis of the nominee process.
http://www.uscourts.gov/faq.html
U.S. courts frequently asked questions site. Explains the process of federal judge selections in a concise way.

The following debates in the Pro/Con series may also be of interest:

In this volume:
Topic 1 Is the Supreme Court too activist?

The Bork nomination, pages 72–73

Topic 6 Should federal judicial applicants have to meet a formal set of requirements?

ARE POLITICS TOO INFLUENTIAL IN THE SELECTION OF FEDERAL JUDGES?

YES: The complicated and nasty confirmation hearings has sometimes put off the best judicial candidates

YES: Robert Bork's hearings were unprecedented and were the first time that interested parties used the media to such a degree to discredit a candidate

DIFFICULTY
Have the confirmation hearings often stopped the best candidates from being nominated ?

INTEGRITY
Did federal judicial proceedings become more political after Bork?

NO: The confirmation hearings just act as another check that the best candidates are appointed— they are rigorous, but the appointments are for life and are extremely important

NO: The process has always been political, from George Washington's presidency onward

YES: Supreme Court Justice Rehnquist once suggested this would make the process more efficient and get better results

YES: Many judicial candidates have been discounted in the past because their political ideology clashed with that of certain senators. Their experience and qualifications have not been taken into account, and that has led to bad appointments.

ARE POLITICS TOO INFLUENTIAL IN THE SELECTION OF FEDERAL JUDGES?
KEY POINTS

DELAYING TACTICS
Should the confirmation proceedings be time specific to avoid calculating delaying tactics by senators?

QUALIFICATIONS
Should federal judicial appointments be made on merit and experience rather than political ideology?

NO: Sometimes it takes a lot of time to research the background, ideology, and qualifications of a candidate. It is such an important appointment that the process should not be rushed.

NO: Ideology cannot be disregarded. The decisions made by federal judicial appointees will affect every aspect of U.S. society.

Topic 3

SHOULD FEDERAL JUDGES BE APPOINTED FOR LIMITED TERMS?

YES

FROM "SHOULD U.S. SUPREME COURT JUSTICES BE TERM-LIMITED?: A DIALOGUE"
WWW.FINDLAW.COM, AUGUST 23, 2002
AKHIL REED AMAR AND VIKRAM DAVID AMAR

NO

"STATEMENT OF CHIEF JUSTICE WALTER L. MURPHY OF THE SUPERIOR COURT BEFORE THE
HOUSE SUBCOMMITTEE ON JUDICIAL SELECTION AND RETENTION"
OCTOBER 4, 2001
WALTER L. MURPHY

INTRODUCTION

Since President Clinton (1993–2001) nominated Judge Stephen G. Breyer to the Supreme Court in May 1994—and his nomination was approved by Senate in August that year—there have been no vacancies on the court. In fact, the same group of justices serving the nation's highest court have now served together for the longest period of time since the early 19th century. Among the current justices are 79-year-old Chief Justice William H. Rehnquist, who was appointed by President Richard Nixon (1969–1974) in 1971, and 84-year-old Associate Justice John Paul Stevens, who was appointed by President Gerald Ford (1974–1977) in 1975.

Only in the judicial branch of federal government are such lengthy terms of office possible. Unlike members of the legislative and executive branches of government who serve for limited terms, federal judges serve for life. There are now about 800 life-tenured judges in the federal judiciary. By contrast, many state and local judges serve fixed renewable terms ranging from 4 to 14 years, and occasionally for life. A further difference is that while some state judges are appointed, the remainder are elected.

Article III of the Constitution states that "judges, both of the supreme and inferior courts, shall hold their offices during good behavior." Apart from the rare possibility of impeachment due to some crime or misdemeanor, this phrase is understood to mean for life. In granting federal judges life tenure, the Framers believed that they were ensuring an independent judiciary. Some legal commentators argue that the Constitution should be amended to limit the terms of federal judges. Others, meanwhile, contend that life tenure protects judges from political pressures. Life tenure is the most controversial aspect of selecting judges.

It is a contentious matter because it is such an important one. Federal judges—who interpret the law—have the last word on practically every issue of concern to the American people.

The most enduring argument for the life tenure of federal judges was made by statesman Alexander Hamilton (1755-1804) in The Federalist Papers. He argued (against those who opposed ratification of the Constitution, the anti-Federalists) that the judiciary posed no threat to republican liberty because it is the weakest of the three branches of government. Judges can declare laws unconstitutional only when a case is brought before them. In addition, they depend on the executive branch to enforce their decisions.

> *"The judiciary ... [has] neither force nor will but merely judgement."*
> —ALEXANDER HAMILTON, *THE FEDERALIST NO. 78* (1788)

The judiciary also has the important powers of judicial review to prevent the other two—stronger—branches of government from violating the Constitution. Hamilton argued that it was thus crucial to keep the judiciary relatively separate from politics and any political superior that could compromise its integrity. It is not hard to imagine, for example, a judge whose term is about to end ruling on a case in a politically popular way with an eye to securing his reappointment. According to this argument, then, judges should be appointed for life.

A further argument for life tenure is that the most experienced judges make the best judges. The longer time a judge has served on the bench, the more likely he or she is to have the legal expertise required of federal judges. It is also vital, some say, that judges are appointed rather than elected. If judges were regularly elected, they would be more likely to feel that they have a personal stake in the outcome of a case. Judges, it is argued, should apply the law and not their own values.

Other commentators, however, believe that the Constitution should be amended to limit the terms of federal judges. Life expectancy is much longer now than it was at the end of the 18th century when the Constitution was written. As a result, judges can serve for several decades. Chief Justice Rehnquist, for example, has held a seat on the Supreme Court for more than three decades. This has led to calls for a mandatory retirement age for judges. Rehnquist and several other justices are expected to retire in the near future. Some people believe that these justices are waiting for the presidential election before making any announcement. Indeed, research by political scientist Patrick Marecki has indicated that Supreme Court justices tend to pick "a retirement date during the administration of a president that shares his or her political philosophy." For example, the most recent retiree in 1994, Harry Blackmun, made no secret of the fact that he worried about dying in office while a conservative president had the power to name his successor. Limiting the term of office for federal judges, proponents argue, would prevent politically timed retirements.

The following articles look at this debate in more detail.

SHOULD U.S. SUPREME COURT JUSTICES BE TERM-LIMITED?: A DIALOGUE
Akhil Reed Amar and Vikram David Amar

Akhil Reed Amar is Southmayd professor of law at Yale University. Vikram David Amar is a professor of law at the University of California. Both have served as law clerks to high court judges. This column originally appeared on www.findlaw.com.

YES

Vikram David Amar: In our column two weeks ago, we analyzed a recent Supreme Court case, *Republican Party of Minnesota v. White*, involving state judicial elections. That same day I noticed that you and Steve Calabresi published an op-ed in the *Washington Post* on a related topic: life tenure for federal judges, who of course are not elected, but appointed.

Akhil Reed Amar: You're right to see the topics as related. Lots of critics think judicial elections threaten judicial impartiality and the appearance of impartiality. Justice O'Connor, in fact, wrote a separate opinion in *White* criticizing this entire mode of picking judges, and praising the federal model of executive appointment, senate confirmation and life tenure as a far better way to secure judicial impartiality and its appearance.

And that's where the *Washington Post* piece comes in. Steve and I argue that—contrary to Justice O'Connor's view—in some ways, the federal model of life tenure, at least for the Supreme Court, is a suboptimal way of achieving judicial impartiality and its appearance.

Begin by noting that only one of the fifty states copies the federal life-tenure model for its highest court, and that none of the major world democracies abroad does so. That is at least suggestive that perhaps the federal system isn't as wonderful as Justice O'Connor seems to think.

Should it matter to us how other countries organize their legal systems?

For a discussion on this subject see Volume 2, Government, Topic 13 Should the electoral college be abolished?

Vik: We've made a similar argument about the electoral college: if it's so great, why is it the case that not a single state copies it for the governor's election, nor does a single other major world democracy use it to pick its president? But surely you don't think that federal judges should be elected the way many state judges are?

Akhil: No, I don't. Steve and I were arguing for something much less drastic: keep presidential selection, and senate confirmation (and the protections against retaliatory pay cuts), but move towards fixed terms rather than life tenure: after, say, 18 years, a Justice should automatically step down. This is how many states and other world democracies protect judicial independence and its appearance.

Vik: What's the difference between the consequences of life tenure and those of a relatively lengthy fixed term…?

Akhil: Here's the irony: life tenure is supposed to insulate federal judges from politics so that they will act apolitically in deciding cases. In reality, though, life tenure encourages Supreme Court Justices to be overly mindful of politics—in particular the partisan political landscape of the White House and the Senate—in deciding when to retire.

For a debate on the selection of Supreme Court justices see Topic 5 Should Supreme Court candidates be asked their views on legal issues during confirmation proceedings?

Consider, for example, the Court's three most senior Justices. Justice Stevens holds views unlikely to be shared by any person President Bush would appoint to replace him. Isn't he understandably tempted to delay his retirement—if he possibly can—until a Democrat or more moderate Republican occupies the Oval Office? On the other side, both Chief Justice Rehnquist and Justice O'Connor might be tempted to hold on, for now, to give the Republicans a chance to regain control of the Senate this November and thus give President Bush more latitude in judicial appointments than he now has with the Senate in the hands of the Democrats.

The nomination and selection of judges is always more crucial when the president and majority of the Senate are from different political parties.

In previous columns, you and I have mapped out some of the ground rules of the appointments game between partisan Presidents and partisan Senators; but I wonder whether the Justices should be playing this game…. And even if these incentives I'm talking about don't actually affect judicial resignation decisions … the public perception of their doing so is inescapable…. Remember, many of the Justices in *White* were worried not just about the reality of judicial impartiality but also its appearance. But all these problems would be solved if we moved to fixed terms so that Justices would be limited in their ability to politically time their exits.

Do you think senior judges should be able to politically time their exits? Should there be a mandatory retirement age for judges?

Vik: You and Steve made another interesting point when you observed that no one on the Court has stepped down in the last eight years and that never before in history have the same nine Justices served together so long.

Akhil: Of course, there was an even longer stretch between appointments in the early 1800s, but the Court was smaller then, with fewer possibilities for vacancies.

The longest stretch in time between Supreme Court appointments was between 1812 and 1823.

Vik: Here are some additional facts about vacancies that I've dug up…. Between 1789 and 1970, the average time between Supreme Court vacancies was 1.93 years; between 1971 and 2000, it went up about 50% to 2.98 years.

The big reasons for that, of course, are that Justices are living—and thus serving—much longer. The average age at departure for Supreme Court Justices from 1789 to 1970 was 68.5 years; whereas from 1971 to 2000, it was 78.8 years. From 1789 to 1970, the average Justice served on the Court 15 years, whereas from 1971 to 2000, Justices who left had served an average of a whopping 25.5 years.

While perhaps the predictable result of advances in medicine and healthier lifestyles, these changes are troubling in a number of ways. Because Presidents have few chances to affect the Court, they may be inclined to act more ideologically with each chance they get.

Akhil: And they also may tend to pick very young … candidates … to extend their legacy as much as possible. This problem, too, would be solved by an 18-year term limit.

Vik: O.K. Let's talk about ways to implement term limits for Supreme Court Justices. Amending the Constitution right away isn't necessary. A clever statutory solution might satisfy the Constitution. Under the statute, judges would technically sit on the Supreme Court "by designation" for a fixed number of years after which they would have the option to serve the remainder of their life tenure on some lower federal court. The Justices would be federal judges with life tenure—but not all of that tenure would be served on the Supreme Court.

Akhil: And as [journalist and editor] Gregg Easterbrook has reminded me, any such approach may benefit the lower federal courts, by having former Supreme Court Justices sharing their talents and experiences with the judges whose decisions are reviewed on high.

Vik: Perhaps. And there are other, non-constitutional, fixes that may be possible. The Senate could insist that all future Court nominees publicly agree to term limits, or risk nonconfirmation. While legally unenforceable, such commitments by Justices would likely be honored.

And unlike promises to rule certain ways on certain cases—which you and I have criticized elsewhere—a term limits pledge would not raise judicial independence or due process problems. Congress could also restructure salaries,

Careful use of statistics can add weight to your argument. Here they illustrate the author's point about the consequences of life tenure as the age expectancy of judges has become longer.

Amending the Constitution is very difficult, and most people agree that is right considering what is at stake. Go to http://www.usconstitution.net/constam.html to find out more about amending the Constitution.

A common criticism of how Supreme Court judges are appointed and of the length of time they serve is that it encourages an elitist group of senior judges.

What are the dangers of getting judges to promise to rule certain ways on certain cases?

pensions, office space and other perks to give future justices incentives to live by their word.

Akhil: You were right to say "future justices." Any changes should be completely prospective, rather than retrospective: they should be applicable only to the future nominees of both parties and all ideologies, and to no present sitting Justices. This will avoid any perception that the term limits idea is being used to oust disliked current Justices.

Indeed, ideally, politicians should declare their preference for Supreme Court term limits before the next Court vacancy comes up, so as to avoid even the appearance of outcome-manipulation. This should be an issue on which the parties can agree: One of the reasons Steve and I decided to coauthor our OpEd was to make clear that ours is not a partisan proposal. He's a Reagan Republican and I'm a registered Democrat.

> "OpEds" are opinion editorials that are published in newspapers and magazines. They add to debate on particular issues and can play a part in campaigns to change laws and systems.

Vik: Even if you had such a system in place, couldn't Justices still act strategically by leaving BEFORE their 18 years were up, if to do so would be to give their seat to a "friendly" President and Senate?

Akhil: They could, in the same way that Presidents Reagan and Clinton COULD have resigned in the last years of their second terms to give their Vice Presidents the mantle of incumbency when those Vice Presidents themselves ran for the White House the next year. If overtly political Presidents can be encouraged not to act in this manipulative way, surely we can … expect the same from our Supreme Court Justices.

Vik: Some people might say *Bush v. Gore* suggests otherwise. Anyway, how likely do you really think these changes are to come about? For better or worse, Americans are reluctant to tinker with the Constitution.

> Some people argue that the Supreme Court intervention in the 2000 postelection controversy over which candidate had the most votes brought disgrace on the court. Go to http://www.commondreams.org/views/01/1209/03.htm for an article about this. Do you agree?

Akhil: That is precisely why we should think about ways to work within the Constitution itself. The Congressional fixes we have been discussing—and perhaps an alternative, or complementary, solution in which the Court itself develops some of its own retirement guidelines to change the culture and tradition of the place—would be just as effective as a ramped-up amendment process. Just as our previous column on Minnesota's judicial election regime pointed out, there's almost always more than one way to get where you want to constitutionally go.

STATEMENT ... BEFORE THE HOUSE SUBCOMMITTEE ON JUDICIAL SELECTION AND RETENTION
Walter L. Murphy

The author of this article, Walter L. Murphy, served 20 years as a state trial judge in New Hampshire. He was chief justice of the Superior Court for three of those years.

The Federalist Papers were written by Alexander Hamilton (1755–1804), who later served in the Cabinet, James Madison (1751–1836), who became the fourth president (1809–1817), and John Jay (1745–1829), who became the first chief justice of the Supreme Court.

Using powerful quotations from authoritative sources can strengthen your argument.

NO

There is no greater threat to the independence of the New Hampshire Judicial Branch than the proposal to amend the constitution to impose term limitations on judges. The institution of term limits for judges goes against the very grain of the state which proudly proclaims as its motto, "Live Free or Die", as it is for the protection of the people's rights to have their issues litigated by judges who are "as impartial as the lot of humanity will admit." As Article 35 of the state constitution articulates: "... it is not only the best policy, but for the security of the people" that judges hold their offices so long as they behave well. As Alexander Hamilton so aptly put it in the Federalist papers, "... adherence to the rights of the Constitution and of individuals indispensable to the courts of Justice, can certainly not be expected from judges who hold their offices by a temporary commission." Likewise, in providing life tenure for federal judges under the United States constitution, John Adams said of judges that "their minds should not be distracted with jarring interests; they should not be dependent upon any person or body of persons."

Life tenure protects the people

Lifetime tenure is not in place to protect judges; it is for the protection of the people.

A promise was made by the late Chief Justice Frank Kenison of the New Hampshire Supreme Court that the judiciary of this State "... will continue to maintain its House of Justice for the humble as well as the powerful, for the poor as well as the rich, for the minority as well as the majority, and the unpopular as well as the popular."

Decisions of a court of law must not be based upon what is popular or unpopular at the moment, nor what the media thinks, nor what politics might dictate, nor by the fear that one's position might be lost as a result of a judge's determination.

Chief Justice William Rehnquist heads the U.S. judiciary. He became a Supreme Court justice in 1972 and has been chief justice since 1986. Some legal commentators argue that federal judges serving such long terms is not good for the independence of the judiciary.

Specifically, I am concerned about the quality of persons who would be willing to dedicate their lives to public service as a judge if he or she is not assured that his or her position would not be lost because of some political interests which oppose a decision made by the judge. When an established attorney accepts judicial office, she gives up the opportunity to earn significantly more money in private practice, which less persons will be willing to do if their continuation in office could be in jeopardy after a term of seven or ten years.

Worries about judicial selection process

The repeated use of a word or phrase can make your argument resonate more powerfully with the audience.

I worry about having two separate categories of judges, those with life tenure and those without and the attempts on the part of some litigants or their counsel to shop for a judge who might be more sympathetic to a person's cause because of perceived public sentiment. I worry about those judges whose appointments are coming up for review being able to withstand the pressure of the process, or who might be tempted to evade the tough issues by referring the "hot potato" case to a colleague who is not up for renewal. I worry that judges might be inclined to look over their shoulders to test the winds of public opinion rather than objectively apply the law. I worry that those who are supposed to rule objectively and fairly might have their thoughts elsewhere such as currying the favor of a particular litigant or law firm in which he or she may take refuge in the event that his or her term of office is not renewed. I also worry that the public may misconstrue the rationale behind judges' decisions, and sense that the decision was made, not as a result of considered judgment, but as a result of inappropriate influence.

Go to http://www.salemweb.com/guide/witches.html for more about the witch trials in Salem, Massachusetts.

One only has to look at the history of this nation to discern many instances in which the popular sentiment of the times, the majority public opinion, was at odds with reason. In Salem in the seventeenth century, hundreds of people, mostly women, were burned at the stake because of suspected witchery. Nor is more recent history in this country lacking in such examples: persons of color not being able to vote, attend public schools, or ride in public transportation, against a backdrop of murders, lynching, and church bombings, all in the name of what the majority perceived as racial superiority. Thanks to an independent judiciary, that is federal judges with lifetime appointments, those dark days are a thing of the past. One doesn't have to wonder much if the results would have been the same had the judges considering the civil rights issues of the 1960's been subject to a review process after their initial term of office. It is obvious from these lessons of the past that judges should be free from the popular pressures of the moment and that their decisions should be made without regard to the popularity of the decision.

Is it possible for judges to be truly free of popular pressures if they are living in the real world?

The people's right to an impartial judiciary
My worries are not personal, as any changes will not affect my term of office; but they should be the concerns of all the citizens of the State as it is their right to an impartial judiciary which will be affected. A judge should have no personal interest in the outcome of any litigation. The only way to ensure that judges are free from outside influence is to maintain lifetime tenure which has withstood the test of time over the past two plus centuries. Please consider any proposed change with extreme caution, as the rights, not of the judges themselves, but those of your constituents, the people of this state, hang in the balance.

There are those among you that claim that the public demands change; it is up to us all to see to it that the public is fully informed of all of the consequences of the efforts to initiate this type of proposal. Among those consequences is a loss of an independent judiciary so vital to their rights as citizens to be tried by judges as free from influence as humankind admits.

Chief Justice Walter L. Murphy made this statement to the House Subcommittee in 2001. He retired in December 2003.

Summary

Law academics Akhil Reed Amar and Vikram David Amar argue that Supreme Court justices at least should be limited to fixed terms of 18 years. "[T]he federal model of life tenure," Akhil says, "is a suboptimal way of achieving judicial impartiality and its appearance." Life tenure was originally intended to insulate federal judges from the political fray, but, Akhil contends, it has had the opposite effect of making them "overly mindful of politics" in deciding when to retire. Also, the average number of years a Supreme Court justice serves has jumped in the last 30 years to ten years more than what it has ever previously been. Vikram points out that this affects who gets nominated for the Supreme Court: Since presidents have fewer opportunities to nominate justices, "they may be inclined to act more ideologically with each chance they get."

Former New Hampshire Chief Justice Walter L. Murphy strongly opposes any move to limit the terms of federal judges, including Supreme Court justices. He advocates the thinking of Alexander Hamilton, who argued that life tenure is the best way to ensure an independent judiciary faithfully performing its constitutional responsibilities. Chief Justice Murphy argues that life tenure is in place not to protect judges but to protect the people. He quotes another chief justice who held that a court of justice should function "for the humble as well as the powerful, for the poor as well as the rich, for the minority as well as the majority, and the unpopular as well as the popular." Murphy believes that a court of law must be immune from public, media, and political opinion and life tenure for federal judges achieves this.

FURTHER INFORMATION:

Books:

Sheldon, Charles H., and Linda S. Maule, *Choosing Justice: The Recruitment of State and Federal Judges*. Pullman, WA: Washington State University Press, 1998.

Useful websites:

http://electionlawblog.org/archives/000129.html
Article on "Time to End Life Tenure of Federal Judges."
http://faircourts.org/newsViewer.asp?breadcrumb=7&docID=1981
2003 article "Life Tenure for Judges Ensures Better Courts," part of the Justice at Stake campaign.
http://www.gradesaver.com/ClassicNotes/Titles/federalist/summ78.html
Explanation and summary of Alexander Hamilton's *The Federalist No. 78* on the life tenure of federal judges.

http://www.uscourts.gov/understand02/content_5_0.html
U.S. government site geared to understanding the federal courts and how they work.

The following debates in the Pro/Con series may also be of interest:

In this volume:

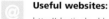 Part 1: The federal judiciary: Checks and balances

 Topic 8 Should state court judges be appointed rather than elected?

SHOULD FEDERAL JUDGES BE APPOINTED FOR LIMITED TERMS?

YES: It will remove judges who act politically and bring new blood to the bench

YES: This cannot be a good model since only one U.S. state and none of the major world democracies follow it

IMPARTIALITY
Will fixed terms of office ensure an impartial judiciary?

GOOD MODEL?
Does the life-tenure model politicize the judicial process?

NO: Limited terms will not shield the judiciary from popular political pressures of the moment. Judges have to objectively apply the law regardless of outside influence.

NO: Lifetime appointments mean that judges do not feel they have a personal role in the outcome of high-profile cases. The life-tenure model protects judges from acting politically and has withstood the test of time.

SHOULD FEDERAL JUDGES BE APPOINTED FOR LIMITED TERMS?

KEY POINTS

YES: Justices are now serving for several decades. The bench needs the vitality of new and younger judges. A mandatory age will help stop judges from politically timing their exits.

YES: Lifetime appointments encourage justices to pay too much heed to politics. Fixed terms will remove the political players from the bench.

RETIREMENT
Should there be a mandatory retirement age for federal judges?

BETTER JUDGES
Would fixed terms ensure better judges?

NO: The Constitution says that federal judges should keep their position so long as they behave well. This usually means for life.

NO: Life tenure ensures that the most experienced judges, with the best legal knowledge, sit on the highest courts

Topic 4

IS IT TOO DIFFICULT TO IMPEACH FEDERAL JUDGES?

YES

"WE HOLD THESE TRUTHS: THE CASE FOR IMPEACHING ROGUE JUDGES"
POLICY REVIEW: THE JOURNAL OF AMERICAN CITIZENSHIP, MAY–JUNE 1997, NO. 83
DENNIS SHEA

NO

"THE SENATE'S EPIC HYPOCRISY"
WWW. WORLDNETDAILY.COM, JANUARY 11, 1999
GEOFF METCALF

INTRODUCTION

In 1986 Harry E. Claiborne, judge of the District Court for Nevada, was impeached—accused of misconduct by the House of Representatives and made to stand trial in the Senate. Claiborne was convicted and removed from office for failing to report more than $107,000 on his 1979 and 1980 federal income tax returns. At the time, he was the first judge in more than 50 years—and one of only a small handful of federal officials—to be removed from office through impeachment. Claiborne's case highlighted the fact that very few judges have actually been removed from office despite reports that some of them have abused their power or behaved inappropriately while in office. Some commentators have therefore questioned if it is simply too difficult to impeach federal judges.

Although the constitutional system of checks and balances places restraints on federal officials, the ultimate check on judicial abuse of power—or other

serious misconduct in office—is impeachment, which is established by the Constitution. According to Article II, section 4, the president, vice president, and "all civil officers of the United States," including federal judges (who serve during "good behavior"), can be removed from office for "treason, bribery, or other high crimes and misdemeanors."

Article I, sections 2 and 3, outline the two-step procedure for removing a federal official from office. Impeachment first of all requires a majority vote by the House of Representatives. Afterward the impeached officer is tried in the Senate, which sits as a court, hears all the evidence, and makes its decision under whatever rules it wishes to adopt. In order to convict the accused and remove him or her from office, a two-thirds majority "of the members present" in the Senate is required. In an impeachment case involving the president, the Constitution stipulates, the chief justice of the Supreme Court has to preside over the trial in the Senate. According to the Constitution, "judgment in cases of impeachment shall not extend further than to removal from office, and disqualification to hold and enjoy any office of honor, trust or profit under the United States." A person removed from office is thus subject "to indictment, trial, judgment, and punishment, according to the law."

"Congress has given up its responsibility in [overseeing] judges and their performances on the bench … we intend to … go after them in a big way."
—CONGRESSMAN TOM DELAY ON THE IMPEACHMENT OF ACTIVIST FEDERAL JUDGES (1997)

Since 1789, the year that the Constitution was ratified, only 12 federal judges have been impeached by the House of Representatives: Seven were convicted and removed from office, and five were acquitted. These low figures have led some critics to claim that the impeachment rate is merely a token one, and that judges are only impeached when the House of Representatives has no other option.

Advocates who believe that the system works cite the example of Walter L. Nixon, judge of the District Court for Mississippi. Nixon was impeached and removed from office in 1989 for lying about interfering in the criminal prosecution of his business partner's son, who had been accused of drug smuggling. Nixon's removal shows, proponents argue, that the system does work. Some of them even claim it would be a good thing if the impeachment system regulating presidential behavior worked even half as well. They assert that while Nixon was essentially impeached and removed from office for committing perjury, President Bill Clinton, who basically committed a similar if not more serious crime, was not impeached. They argue the application of the impeachment system is therefore not only unfair but extremely hypocritical, especially since a number of the senators who contributed to Nixon's fall from grace— including Al Gore—voted against Clinton's impeachment just years later.

Some people, however, believe that the system for impeaching judges is sometimes abused. In 1997 N. Lee Cooper, former American Bar Association president, alleged that some congressmen were using impeachment to threaten judges whose court decisions they disagreed with. Stephen W. Fitschen, president of the National Legal Foundation, also claimed that the religious right had launched an impeachment movement in response to the Supreme Court's decision in *Romer v. Evans*. The court ruled that the state of Colorado could not amend the Constitution to prevent homosexuals from being granted special rights or minority status. Some conservative groups called for the impeachment of the judges involved; they argued that the decision was unconstitutional and threatened the moral fabric of society.

The following articles present two very different answers to this question.

WE HOLD THESE TRUTHS: THE CASE FOR IMPEACHING ROGUE JUDGES
Dennis Shea

Dennis Shea is a contributor to the cable news network MSNBC. He was also former deputy chief of staff to Senator Robert Dole.

Is it right to impeach a judge just because a person disagrees with a court decision? Would this be a valid reason according to the Constitution?

Do you think lifetime appointments are a good or bad thing? Are there enough checks and balances to prevent judicial abuse or misconduct?

YES

Federal judges are about as popular today as auditors from the Internal Revenue Service. And for good reason.

In case after case, federal judges are expressing contempt for democracy, overturning laws passed by state legislatures or adopted directly by the people through the initiative process. In recent years, federal judges have blocked the implementation of two California ballot initiatives, one that denies government services to illegal immigrants and one that bans racial and ethnic preferences. In Washington state and New York, federal judges have overturned state laws banning physician-assisted suicide. And the Supreme Court overturned a Colorado initiative to deny giving special legal preferences to homosexuals.

The American people are asking themselves, why bother voting when the judiciary can knock down laws like so many bowling pins?

Term limits?

In conservative circles, exploring ways to curb the activism of some of our federal judges has also become a hot topic. One suggestion that seems to be gaining currency is limiting the terms of federal judges, who now enjoy lifetime appointments....

For starters, imposing term limits on judges would be difficult. Article III, section 1 of the Constitution states that federal judges are to hold their offices "during good Behaviour." Changing this provision would require a constitutional amendment. In recent years, Congress has proposed dozens of constitutional amendments on everything from balancing the federal budget and campaign spending limits to flag desecration and voluntary school prayer.

Unlike many of these proposed constitutional amendments, which are mainly designed to overturn specific decisions by the Supreme Court, an amendment to impose term limits on federal judges would alter the fundamental structure of our system of government. Anticipating that the judiciary would be the weakest of the three branches, the Framers explicitly granted federal judges lifetime tenure so that they would be able to protect the Constitution against "legislative encroachments."

As Alexander Hamilton explains in *Federalist* No. 78, "nothing will contribute so much as [lifetime tenure] to that independent spirit in the judges which must be essential to the faithful performance of so arduous a duty." Is it smart to monkey with the fundamental mechanics of our constitutional structure? Do we really want to second-guess the Framers?…

Some argue that term limits should be linked to reappointment: When a federal judge's term expires, he or she would be eligible for reconfirmation by the U.S. Senate. But what would this accomplish? Anxious about reappointment, judges might tack their decisions to the prevailing political winds as the expiration of their terms grew near. Would judges resort to lobbying the Senate for reappointment? What kind of deals would be made? And what about a conservative judge, properly committed to the principle of judicial restraint, who must face reappointment by a hostile Senate controlled by liberals?

For shame!

Finding the right balance between judicial independence and judicial accountability is difficult. But there is a way. It's called shame. Shame is one of the most underutilized checks on a runaway judiciary. Remember Harold Baer, the federal district court judge in New York, who suppressed more than $4 million worth of drugs seized as evidence by the New York City police? Baer claimed that the police lacked a "reasonable suspicion" that a crime was occurring, even though they observed four men at 5 a.m., in an area notorious for drug-dealing, load bags into the trunk of a car without speaking to its driver, and then run away after noticing the cops. According to Baer, it was perfectly normal for them to flee from the police since "residents in this neighborhood tended to regard police officers as corrupt, abusive, and violent."

The foolishness of this ruling transformed Baer into the poster child for an out-of-control and out-of-touch federal judiciary. After being publicly denounced by both President Clinton and Senator Dole, the judge hastily reversed himself.

Even the Supreme Court has recognized that "[t]he operation of the courts and the judicial conduct of judges are

Alexander Hamilton (1755–1804) was one of the Framers of the Constitution. He produced a series of essays with John Jay and James Madison called The Federalist Papers to explain the Constitution. Go to pages 78 and 81 in Volume 2, Government, for more information on Hamilton and The Federalist Papers, and page 27, Volume 7, The Constitution, for more information on Hamilton and the judiciary.

Is shaming someone an appropriate way to deal with judicial misconduct?

Harold Baer, Jr. (1933–), received a federal judicial nomination from Bill Clinton in 1994. He is judge on the District Court, Southern District of New York.

matters of utmost public concern." When a federal judge issues a "prison cap" order, resulting in the early release of hundreds of violent criminals, that's a matter of real public concern that should concern politicians too. The same can be said when a federal judge strikes down a popularly enacted ballot initiative using half-baked constitutional analysis. Elected officials at all levels of government have an obligation to speak out when a judge crosses the line. ...

Too often today lower federal court decisions are issued without much public notice. They are tucked away in court reports, inaccessible to the public. And don't expect the liberal and often lazy mainstream press to bring these decisions to light.... The congressional leadership should ... consider passing, on a routine basis, nonbinding resolutions expressing disapproval of those decisions that show a clear disregard for established law. The purpose ... would not be to change the outcome of any particular case, but to serve as a warning to renegade federal judges that the people's elected representatives are monitoring their conduct....

What about impeachment?

In those extraordinary cases where a federal judge has clearly, deliberately and consistently exceeded his authority, there is also another option. Let's take our cue again from Alexander Hamilton, this time in *Federalist* No. 81. In it, Hamilton woefully underestimates the mischief judges might cause in the future: "Particular misconstructions and contraventions of the will of the legislature may now and then happen; but they can never be so extensive as to amount to an inconvenience, or in any sensible degree affect the order of the political system." But then he redeems himself by suggesting an antidote to those rare occasions of chronic judicial arrogance: impeachment. As he explains, "There never can be danger that the judges, by a series of deliberate usurpations on the authority of the legislature, would hazard the united resentment of the body entrusted with it, while this body was possessed of the means of punishing their presumption by degrading them from their stations."

In other words, Hamilton and the Framers envisioned that any judge who consistently and deliberately exceeded his judicial authority would be given a pink slip. The impeachment process should be regarded as the ultimate check on a rogue judiciary.

Representative Tom DeLay of Texas performed a public service recently by suggesting that renegade federal judges could be removed from office through the impeachment

By quoting extensively from Hamilton, the author gives his argument authority.

Some people believe that DeLay's suggestion is unconstitutional since impeachment on the grounds of judicial decisions is not included in the Constitution.

process. Not surprisingly, this suggestion has met with fierce criticism. Even some of DeLay's Republican colleagues have dismissed the impeachment remedy out of hand.

Not so fast. Congress should first sort out and evaluate the competing arguments over impeachment. Article II, section 4, of the Constitution provides that "[t]he President, Vice President and all civil officers of the United States, shall be removed from Office on Impeachment for, and conviction of, Treason, Bribery, or other high Crimes and Misdemeanors." Some observers have cited the "high Crimes and Misdemeanors" phrase to argue that only an indictable criminal act, not a ruling in a contested case, can be grounds for impeaching a federal judge. This view, however, is not universally shared. In 1833 the famed Justice Joseph Story explained in his Commentaries on the Constitution that "misdemeanor" refers to forms of misbehavior well beyond indictable criminal acts. According to Story, the impeachment power applies to "what are aptly termed, political offenses, growing out of personal misconduct, or gross neglect, or usurpation, or habitual disregard of the public interests." More recently, law professor Raoul Berger points out that "impeachment itself was conceived because the objects of impeachment for one reason or another were beyond the reach of ordinary criminal redress."

Yes, the most recent examples of judicial impeachments have all involved indictable criminal behavior on the part of the impeached judge. But in 1803, one of the impeachable offenses cited against Judge John Pickering was his failure to adhere to the requirements of an act of Congress, hardly a criminal act.…

Ultimately, it's up to the Congress to determine the proper grounds under the Constitution for impeaching a federal judge. The Supreme Court ruled just four years ago that matters governing impeachment are left to Congress and that the courts are powerless to review impeachment decisions (*Nixon v. United States*, 1993). Writing for the majority, Chief Justice William Rehnquist reasoned: "[j]udicial review [of impeachments] would be inconsistent with the Framers' insistence that our system be one of checks and balances. In our constitutional system, impeachment was designed to be the only check on the judicial branch by the Legislature.æ

As the 105th Congress looks at ways to curb the "imperial judiciary," it should consider breathing new life into its own impeachment authority. A very careful and highly selective use of this authority would send a powerful message to the federal bench that its renegade days are over.…

Joseph Story (1779–1845) is one of the most famous commentators on the Constitution. He was appointed to the Supreme Court by James Madison in 1811, the youngest person to be appointed to that position.

In the last days of his presidency John Adams, anxious to have judges sympathetic to his opinions in office, made many federal judicial appointments. His successor, Thomas Jefferson, opposed them and used impeachment to try to remove judges from office. John Pickering was the first judge to be impeached and convicted. In 1803 he was found guilty. He is believed to have been insane.

THE SENATE'S EPIC HYPOCRISY
Geoff Metcalf

Geoff Metcalf is a contributing writer for www.worldnetdaily.com and former talk-show host for TalkNetDaily.

NO

The duplicity and unbridled hypocrisy being demonstrated by United States Senate is sufficient to gag a maggot. Years ago an old family friend in the Senate presumed to clarify for me the difference between the House and Senate. He said, "The House of Representatives is inhabited by politicians ... the Senate is a collection of statesmen." What a pretentious, arrogant and flat out wrong claim.

Those Americans (both of you) who thought that the U.S. Senate would approach the most historically significant congressional event in 131 years with at least the perception of nonpartisan objectivity are in for a cruel reality check.

Before we even got to this muddy, tenuous and fuzzy procedural point, the stench of partisanship was wafting through the hollowed halls of Congress. Reportedly, the Senate has now (kinda, sorta) agreed to agree, on "something." The real trial of the century has begun. However, we as observers are not only witnesses to history, but an example of how "statesmen" herd cats.

The author uses strong language to portray his disgust with the system. He is critical without being offensive. Is he successful?

Last week Democrats were apparently prepared to punish a Democratic president of the United States without providing him the opportunity to hear and refute evidence and witnesses. Republicans were apparently prepared to offer the form of a trial, but with no resultant punishment. Now, in the wake of all the rancor, itching and moaning, they have agreed to agree to agree to change what they have agreed to ... maybe, as the process unfolds.

Judge Walter Nixon

One of the best examples of the disingenuous duplicity of the Democrat defenders of the indefensible was revealed in the January 1 Human Events piece about the impeachment of federal district Judge Walter Nixon. In 1989 the Senate voted 89–8 to approve an article of impeachment removing Nixon from the bench for making "false or misleading statements to a grand jury." Gee, that sounds familiar. So, in 1989, 27 of the 45 Democrats, who will sit in the next Senate to try William Jefferson Clinton, voted to remove Judge Nixon for ostensibly the same offenses they now claim are not sufficient to

The president in question was Bill Clinton. Go to Volume 2, Government, pages 200–201 for more information on this subject.

Senator Edward Kennedy is a member of the Senate Judiciary Committee. He voted to impeach Judge Walter L. Nixon in 1989.

Go to
www.google.com,
and search for
articles on both
Walter L. Nixon
and Bill Clinton.
Was Nixon treated
unfairly? Go to
http://www.npr.
org/news/national/
articlesofimpeach.
html—should
Clinton have been
impeached?

remove Billy Jeff. It is especially significant (at least to me) the similarity of the charges Judge Nixon was brought up on, and the charges against President Clinton, specifically: 1. Perjury and; 2. Obstruction of Justice.

OK, so who where these alleged "statesmen" who considered perjury and obstruction of justice impeachable offenses which warranted removing a federal judge from office? Some of them are conspicuous because of their stated positions on the current impeachment process. It is interesting (and hypocritical) that many of those 27 who voted to kick out Judge Nixon, now claim that although the president's conduct has been "reprehensible and egregious," there is (they claim) not sufficient reason to remove Clinton from office. Sen. Tom Daschle has been struggling to maintain the partisan iron curtain. Daschle voted to dump Judge Nixon for lying to a grand jury. Sen. Joe Biden has been petulant, adversarial, and absurd in his impeachment comments. Biden voted to dump Judge Nixon in 1989. Some of those who are posturing as reasonable and statesmanlike (like Sen. Robert Byrd, Sen. Joseph Lieberman, the Sens. Kerry, Joe and Bob) also voted to impeach in 1989 because Judge Nixon lied to a grand jury.

Should senators
who fail to do their
duty be removed
from office?

Alright, so here are the names of 27 Democratic senators who voted to impeach federal district Judge Walter Nixon for lying to a grand jury. I suggest that you contact these senators. They should to be hearing from all of us congratulating them on the wisdom of their vote to impeach in 1989 and demanding that they hold the president of the United States to at least the same high standard that they have set for federal district judges. If you are uncomfortable "demanding" perhaps you could ask them to explain the difference between their 1989 vote and their current position?

Jury tampering?

Eventually someone will challenge this as potential jury tampering. However, here is the dilemma of the political trial as opposed to a normal judicial proceeding. The White House will maintain communication with the Senate (the jury). They will claim the executive branch has not only the right but the fiduciary responsibility to communicate with Congress on non-impeachment matters. Presidential defenders will argue the impeachment proceedings should not gridlock routine business. Sen. Barbara Boxer, who claims there is no need for her to recuse herself because of the family connection recently had dinner with the president to

California
Democrat Senator
Barbara Boxer was
labeled a hypocrite
when she failed to
condemn President
Clinton's sexual
misconduct. Boxer
had earlier
criticized Supreme
Court nominee
Clarence Thomas
for very similar
behavior. Some
critics believe that
Boxer's views may
have been
influenced by
the fact that her
daughter is
married to Tony
Rodham, Hillary
Clinton's brother.

celebrate her husband's 60th birthday. Well, they can't (or should not) get to have it both ways. If the president is to be permitted to communicate with the senators who will sit as his jurors, then constituents should likewise have the right to communicate with their elected representatives.

These senators need to be reminded of how they voted for conviction of Judge Nixon and that to treat President Clinton (who has admitted his crime of perjury before the American people) to a lower standard is, at best, inappropriate, and at worst, hypocritical. His actions and those of the White House also clearly implicate him in obstruction of Justice as well.

The 27 Democratic senators who voted to impeach Judge Walter Nixon in 1989 are [included in the table below]:

SENATOR	STATE	SENATOR	STATE
Max Baucus	Mont.	Bob Kerry	Neb.
Joseph Biden	Del.	John Kerry	Mass.
Jeff Bingaman	NM	Herb Kohl	Wis.
John Breaux	La.	Frank Lautenberg	NJ
Richard Bryan	Nev.	Patrick Leahy	Vt.
Robert Byrd	WV	Carl Levin	Mich.
Kent Conrad	ND	Joseph Lieberman	Conn.
Tom Daschle	SD	Barbara Mikulski	MD
Chris Dodd	Conn.	D. Patrick Moynihan	NY
Bob Graham	FL	Harry Reid	Nev.
Tom Harkin	Iowa	Chuck Robb	VA
Fritz Hollings	SC	Jay Rockefeller	WV
Daniel Inouye	Hawaii	Paul Sarbanes	MD
Teddy Kennedy	Mass.		

By the way ... Vice President Al Gore was also in that senate, and HE voted to convict Judge Nixon.

Hypocrisy: "the act or practice of pretending to be what one is not or to have principles or beliefs that one does not have." Gee, that definition seems to not only crystallize the current status of the U.S. Senate, but also, defines a politician.

By quoting a definition of hypocrisy, the author underlines his point that the senators used double standards in the impeachment process.

Summary

These two articles offer two very different answers to the question: Is it too difficult to impeach federal judges?

In the first piece Dennis Shea worries that Congress has come to define too narrowly what constitutes an impeachable offense by federal judges. Whereas the most recent examples of judicial impeachments have involved indictable criminal behavior, as we have seen, Shea points out that in 1803 one of the articles of impeachment against John Pickering, the first federal judge to be removed from office through the impeachment process, was not a criminal act but rather his "failure to adhere to the requirements of an act of Congress." According to Shea, the impeachment process should be regarded as the "ultimate check" on what he calls the "imperial judiciary," the branch of government that in his view has repeatedly thwarted the will of democratic majorities on a range of policy matters.

Geoff Metcalf, on the other hand, compares the 1989 impeachment and removal from office of Judge Walter L. Nixon to the Senate acquittal 10 years later of President Bill Clinton on roughly similar charges—perjury and obstruction of justice. Metcalf chastises the 27 Democratic senators who voted for the conviction and removal from office of Judge Nixon yet were unwilling to do the same in the case of President Clinton. In sharp implicit contrast to Shea, Metcalf argues that the impeachment of federal judges, as opposed to the president, is not difficult because they are held to such a high standard of conduct.

FURTHER INFORMATION:

Books:

Goldman, Sheldon, *Picking Federal Judges: Lower Court Selection from Roosevelt through Reagan*. New Haven, CT: Yale University Press, 1997.

Useful websites:

http://www.artsci.wustl.edu/~polisci/calvert/PolSci3103/judiciary.html#impeaching
Looks at the impeachment of federal judges in the 19th century. Includes some useful links to articles.
http://www.eagleforum.org/psr/1997/mar97/psrmar97.html
Article that examines why it is time to hold federal judges accountable.
http://www.nlf.net/brief.html
Stephen W. Fitschen, president of the National Legal Foundation, looks at impeaching federal judges in this 27-page article.

The following debates in the Pro/Con series may also be of interest:

In this volume:
Part 1: The federal judiciary: Checks and balances,
pages 8–9

Topic 1 Is the Supreme Court too activist?

In *Government*:
The case of President Clinton: Politics and morality,
pages 200–201

IS IT TOO DIFFICULT TO IMPEACH FEDERAL JUDGES?

YES: There are many more reasons why a judge should be impeached than those outlined in the Constitution

YES: Only 12 judges have been impeached since the Constitution was ratified

CONSTITUTION
Is the Constitution too restrictive in the reasons why judges can be impeached?

FEW NUMBERS
Do the relatively few successful impeachments since 1789 prove the system is ineffective?

NO: Several successful impeachments of federal judges, including that of Judge Walter Nixon, prove that the system works—far better than the presidential impeachment system

NO: Although judges may sometimes act inappropriately, this is not good enough grounds for impeachment. It would be far too easy for the system to be abused if it were made easier.

IS IT TOO DIFFICULT TO IMPEACH FEDERAL JUDGES?
KEY POINTS

YES: Many judges make inappropriate or incorrect judgments. If senators have the right to impeach on these grounds, it would benefit the judiciary.

YES: Many judges should not be still sitting on the bench—if they are corrupt themselves, how can they make judgments on other people's conduct?

THREATS
Should senators be able to start impeachment proceedings against judges based on alleged bad court decisions?

NEGATIVE EFFECT
Has the difficult system of impeachment had a negative effect on the federal judiciary's quality?

NO: This is completely unconstitutional and would just end up being ammunition that could be used against more liberal judgments

NO: Impeachment acts as a deterrent. Active judges are well suited to do their jobs.

Topic 5

SHOULD SUPREME COURT CANDIDATES BE ASKED THEIR VIEWS ON LEGAL ISSUES DURING CONFIRMATION PROCEEDINGS?

YES
"THE RIGHT TO ASK"
NCJW JOURNAL: THE FIGHT FOR CHOICE, SPRING 2002
MARCIA GREENBERGER

NO
"WHY LITMUS TESTS THREATEN THE INTEGRITY OF OUR COURTS"
OCTOBER 1999
BRENNAN CENTER FOR JUSTICE

INTRODUCTION

Article II, section 2, of the Constitution specifies that the president "shall nominate, and by and with the Advice and Consent of the Senate, shall appoint … Judges of the Supreme Court." This means that when there is a vacancy on the Supreme Court, the president names potential candidates to fill the position, and the Senate Judiciary Committee conducts confirmation hearings to ascertain the nominee's suitability before sending it to a vote on the full Senate floor.

There has, however, been much debate over the type of questions that senators should be allowed to ask candidates during these proceedings. In particular, commentators query the legitimacy of senators asking probing questions on controversial issues and cases. Some critics argue that such

behavior drags political partisanship into the process and thus undermines judicial independence. Others counter that senators have a constitutional obligation to make sure that the candidates are suitable for confirmation.

The appointment of a justice to the Supreme Court is a matter of crucial importance. Whereas a president serves eight years at most, justices have life tenureship. Moreover, the decisions that the Supreme Court makes affect many aspects of American life. A new justice may have a role in determining issues such as whether abortion remains legal, or whether considerations about race can be used in college admissions.

With so much at stake, some commentators insist that senators have every right to carefully scrutinize the judicial philosophy of a Supreme Court nominee. They support the practice of "litmus testing" a candidate—that is, asking the nominee his or her views on hot-button questions of law in order to elicit how he or she would decide particular cases. For example, a common litmus test is to inquire of candidates whether they have made a commitment to upholding *Roe v. Wade*, the 1973 ruling that gave women the constitutional right to have an abortion.

> *"What we want in our federal judges are people who have strong opinions about the law and the Constitution."*
>
> —MATTHEW J. FRANCK,
>
> POLITICAL SCIENTIST (2003)

Critics protest that such aggressive questioning amounts to using political ideology to screen judicial nominees. They claim that this threatens the impartiality of the Supreme Court. Critics insist that candidates should refrain from answering politically loaded questions since they could be accused of prejudging a case that may subsequently come before them in court. They say that for a judge to reveal his or her views on a legal issue goes against the fundamental principle of approaching each new case with an open mind. They suggest that senators should instead pay more attention to a candidate's experience, intellect, and character. In the past, senators relied on a nominee's reputation and written record of decisions for purposes of

confirmation; it is only since the mid-20th century that nominees have routinely testified before the Judiciary Committee. Some commentators say that Supreme Court candidates have been particularly wary of voicing an opinion on any important legal topic in confirmation hearings since the Senate rejected outspoken conservative candidate Robert Bork in 1987 (see pages 72–73).

However, advocates contend that ideological litmus tests promote honesty and transparency in a process that is inescapably political. They argue that is especially important to establish a candidate's position on controversial legal issues in cases in which a candidate lacks a "paper trail"—a history of published decisions or articles. Proponents also claim that litmus testing nominees is the only way to ensure that senators confirm justices who will preserve the people's hard-won civil rights and individual liberties. They point to the confirmation hearings of Justice Clarence Thomas in 1991. Thomas repeatedly insisted that he had not formulated an opinion on legal abortion. But just months after his appointment to the Supreme Court he stated that *Roe v. Wade* was wrongly decided. Since then some politicians and lawyers have stressed the need to question judicial nominees more rigorously. After all, they say, it is not plausible that an experienced judge has no views on a decision as contentious as *Roe*. Others argue, however, that there is a danger that nominees will simply say whatever they think senators want to hear and then seek to reverse legal decisions once they are on the bench.

The following articles examine these issues in further detail.

THE RIGHT TO ASK
Marcia Greenberger

Marcia Greenberger is copresident of the National Women's Law Center. The information in this article, which appeared in the spring 2002 issue of NCJW Journal: The Fight for Choice, was first presented by Greenberger to the Senate Judiciary Subcommittee on Administrative Oversight and the Courts in June 2001.

YES

Scholars and commentators across the ideological spectrum agree that it is appropriate, and indeed necessary, for senators to inquire into, and base their confirmation votes on, judicial nominees' positions and views on substantive areas of law. This is nothing new. There is ample historical precedent for the Senate to consider judicial philosophy in considering judicial nominations—dating back to George Washington's nomination of John Rutledge as Chief Justice in 1795 and his rejection by the Senate on the basis of his views. The "advise and consent" language of the Constitution itself, and the history of the framers' adoption of this formulation, make it clear that the Constitution creates an independent role and set of responsibilities for the Senate in the confirmation process.

As in so many other ways, the framers of the Constitution were right. The judiciary, after all, is independent from the Executive and Legislative branches, and indeed is sometimes called upon to resolve disputes between the two. If the President were given a superior role in judicial appointments, it would upset the neutrality of the judiciary and the system of checks and balances of which it is a part. Unlike Cabinet members or other appointments to the Executive branch, judges do not work for the President or serve at the pleasure of the President only while he (or someday, she) is in office. So while it may be appropriate for senators to give deference to a President's choices of the personnel who will work for him and implement his policies in the departments and agencies of the federal government, it would be entirely inappropriate to give deference to the President's selection of judicial candidates.

Statistics show that as of mid-2004, the Senate had rejected 27 of 148 Supreme Court appointments, but only 9 of more than 700 cabinet appointees. Go to http://www.senate.gov/artandhistory/history/common/briefing/Nominations.htm for more information.

The standards senators should apply

Senators hold the tremendous power and responsibility to "advise and consent" on federal judicial nominees. How they exercise that power and responsibility, the degree to which they are demanding and thorough in examining the records and views of the nominees that come before them, and the extent to which they are willing to assert their Constitutional prerogative to say "no" when appropriate, will have a tremendous impact on the lives of American citizens for many years to come.

In light of all that is at stake, and the Senate's constitutional responsibility to determine who will be entrusted with life tenure on the bench, the Senate must scrutinize the fitness of judicial nominees with extraordinary care. In addition to meeting the necessary requirements of honesty, integrity, character, temperament, and intellect, to be confirmed to a federal judgeship a nominee should be required to demonstrate a commitment to protecting the rights of ordinary American citizens and the progress that has been made on civil rights and individual liberties, including those core constitutional principles that protect women's legal rights under the Equal Protection Clause and the right to privacy (which includes contraception and abortion) as well as the statutory provisions that protect women's legal rights in such fundamental areas as education, employment, and health and safety.

Tackling "the large issues of the day"

Senators therefore have a duty to study a nominee's record and to probe during the confirmation hearing in order to form a judgment about what kind of jurist the nominee will be, based on judicial philosophy and the nominee's views on what are called "the large issues of the day." This does not mean asking a nominee for his or her personal views on questions of religion or morality or how he or she has voted on ballot measures in the privacy of the voting booth. But it does mean, as reflected in past practice, probing into a nominee's views on the correctness of important Supreme Court precedents establishing the right to privacy and its application in *Roe v. Wade* (1973), or the appropriate standard of scrutiny under the Equal Protection Clause for sex- or race-based classifications. A nominee's previous writings or statements should be taken seriously.

Carrying out the Senate's responsibility also means that if a nominee has little or no relevant record, he or she bears the burden of assuring the Senate of his or her commitment on key issues and principles. This is particularly important when, as is currently the case, there is a President in office who has made clear that he is looking for judicial nominees of a particular type, in this case those in the mold of Justices Thomas and Scalia. The White House and Justice Department have the opportunity and ability to thoroughly vet potential nominees, before they are sent to the Senate, to ensure that

The Equal Protection clause of the Fourteenth Amendment prohibits states from denying any person within its jurisdiction the equal protection of the law. This means that the laws of a state must treat an individual in the same manner as others in similar conditions and circumstances. The clause is crucial to the protection of civil rights.

Do you think it is difficult for a judge to separate his or her legal opinion on an issue such as abortion from his or her moral view?

As a presidential candidate in 2000, George W. Bush said he would try to fill any Supreme Court vacancy with judges like Antonin Scalia (1936–) and Clarence Thomas (1948–), who are widely accepted to be the most conservative on the bench.

COMMENTARY: The Thomas hearings

In July 1991 President George Bush nominated Clarence Thomas (1948–), a judge on the U.S. Court of Appeals for the District of Columbia Circuit, to be an associate justice on the Supreme Court, replacing Thurgood Marshall (1908–1993). In his previous positions as assistant secretary for civil rights in the Education Department and chairman of the Equal Employment Opportunity Commission Thomas had become known as an outspoken conservative. Some people feared that his stance on issues such as affirmative action would reverse the progress on civil rights that Marshall had fought to achieve during his time on the bench.

The Senate Judiciary Committee conducted confirmation hearings during September 1991. Thomas himself testified for five days. Controversy about whether he was sufficiently qualified to serve on the Supreme Court split the committee's vote, and it sent the matter to the Senate floor without endorsing the nomination. Meanwhile, Anita Hill (1956–), a professor of law at the University of Oklahoma, had come forward with allegations that Thomas had sexually harassed her when she was his assistant in the 1980s.

"High-tech lynching"

The FBI interviewed both Hill and Thomas, and sent a report to the Judiciary Committee. Hill's allegations became public after part of the report was leaked, forcing the committee to reopen hearings in October. Amid great media interest Thomas, Hill, and other witnesses testified before the committee for several days. Thomas, who strenuously denied the allegations, likened the televised proceedings to a "high-tech lynching for uppity blacks." The full Senate debated the nomination and finally confirmed Thomas as associate justice on October 16, 1991, by a vote of 52 to 48—the closest margin in a century. Some women expressed dismay over the appointment. They felt that the Senate, which was 98 percent male, had not taken Hill's claims seriously.

> Greenberger implies that politics can never be entirely removed from the process of nominating and confirming federal judges; do you agree?

those nominees do indeed fit the President's judicial philosophy requirements. Thus, it is fair to assume that a judicial candidate who appears in his or her confirmation hearing to be a blank slate has revealed him or herself to be nothing of the kind. The Senate, then, must satisfy itself as to the nominee's views on critical issues. Nominees who refuse to provide insights into their judicial philosophy have failed to meet their burden.

A case in point

These points can be illustrated with a brief look at the confirmation hearings of Clarence Thomas to the Supreme

Court (before Anita Hill's allegations of sexual harassment surfaced), and specifically what happened when he was asked about his views on *Roe*. Then-Judge Thomas had a prior written record of his views on *Roe* but attempted to explain them away during his hearing. Asked about his enthusiastic praise of an antiabortion polemic by the Heritage Foundation's Lewis Lehrman he explained that he had merely skimmed the article and was praising it for a different reason. Other writings he disowned by explaining that he wasn't a Supreme Court Justice when he wrote them, so they had no relevance to what he would do on the Court. At the same time, Justice Thomas repeatedly insisted that he had no ideological agenda on the right to choose and had a completely open mind. Others pressed him again and again, and he simply refused to say what he thought.

In the face of all of these assurances of a completely open mind, a mere eight months after this testimony Justice Thomas joined Justices Rehnquist, Scalia, and White in a Rehnquist opinion that said, "We believe that Roe was wrongly decided, and that it can and should be overruled consistent with our traditional approach to stare decisis in constitutional cases." And he has not wavered from this view. Just last year Justice Thomas wrote that Roe was "grievously wrong."

Conclusion

The stakes are too high—especially on such a closely-divided Supreme Court, and Courts of Appeals that already reflect an imbalance to the right—to allow nominees to walk away from their pasts or to shield their views and ideology from Senate and public scrutiny. Most dramatically, *Roe v. Wade* now has only a 5–4 majority in the Supreme Court. (And since the Supreme Court considers only a tiny fraction of the cases sent to it by the appellate courts, judges on the Courts of Appeals have enormous power.) No judicial nominee enjoys a presumption in favor of confirmation. Rather, as numerous legal scholars have shown, it is the nominee who carries the burden of convincing the Senate that he or she should be confirmed, and any doubts should be resolved against confirmation. No person has an entitlement to a lifetime seat on the federal bench, and if a nominee cannot clearly satisfy the Senate that he or she meets all of the criteria for confirmation, the American people should not be asked to bear the risk of entrusting that individual with the reigns of judicial power.

The Heritage Foundation (www.heritage.org) is a right-wing think tank. It was founded in 1973.

The subject of Roe arose again in 2003 during the confirmation hearings of Miguel Estrada, a conservative who was nominated for a seat on the influential U.S. Court of Appeals for the District of Columbia Circuit by President George W. Bush. Like Thomas, Estrada was not forthcoming with his legal opinion of Roe. Go to http://writ.corporate.findlaw.com/lazarus/20030220.html for an analysis by Edward Lazarus.

According to some estimates, the court hears fewer than 250 cases every year, which is less than 5 percent of the total number that it is petitioned to review.

WHY LITMUS TESTS THREATEN THE INTEGRITY OF OUR COURTS
Brennan Center for Justice

The Brennan Center for Justice at New York University School of Law is a nonpartisan institute that aims to find solutions to problems in the areas of democracy, poverty, and criminal justice. This article, dated 1999, appears on the center's website (www. brennancenter.org).

NO

The next President of the United States may have the opportunity to appoint several Supreme Court Justices, and will almost certainly appoint hundreds of lower federal court judges, thereby establishing a judicial legacy for decades to come. With so much at stake, the Brennan Center for Justice at NYU School of Law has examined the candidates' positions on judicial selection. Regrettably, one of the most frequent refrains emerging from the presidential campaigns is the uncritical endorsement of "litmus tests," a selection method that undermines the independence of our third branch of government.

The use of litmus tests is also increasingly common in the U.S. Senate. The Constitution empowers the Senate to provide "Advice and Consent" with respect to judicial nominations but leaves that power undefined. Senators seeking to advance their own political agendas have therefore pushed the limits of their constitutional authority by making ideological orthodoxy on controversial issues a prerequisite for judicial confirmation.

"It is unclear whether the presidential candidates and the Senators who use litmus tests appreciate the grave risks such tests present to our constitutional democracy," said Brennan Center staff attorney Mark Kozlowski, who writes frequently on issues of judicial independence. "Our Constitution establishes not only the executive and legislative branches of government, but also an independent and co-equal judiciary." As the Brennan Center explains below, litmus tests threaten the integrity of our courts and are therefore fundamentally inconsistent with that constitutional mandate.

The author structures the debate by organizing the main issues under subheadings in the form of simple questions. This can be an effective way to make your points clear to the audience.

What is a litmus test?

A litmus test is a standard that qualifies or disqualifies potential judicial nominees on the basis of the holdings they would issue with respect to a particular case, or a class of related cases, that they may be asked to decide if appointed to the bench. The most common litmus test asks whether potential judges have made a commitment to overrule or

uphold *Roe v. Wade*, the 1973 U.S. Supreme Court ruling that
gave women the constitutional right to an abortion. Another
litmus test evaluates judicial nominees in accordance with
their views about capital punishment. The use of litmus tests
thus politicizes the process of selecting judges who are
supposed to be neutral when deciding cases.

What is judicial independence?

Judicial independence is the freedom of judges to act as
principled decision-makers, approaching the facts of each
case with an open mind and unclouded judgment. When
truly independent, judges are not influenced by personal
interests or relationships, the identity or status of the parties
to a case, or external economic or political pressures.
Achieving this ideal requires a combination of individual
character and societal practices that encourage courts to
decide each case purely on its merits.

> *Do you think any judge can ever truly achieve the ideal approach to deciding a case that the author outlines here?*

What is the problem with litmus tests?

Litmus tests impede judicial independence and undermine
our ability to select the best judges. In particular, litmus tests:

> *By refusing to answer an ideological litmus test, do you think a nominee is being less than honest?*

- distort the Advice and Consent process by fomenting
senatorial debate about how a nominee is likely to rule in
particular cases rather than about the nominee's intellect,
honesty, and other relevant qualifications;
- reduce the pool of distinguished candidates, and thus
depress the quality of the judiciary overall, by discouraging
the nomination of people with a substantial written record
or history of involvement in public affairs that could fuel
opposition to them;
- foster partisan attacks that trivialize the judicial selection
process and undermine confidence in surviving nominees;
- place pressure on judges to act as proponents of ideology
rather than as impartial adjudicators of disputes;
- increase the potential for and appearance of biased
decision-making and thus erode public trust in the
fundamental fairness of our justice system; and
- diminish our ability to rely on the judiciary to defend
individual rights against overreaching by the executive
and legislative branches.

> *Some commentators argue that without the ability to be openly ideological in confirmation hearings, some senators have resorted in the past to blocking a nomination over more trivial matters, such as minor financial improprieties. They claim that this practice is actually more damaging to the reputation of both the Senate and the judiciary. Do you agree?*

Judging is a difficult job. It demands keen intellectual acumen
and an unswerving commitment to justice, fairness, and
human dignity. Judging is also an extremely important job. We
rely on judges to solve our disputes and to protect our hard-

In June 2001 the Senate Judiciary Subcommittee on Administrative Oversight and the Courts, chaired by Democrat Charles Schumer, called to order a hearing entitled "Should Ideology Matter? Judicial Nominations 2001." Its aim was to look at ways to reform the confirmation process. Go to http://judiciary.senate.gov/oldsite/hr062601sc.htm to read the proceedings.

won liberties. Our judicial selection procedures should therefore be designed to identify candidates of the very highest caliber and to safeguard their independence of judgment. Litmus tests do precisely the opposite.

What types of inquiries are acceptable?

The Constitution allows the President and Senate to ask probing questions regarding the nominee's overall legal acumen, judicial philosophy, temperament, and commitment to fairness and impartiality. For example, when a nominee is seeking to advance to a higher court, it is entirely appropriate to examine the nominee's legal reasoning in prior cases for evidence of open-mindedness and willingness to consider each case on its own merits. Inquiries into other relevant aspects of a nominee's character—his or her reputation for probity, patience, discipline, industry, and the like—are also legitimate. In short, questioning should be designed to test whether nominees will conduct themselves as judges in a manner that commands respect and trust.

Compare Thomas's account of his nomination interview with President George Bush with the account that Greenberger gives of his Senate confirmation hearings on page 65.

Are litmus tests a partisan issue?

Litmus tests should be rejected by the left and the right, Democrats and Republicans alike. U.S. Supreme Court Justice Clarence Thomas, a noted conservative, recently praised former President George Bush for not having asked him any questions regarding how he would rule on particular cases that might come before the Court: "At no time did the president have a litmus test.… The president recognized the independence of the judiciary." (*The Des Moines Register*, July 14, 1999, at 6.) Similarly, Stephen L. Carter, a Yale law professor of decidedly more liberal views, argues that, when faced with a litmus test, a judicial nominee should respond, "with respect, I have no settled view on that. When I see the issue fully briefed and argued in the context of a specific case, I will make up my mind." (*The Confirmation Mess*, p. 84.) Clearly, both conservatives and liberals should agree that requiring judges to commit to specific holdings prior to hearing a particular case is bad for our democracy.

If you were interviewing someone for a job, would an answer such as "I don't know" be acceptable to you? Should an exception be made for judges?

Conclusion

James Madison called courts "independent tribunals of justice" that he hoped would serve as "an impenetrable bulwark against every assumption of power" that threatens constitutional rights and liberties. (The Congressional Register, June 8, 1789.) To remain independent, judges must not be subjected to litmus tests on politically-loaded issues.

Clarence Thomas during the Senate Judiciary Committee confirmation hearings in 1991.

As the 2000 election nears, Americans should remain attentive to the statements and actions of both presidential candidates and Senators regarding the judiciary. Politicians who advocate the use of litmus tests in the selection of federal judges should be pressed to explain why their views of the third branch of government differ so starkly from the conviction espoused by the framers of our Constitution.

Summary

Marcia Greenberger argues that it is necessary for senators to inquire into the legal views of federal judicial nominees. She contends that how senators use their great power to "advise and consent" on nominees has a huge effect on people's lives. Greenberger insists that as well as considering the integrity, character, and intellect of nominees, senators should probe into candidates' views on "the large issues of the day." She says that nominees have a burden to demonstrate a commitment to civil liberties and to important precedents, such as the right to privacy and its application to the law on abortion. Greenberger cites the confirmation hearings of Clarence Thomas, who was not forthcoming about his views on abortion but later called the *Roe* decision "grievously wrong." She concludes that it is dangerous to entrust nominees with "the reigns of judicial power" if they do not meet all the confirmation criteria.

The Brennan Center for Justice argues that using ideological litmus tests during confirmation proceedings undermines the independence of the judiciary. Although the Constitution empowers the Senate to advise and consent on judicial nominations, the center holds that it "leaves that power undefined." The center argues that senators who try to advance their own political agendas "have pushed the limits of their constitutional authority by making ideological orthodoxy on controversial issues a prerequisite for judicial confirmation." It concludes that it is appropriate to inquire into a nominee's ability, temperament, commitment to impartiality, and so on, but that litmus tests on politically loaded issues will not lead to an independent judiciary, as envisaged by the Framers.

FURTHER INFORMATION:

Books:

Baugh, Joyce A., *Supreme Court Justices in the Post-Bork Era: Confirmation Politics and Judicial Performance*. New York: Peter Lang, 2002.

Carter, Stephen L., *The Confirmation Mess: Cleaning Up the Federal Appointments Process*. New York: Basic Books, 1994.

Maltese, John Anthony, *The Selling of Supreme Court Nominees*. Baltimore, MD: John Hopkins University Press, 1995.

Useful websites:

http://www.heritage.org/Research/LegalIssues/HL740.cfm

"The State of the Judicial Confirmation Process" by Mitch McConnell.

http://judiciary.senate.gov

Official site of the United States Senate Judiciary Committee, with full reports available.

http://www.theatlantic.com/issues/2003/03/york.htm

"Back to Bork?" by Byron York.

The following debates in the Pro/Con series may also be of interest:

In this volume:
Topic 2 Are politics too influential in the selection of federal judges?

The Bork nomination,
pages 72–73

SHOULD SUPREME COURT CANDIDATES BE ASKED THEIR VIEWS ON LEGAL ISSUES DURING CONFIRMATION PROCEEDINGS?

YES: No judicial nominee is a blank slate. Senators need to satisfy themselves about a nominee's views on critical issues like abortion and affirmative action.

YES: The Senate neglects its duty if it confirms a nominee in ignorance of his or her views, and it cannot "advise" or meaningfully "consent" without relevant information

INDEPENDENCE

Does asking nominees controversial legal questions preserve the independence of the judiciary?

CONSTITUTIONAL DUTY

Do senators have a duty to inquire into nominees' legal views?

NO: It politicizes the process of confirming judges, who are supposed to be neutral, and therefore threatens the impartiality of the judiciary

NO: The Constitution empowers the Senate to "advise and consent" on judicial nominations, but it does not define that power. Senators are pushing the limits of their constitutional authority by using litmus tests.

SHOULD SUPREME COURT CANDIDATES BE ASKED THEIR VIEWS ON LEGAL ISSUES DURING CONFIRMATION PROCEEDINGS?

KEY POINTS

YES: It is essential that nominees demonstrate a commitment to protecting hard-won civil rights and liberties. This necessitates answering questions on the big legal issues of the day.

YES: There have been cases of well-qualified, experienced nominees refusing to answer questions or answering dishonestly at confirmation proceedings. Senators must therefore interview candidates rigorously.

PHILOSOPHY

Is a nominee's judicial philosophy a good indication of his or her suitability as a justice?

NO: Factors such as a nominee's legal acumen, temperament, and commitment to fairness are the best indication of what kind of judge he or she will be

NO: Forcing a candidate to answer politically loaded questions amounts to prejudging cases and undermines the neutrality of the judiciary

THE BORK NOMINATION

"The court plays a bigger role in political matters ... it has to expect to be subject to the types of political checks that other institutions are."
—NORMAN VIERA, *SUPREME COURT APPOINTMENTS: JUDGE BORK AND THE POLITICIZATION OF SENATE CONFIRMATIONS*

Former solicitor general and U.S. Court of Appeals Judge Robert Bork (1927–) is a well-known commentator on U.S. law. Bork has been the focus of media attention on many occasions over the years, but never more so than when President Ronald Reagan nominated him as a Supreme Court justice in 1987. After long and acrimonious proceedings Bork's candidacy was turned down. Many believe that this has had longlasting effects on the nomination and confirmation process.

Public notoriety

Robert Heron Bork was born in Pittsburgh in 1927. He received his law degree from the University of Chicago in 1953. Bork achieved public notoriety when in his capacity as solicitor general he fired special prosecutor Archibald Cox, who was investigating President Richard Nixon's involvement in Watergate (see Volume 2, *Government, The Watergate Affair*, pages 172-173) on Nixon's orders. His action proved fruitless: The full extent of Nixon's involvement became known anyway. Bork remained solicitor general until 1977, after which he taught at Yale Law School. Bork was appointed a judge for the U.S. Court of Appeals for the District of Columbia Circuit in 1982, where he remained until 1988.

Powell's retirement

Following the announcement of Supreme Court Justice Lewis Powell's retirement on June 26, 1987, commentators began to speculate on the identity of his successor. Bork, who was seen as one of the most astute legal scholars of the time, seemed a natural candidate. When President Reagan exercised his constitutional right and nominated him, few were surprised, but many were opposed to it. The position was important: The Supreme Court had grown increasingly more powerful in the postwar decades, and many believed that decisions on key issues—such as contentious civil rights matters—were legislated from the bench. Powell's replacement could overturn controversial but important legal decisions.

In 1987 Bork was already a prominent public figure. He was known for his extremely conservative position on a number of civil rights issues—he had opposed decisions on abortion and the right to privacy in the past. While few doubted Bork's intellectual suitability for the position, his extreme views and often quite narrow interpretation of the Constitution had brought him many critics.

Organized campaigning and Senate intervention

Some commentators have argued that pre-Bork the Senate had a narrowly defined role in confirmation proceedings: For the most part senators considered the nominee's qualifications and integrity, but to a lesser extent his or her judicial opinions or philosophy. Some legal scholars believe that the Senate subjected Bork's judicial ideology to greater scrutiny than ever before. Critics counter that Ronald Reagan's administration opened the doors to do this since, in trying to stem the tide of liberal activism, the Justice Department had introduced an intensive screening of nominees on ideological grounds. When Reagan nominated Bork, the Democrat-controlled Senate delayed the confirmation hearings for two months. The delay gave Bork's supporters—including conservative think tanks and prolife groups—time to arm themselves, but it also gave Bork's critics time to act.

The anti-Bork league comprised a diverse range of groups, some of whom had never been involved in opposing a judicial nominee before. Women's groups joined together with environmental agencies, and health and consumer groups, such as Planned Parenthood and the Sierra Club, fought with them. Both anti- and pro-Bork groups used methods never really seen before in judicial campaigns to fight their battle—including advertising campaigns, direct mail, and fundraising. By the time the hearings began on September 15, 1987, both lobbies had spent over $20 million in either praising or demonizing Bork.

During the confirmation proceedings the Senate called 112 witnesses—a much greater number than usual. Although the witnesses were carefully questioned on a number of issues, and some were critical of Bork's attitudes, commentators believe that it was Bork himself who did the most damage to his nomination. Questioned for five days—longer than any other candidate—Bork moderated his views on several issues. Critics believe that he still appeared arrogant and insensitive— a man so sure of his own opinions that he seemed dismissive of the ideological perspective of others, including those of his own legal peers. When questioned about specific rulings, Bork showed contempt for the judicial reasoning rather than the actual outcome of some court cases—this, some believe, alienated previously sympathetic members of the legal profession. The Senate Judiciary Committee voted against the nomination by 9 to 5 votes. Although it was evident to most people that Bork would lose a full Senate vote, he refused to withdraw his candidacy. In the end the Senate turned down the nomination by 42–58.

The legacy

Political commentators believe that Bork's nomination has had longlasting effects on judicial selection proceedings. Presidents have been more careful to put forward names of more moderate candidates for fear that they might otherwise stir up the same kind of frenzy that followed Bork's nomination. Candidates are more careful about voicing opinions on politically sensitive issues—Clarence Thomas, for example, refused to discuss abortion on the grounds that he had never debated the subject. The most important effect, however, has been the Senate's closer interest in the confirmation process. Critics believe that the increased politicization of the selection procedure has adversely affected the standard of the federal judiciary.

Topic 6

SHOULD FEDERAL JUDICIAL APPLICANTS HAVE TO MEET A FORMAL SET OF REQUIREMENTS?

YES

"BUSH ENDS AMERICAN BAR ASSOCIATION'S PRESCREENING OF JUDICIAL NOMINEES"
WORLD SOCIALIST WEBSITE, APRIL 6, 2001
JOHN ANDREWS

NO

FROM "REMARKS BY THE PRESIDENT ON JUDICIAL INDEPENDENCE
AND THE JUDICIAL CONFIRMATION PROCESS"
OFFICE OF THE PRESS SECRETARY, THE WHITE HOUSE,
IN FOCUS: JUDICIAL NOMINATIONS, MAY 9, 2003
GEORGE W. BUSH

INTRODUCTION

Under the Constitution all Supreme Court justices, court of appeals judges, and district court judges are nominated by the president and confirmed by the Senate. Article II, section 2, of the Constitution gives the Senate responsibility for considering and confirming the president's executive and judicial nominations; Article III guarantees judicial independence by giving judges lifetime appointments and salary security. However, no provision was made for the requirements that judicial nominees should have to meet.

While some people argue that the existing system has worked effectively for centuries and that the president with the help of the Senate makes sure that only the best and most qualified candidates are nominated, others claim that this is not the case. They believe that since these appointments have such an important effect on they way in which U.S. citizens may live their lives, it is crucial that the right people are chosen and that politics stays out of the decision-making process. They claim that a more formal set of criteria for nominee selection is necessary, and that if candidates were to meet universally accepted standards, many of the logjams and problems from which the current system suffers would simply disappear.

For many the American Bar Association (ABA) ensured through its rating system that candidates met the requirements necessary to hold a federal judicial appointment. In 2001, however, President George W. Bush decided that the ABA was not impartial, and he took away its right to be involved in the early evaluation process.

Some critics believe that this occurred because Bush was worried that the ABA would stand in the way of his more right-wing nominations.

Most presidents have nominated candidates sympathetic to their own views: When Thomas Jefferson won the 1800 election, for example, John Adams, the outgoing president, staffed the federal judiciary with judges who would limit the success of Republican legislative reforms, with the result that Jefferson spent much of his own presidency trying to get rid of them. More recently, successive presidents have had their judicial nominations blocked, sometimes by senators from the opposition and other times because the nominee made a court decision to which certain Senate members objected. This politicization of the process has had a negative effect on the quality of the judiciary, critics claim.

> *"The new Senate leadership is racing to confirm judges for lifetime appointments without ... fair consideration to ... their ... philosophy."*
> —MARCIA GREENBERGER, NATIONAL WOMEN'S LAW CENTER

Since the Framers conceived the Constitution in a very different world, some legal scholars believe that they would understand that the judiciary plays a far more important role in U.S. life today than could ever have been imagined possible in 1789. Sanford Levinson, professor of government at the University of Texas, has stated that it would have been impossible then for a supporter of the abstract idea of judicial review to contemplate "the role that courts would come to play in our political life, including decisions ... regarding some of the most important political issues before the country...." Therefore, advocates may argue that the system of selection through a mix of "law and custom" has served the United States well. But if Levinson is right, then it is all the more important to make sure that there is an efficient system of evaluating the nominee's suitability for the job. For many the ABA provided that very solution for almost 50 years.

Although some argue that the ABA was far too liberal and that its ranking of nominees was often biased, supporters claim that the ABA, in considering professional competence, integrity, and judicial temperament, provided nonpartisan law-focused professional advice on nominees. It has never, they claim, considered ideology or philosophy in any evaluation. They also argue that the ABA played a crucial role in giving advice to the president when it judged a nominee to be unsuitable. This allowed the president time to back out of his endorsement gracefully. Although the ABA is still able to give its recommendations at a much later stage, it would not be possible for the president to act on this advice without it affecting his credibility, critics believe. They further claim that the Bush administration's decision to prevent the ABA from vetting nominees at an early stage can only result in a weakening of the federal judiciary and the public's confidence in it over time.

The following extracts examine the issue in greater depth.

BUSH ENDS AMERICAN BAR ASSOCIATION'S PRESCREENING...
John Andrews

John Andrews writes for the World Socialist Website.

YES

The Bush Administration last month broke with the U.S. government's 50-year-old practice of using a special committee of the American Bar Association (ABA) to screen presidential nominees to federal judgeships. The ABA has been reviewing prospective presidential appointees to the federal bench for professional competence prior to their identities being made public since it was first requested to do so by the Eisenhower administration.

ABA: a politically active group?

Bush spokesmen claimed the new administration was discontinuing the ABA review process because it did not want to "grant a preferential, quasi-official role in the judicial selection process to a politically active group." As with most statements emanating from the White House, this rationale is hardly credible. Far from seeking to depoliticize the appointment process, the administration is discontinuing ABA review of judicial nominees to facilitate the appointment of right-wing ideologues to lifetime positions at all levels of the federal judiciary, with minimal regard for judicial competence, integrity or temperament. The result will be to tighten further the extreme right's hold on the federal court system and intensify the attack on democratic rights.

Just because a federal judicial nominee is put forward by a president of a certain political persuasion, does this mean that he or she will necessarily make biased legal decisions?

Historical precedent

The ABA began its review program in 1948 at the behest of the Senate Judiciary Committee, which acted in response to complaints that federal judicial appointments had become too political and ideological, and the quality of federal judges was suffering as a result. In 1953, Republican Dwight D. Eisenhower became the first president to use the ABA to screen potential nominees before submitting them to the Senate for confirmation.

If an outside body is so essential to the nomination vetting process, why did early U.S. presidents not use one to help in judicial nomination decisions?

For the last five decades, the identities of potential nominees have been provided to a 15-member ABA Standing Committee, whose members and staff contact lawyers, judges and other people familiar with the nominee. Eventually the

Standing Committee rates each potential nominee "well qualified," "qualified" or "not qualified." Faced with an unfavorable rating, a president has had the option of declining to nominate the individual, or encouraging the individual to withdraw, thus avoiding an embarrassing public vetting of damaging information.

The ABA, long considered an authoritative voice of the legal establishment, is hardly a captive of liberal or left-wing sentiment. The charge that its review process is biased against right-wing nominees is manifestly false. Some 2,000 nominees have been rated by the ABA. Only 26 have been rated "not qualified," and 23 of those were nominated by Democratic administrations.

… Now, with the ABA no longer pre-screening nominees, the Bush administration will have a freer hand to nominate ideologically extreme judges in their place, whether or not they meet basic standards of competence.

The politicization of the federal judiciary has been instrumental in the right wing's efforts to expand its political influence far beyond its numbers and narrow social base. The strategy paid major dividends last December, when the right-wing majority on the Supreme Court threw aside any pretext of following legal doctrine and halted the vote count in Florida, thus allowing Republican George W. Bush—who lost the national popular vote—to obtain the electoral votes needed to win the White House….

The current majority

The current majority, Rehnquist and Associate Justices Sandra Day O'Connor, Antonin Scalia, Anthony Kennedy and Thomas, are responsible for decisions repudiating much of the precedent favoring civil rights and civil liberties created during the Supreme Court's years under Chief Justice Earl Warren. The current majority, for example, has resurrected the doctrine of "states' rights" to immunize state governments from federal anti-discrimination laws, while limiting state power to enforce anti-discrimination laws in state courts. The high court has also limited federal power under the Constitution's "Commerce Clause" in order to gut laws protecting individuals and the environment. While scaling back privacy rights and the protections afforded people accused of crimes, it has enshrined the "right" of private organizations such as the Boy Scouts to practice discrimination.

Owing his presidency to the right-wing majority on the Supreme Court, Bush will carry out his campaign promise to

What kind of factors do you think would count toward an unfavorable rating? Look up the ABA website on www.google.com to find out.

Do you think unsuitable candidates would be weeded out by the Senate during confirmation proceedings?

Appointed to the Supreme Court in 1953, Earl Warren (1891–1974) became famous for his landmark civil liberties decisions. Sandra Day O'Connor (1930–) was appointed in 1981; she resisted judicial activism. William Rehnquist (1924–) was appointed chief justice in 1986; Antonin Scalia (1931–) was appointed associate justice in 1986; and Clarence Thomas (1948–) was appointed associate justice in 1991. Rehnquist, Scalia, and Thomas are generally thought to form the Supreme Court's right wing.

appoint more judges like Scalia and Thomas. Although the Supreme Court may be the most visible branch of the federal judiciary, there are more than 850 other judges who preside over the district courts, where trials take place, or who review district court rulings in the 12 Circuit Courts of Appeals. Because the Republican leadership on the Senate Judiciary Committee blocked dozens of Clinton's politically moderate nominees, Bush enters office with 94 vacancies ready to be filled.

Do you think there should be an amendment to make it illegal for senators to block nominations on grounds other than their qualifications, knowledge, and experience?

No doubt there will soon be many more vacancies, as conservative incumbent judges make a point of retiring before 2003, when control of the Senate, which must confirm presidential nominees to the federal courts, might return to the Democrats. Until then, the Senate Judiciary Committee's Republican leadership can be expected to rubber stamp every Bush nominee who comes its way. Without a thorough pre-screening by the ABA Standing Committee, it will be much easier for the Bush administration to nominate right-wing extremists. Although the ABA intends to continue to rate nominees, it will do so after the identities have been made public. Review under such circumstances will be more hurried and more subject to political pressures, and the ratings will carry less weight....

If the ABA is still involved at some point, why are critics worried?

An invalid decision

Bush administration spokesmen and their media partisans such as the *Wall Street Journal* have justified the scuttling of ABA pre-review by denouncing the ABA as a "liberal" organization. The ABA is comprised of over 400,000 attorneys, more than half of the lawyers in the United States, and reflects the generally conservative social and political outlook of the privileged middle class layer it represents.

If the ABA is dominated by big business attorneys, might critics argue that they do not have enough experience to be involved in the screening process? Would a completely independent body be more effective?

Like the legal profession as a whole, the ABA is dominated not by personal injury trial lawyers or criminal defense attorneys—the right wing's usual whipping boys—but by attorneys for big business. For example, its current president, Martha Barnett, is a partner in Holland & Knight, a 1,100-attorney Florida-based firm which, according to its website, specializes in representing "banking and finance, utilities, insurance, domestic and foreign governments, media, shipping lines and cruise operators, airlines and aircraft manufacturing, transportation, real estate development, mining, agriculture, trade, intellectual property, health care, construction, entertainment, telecommunications, and hotel, resort and timeshare." The next ABA president will be Robert Hirshon, whose resume states that he "represents banks, insurance companies, trade associations and government entities." How truly narrow the social base of the Bush administration is—and how extreme its politics—is underscored by its inability to coexist with even mainstream establishment organizations such as the ABA.

The right wing's drive to eliminate the ABA pre-screening process began after Ronald Reagan's 1987 nomination of Robert Bork to the Supreme Court. Although rated "well qualified" by the ABA's Standing Committee, four members dissented, claiming that Bork had displayed a lack of integrity and judicial temperament in the course of his career. Independently of the ABA review, Senate Democrats held hearings exposing Bork's extremist right-wing views, and then voted to reject his nomination, igniting a right-wing frenzy that has not subsided to this day. Just last week, the *Wall Street Journal* called the anti-Bork vote a "jihad."

For more information on the Bork nomination go to pages 72–73.

In fact, the Senate's rejection of Bork was entirely appropriate.... Both before and after Watergate, Bork published right-wing tracts, invariably drafted in the most pretentious and ponderous style. To cite one example among many, in 1963 Bork denounced the federal Public Accommodations Act, the landmark civil rights law enacted to eliminate Jim Crow segregation by prohibiting businesses engaged in interstate commerce—hotels, restaurants and the like—from refusing to serve black people.... In 1996 Bork published a screed entitled *Slouching Towards Gomorrah: Modern Liberalism and American Decline.* In it ... Bork rejects the Declaration of Independence, denounces "the proposition that all men are created equal" as "profoundly unfortunate," and claims his book demonstrates "the pernicious effects of our passion for equality and the lack of any intellectual foundation for that passion."

The loudest cheers for Bush's elimination of ABA pre-screening came, not surprisingly, from the *Wall Street Journal*, the most rabid supporter of Bush's right-wing trajectory. The paper praised Bush for having "done what even the Gipper [Ronald Reagan] never could: He told the American Bar Association to take a hike." ...

Former Hollywood star Ronald Reagan (1911–2004) was 40th president from 1981 to 1989. He acquired the nickname "Gipper" after playing dying George "The Gipper" Gipp in the movie Knute Rockne All American (1940), the story of famous football coach Knute Rockne. Gipper's tagline was "win one for the Gipper."

… ON JUDICIAL INDEPENDENCE AND THE JUDICIAL CONFIRMATION PROCESS
George W. Bush

43rd President George W. Bush (2001–) made this speech on May 9, 2003.

NO

… Welcome to the White House and the Rose Garden. I'm pleased all of you could be here to stand for a truly independent federal judiciary. The Framers of the Constitution knew that freedom and justice depend on fair and impartial judges. To ensure judges of the highest quality, integrity, they designed a system in which the President would nominate judges and the Senate would vote up or down on the nominees.

Today, we are facing a crisis in the Senate, and therefore, a crisis in our judiciary. Highly qualified judicial nominees are waiting years to get an up-or-down vote from the United States Senate. They wait for years while partisans search in vain for reasons to reject them. The obstructionist tactics of a small group of senators are setting a pattern that threatens judicial independence. Meanwhile, vacancies on the bench and overcrowded court dockets are causing delays for citizens seeking justice. The judicial confirmation is broken, and it must be fixed for the good of the country.…

Do you agree that the judicial system as a whole suffers from senators' delaying tactics?

Nominees

Exactly two years ago, I announced my first 11 nominees to the federal appeals court. I chose men and women of talent and integrity, highly qualified nominees who represent the mainstream of American law and American values. Eight of them waited more than a year without an up-or-down vote in the United States Senate. As of today, three of that original group have waited two years. Their treatment by a group of senators is a disgrace. Overall, I have sent to the Senate 42 superb nominees for federal courts of appeal. Eighteen of them are still waiting for a vote in the Senate; and eight of those 18 have been waiting more than a year. More appeals court nominees have had to wait over a year for a hearing in my presidency than in the last 50 years combined. This is not just business as usual; this is an [abnegation] of constitutional responsibility, and it is hurting our country.

If federal judicial appointments are for life and the appointees have the power to influence what civil liberties citizens may enjoy, should the nomination system be more rigorous than just the president nominating candidates with the Senate's advice and consent?

As President, I have the constitutional responsibility to nominate excellent judges. And I take that responsibility

seriously. The men and women I have nominated are
an historically diverse group, whose character and credentials
are impeccable.

This group includes Miguel Estrada, my selection for the
D.C. Circuit Court of Appeals. Miguel Estrada has served in the
Justice Department under Presidents from both political
parties. He has argued 15 cases before the U.S. Supreme
Court. He has earned the American Bar Association's highest
mark, a unanimous rating of well qualified. If confirmed,
Miguel would be the first Hispanic American ever to serve on
the court that is often considered the second highest in the
land. Miguel Estrada's nomination has strong support from
citizens and leaders in both political parties. And he has
support from a majority in the United States Senate. Yet, after
two years, he still cannot get an up-or-down vote on the floor
of the Senate. A group of Democratic senators has insisted
that Mr. Estrada answer questions that other nominees were
not required to answer. These senators have sought
confidential Justice Department memos not sought for other
appeal court nominees—a request opposed by all living
former Solicitor Generals because of the damage it would do
to our legal system. These senators have also filibustered for
three months to prevent a vote on Miguel Estrada's
nomination. Never before has there been a successful
filibuster to prevent an up-or-down vote on an appeals court
nominee. This is an unprecedented tactic that threatens
judicial independence and adds to the vacancy crisis in our
courts. And it is wrong.

Justice Priscilla Owen, whom I have nominated to the
Fifth Circuit Court of Appeals, also has the support of the
majority of United States senators. And she, too, has become
the target of a filibuster. Justice Owen is an extraordinarily
well qualified nominee, who has served with distinction on
the Texas Supreme Court since 1995. Like Miguel Estrada,
 she has earned the American Bar Association's unanimous
rating of well qualified. She has strong bipartisan support,
including endorsements from three Democrats who served
with her on the Texas Supreme Court; and endorsements
from 15 past presidents of the Texas bar. Yet, Justice Owen
has been waiting two years—two years—for an up-or-down
vote on the Senate floor.

The list goes on. And the trend is clear: Of the 18 appeals
court nominees awaiting a vote, all who have been rated by
the American Bar Association have received well qualified or
qualified ratings. Some Democratic senators have referred to
those ratings as the gold standard. But those same senators

*In September 2003
Miguel Estrada
withdrew his
nomination. Critics
argued that
the senatorial
filibustering had
caused this action.*

*Critics objected to
Priscilla Owen's
nomination on the
grounds that
she is extremely
conservative and
is opposed to
sensitive issues such
as abortion.*

have ignored those high marks, and instead of applying the gold standard, have applied a double standard to some of my nominees. The Senate has a constitutional responsibility to hold an up-or-down vote.

Throughout most of our history, the Senate has exercised this responsibility and voted promptly on judicial nominees. During the administration of former Presidents Bush and Clinton, however, too many appeals court nominees never received votes. And today the situation is worse than ever, making the need for reform greater than ever.

Do you think that George W. Bush's alleged association with the religious right may have exacerbated opposition to his judicial nominees? Go to page 49 for more information on this subject.

While senators stall and hold on to old grudges, American justice is suffering. Dockets are overcrowded, judges are overworked, and citizens are waiting too long for their cases to be heard. The regional appeals courts have a 12 percent vacancy rate. And filings in those courts have reached an all-time high, again last year. The Sixth Circuit, which covers Ohio and Michigan and Kentucky and Tennessee has four vacancies on a 16-judge court. The D.C. Circuit has three vacancies on a 12-judge court. Of the eighteen open seats that could be filled by the nominees waiting for Senate confirmation, 15 have been classified as judicial emergencies by the Judicial Conference of the United States. The American Bar Association has called this an emergency situation. And the Chief Justice recently said that these vacancies and rising caseloads threaten the proper functioning of federal courts and asked the Senate to give every nominee a prompt up-or-down vote.

Framer Alexander Hamilton once commented that the judiciary is the weakest branch of government. Go to http://www. landmarkcases. org/marbury/ judicialpower.html to read Hamilton's analysis of the judiciary. Are his arguments still valid?

The bitterness and partisanship that have taken over the judicial confirmations process, also threaten judicial independence. Some senators have tried to force nominees to take positions on controversial issues before they even take the bench. This is contrary to the constitutional design of a separate and independent judicial branch.

Bush's suggestion

Do you think Bush's concern with the "vacancy crisis" has to do with the presidential election?

Six months ago, I proposed a plan to end the vacancy crisis and make the process work again. This plan would apply no matter who lives in the White House or no matter which party controls the United States Senate. Here's how it works: Judges on the federal appellate and district courts would notify the President of their intentions to retire at least a year in advance whenever that is possible. The President would then submit a nomination to the U.S. Senate within 180 days of receiving notice of a vacancy or intended retirement. The Senate Judiciary Committee would hold a hearing within 90 days of receiving a nomination. And the full Senate would vote on a nominee no longer than 180 days after the nomination is submitted. The goal is to have a new judge ready to take the bench on the same day the sitting judge retires. Since I announced this plan, the Judicial Conference has done its part by strongly urging judges to give a one-year advance notice of retirement. I've done my part with an executive order issued today formalizing my commitment to submit nominations within 180 days after notification of a vacancy. And now we're waiting for the Senate to do its duty and ensure timely up-or-down votes for every single nominee.

Senators have other duties too. Do you think that this would give them enough time to research candidates thoroughly?

Majority Leader Frist and Judiciary Chairman Hatch are pushing hard for progress on this issue. They are reformers. And I thank you for your hard work. U.S. Senator Arlen Specter and U.S. Senator Zell Miller have proposed reforms to fix the problem. And I thank you for your leadership. I'm very pleased that 10 freshmen senators of both parties have come together to demand the return of dignity and civility to the process. As newcomers, they see the futility of endless bickering that blocks good judges from the bench.

Under the leadership of John Cornyn and Democrat Mark Pryor, these senators sent a letter to the Senate leadership last week. And this is what it said: None of us were parties to any of the reported past offenses, whether real or perceived. None of us believe that the ill will of the past should dictate the terms and direction of the future. Each of us firmly believes the United States Senate needs a fresh start.

Some commentators believe that Bush is suffering a backlash to the blocking of Bill Clinton's nominees during his presidency.

I completely agree, and so do the American people. I believe a fresh start is possible. And we will stand with these senators to bring needed reform on behalf of the American people. And I ask for your help—I ask for your help to make sure our judiciary functions in a way that will make the people proud. I ask for your help in talking to senators as we convince them that obstructionist policies harm the American people. It hurts the justice system that makes us the envy of the world. I know we can move forward. I look forward to the day when a good nominee gets a vote—up or down, in timely fashion—on the floor of the United States Senate. Thank you all for coming. And God bless....

Do you agree that the U.S. justice system is the "envy of the world"? Look at www.cnn.com and www.bbc.co.uk, and compare coverage of the U.S. legal system.

Summary

Although the Constitution establishes that the president with the advice and consent of the Senate should nominate federal judicial candidates, it does not set any criteria for selection. Some people believe that creating a formal set of qualifications that candidates must meet would help avoid some of the delays and obstructions to appointments. Others argue this already exists. In the first article John Andrews of the World Socialist Website examines the role that the American Bar Association (ABA) played for almost 50 years in making sure that federal judicial candidates were adequately qualified. Using a rating system, the nonpartisan ABA rigorously examined nominees to make sure that they fit certain criteria and advised the president if a nominee was unsuitable. By removing the ABA from this process, George W. Bush has, Andrews argues, taken away a necessary check on quality.

The second article is a transcript of a 2003 speech by President Bush on judicial independence and the confirmation process. Bush states that his nominees are chosen only for their distinction as lawyers and blames the delays in their appointment on a politically motivated Senate. He states, "As president, I have the constitutional responsibility to nominate excellent judges. And I take that responsibility seriously. The men and women I have nominated are an historically diverse group, whose character and credentials are impeccable." He claims the problems in federal judicial appointments lie in a crisis in the Senate and suggests a plan to impose a time limit on appointments, which would help end logjams.

FURTHER INFORMATION:

Books:

Carter, Stephen L., *The Confirmation Mess.* New York: Basic Books, 1994.

Useful websites:

http://www-camlaw.rutgers.edu/organization/o-fed/bias_article.html
Examines bias in judicial nominees ratings.
http://www.fed-soc.org/Publications/ABAwatch/March1997/standards.htm
American Bar Association standards for evaluating federal judicial candidates.
http://www.lawforkids.org/QA/Other/Other218.cfm
Law For Kids page on federal judicial selection.
http://www.worldnetdaily.com/news/article.asp?ARTICLE_ID=13239
Article that examines the sort of questions about the quality of Supreme Court judges.

The following debates in the Pro/Con series may also be of interest:

In this volume:

Part 1: The federal judiciary: Checks and balances, pages 8–9

Topic 2 Are politics too influential in the selection of federal judges?

The Bork nomination, pages 72–73

SHOULD FEDERAL JUDICIAL APPLICANTS HAVE TO MEET A FORMAL SET OF REQUIREMENTS?

YES: Around 200 lawyers wrote to the Senate to set out the requirements federal judicial nominees should meet

YES: Candidates would have to prove that they are properly qualified to do the job

SELF-DETERMINATION
Should judges be chosen by lawyers?

DEMOCRATIC LAW
Would election be a better method of appointing federal judges?

NO: It is the president's constitutional right to nominate candidates with the advice and consent of the Senate

NO: The current system has worked for centuries—to change it would involve amending the Constitution

SHOULD FEDERAL JUDICIAL APPLICANTS HAVE TO MEET A FORMAL SET OF REQUIREMENTS?
KEY POINTS

YES: For almost 50 years the ABA made sure through its rigorous process that only those candidates who were best qualified were nominated

YES: The ABA acted as a check on the overpoliticization of the selection process through its rating system

AMERICAN BAR ASSOCIATION
Did the ABA ensure that nominees were suitable through the rating system?

NO: This was a biased preferential system that George W. Bush was right to stop

NO: The ABA's ratings were not nonpartisan as many people argue. Research has shown that the ABA has shown bias in its rating of judges.

INTRODUCTION

About 5 percent of prosecutions in the United States are for violation of federal criminal law. The responsibility for sentencing federal offenders has never been the exclusive province of any of the three branches of federal government. Just as Congress can pass statutes defining federal crimes, it can also set the sentences for these crimes. Recent legislation that restricts the sentencing discretion of federal judges has, however, prompted wide debate. While some people applaud Congress's attempt to apply U.S. law evenly across all jurisdictions, others counter that legislators are violating the principle of separation of powers by launching an attack on judicial independence.

In 1984 Congress passed the Sentencing Reform Act, which created the U.S. Sentencing Commission. The commission was charged with formulating national guidelines for the federal judicial branch to follow in its sentencing decisions. Before 1984 federal judges had broad discretion in determining the length of sentences of those convicted in their courts. This system had become increasingly controversial. Critics argued that it created serious sentencing disparities. They also believed that many sentences were too light, and this, they claimed, was contributing to rising crime rates.

The federal sentencing guidelines came into effect in 1987: They prescribed sentencing ranges based primarily on the type of offense and on the defendant's criminal history. Many advocates praised the new scheme for eliminating confusion and for promoting fair and consistent sentencing. However, the commission did not completely remove judicial sentencing discretion: Judges could depart downward from the mandatory minimum sentences if they considered there to be mitigating circumstances not covered by the guidelines.

Between 1991 and 2001 the number of downward departures rose from less than 6 percent to 18.8 percent. Some commentators point out that the bulk of this increase came from the Justice Department's own request to reward defendants for cooperating with the government. But the department itself and several members of Congress became dissatisfied with what they perceived to be too lenient sentencing.

"Judicial discretion ... is the heart and soul of our criminal justice system...."

—MARY PRICE, GENERAL COUNSEL, FAMILIES AGAINST MANDATORY MINIMUMS (2003)

In April 2003 Congress passed the Feeney Amendment, a late addition to the PROTECT Act, which targets crimes against children. Among other things it directed the Sentencing Commission to revise its guidelines in order both to reduce the number of downward departures in general and also to bar them in cases of child abduction and sexual assault unless the departure was based on factors expressly authorized by the sentencing guidelines. In addition federal judges were required to report downward departures to the Sentencing Commission. The Justice Department also gained access to the commission's data.

The legal community widely condemned the Feeney Amendment, and some of its strongest critics were federal judges. They urged Congress to overturn the amendment since the judiciary had been given no advance warning nor an opportunity to comment. Some experts claim that federal guidelines now too sharply curtail the discretion of judges to impose sentences. They argue that it would be impossible for any sentencing system to predict every offense or provide for all relevant features of criminal behavior. They contend that judges remain the most competent people to consider individual circumstances and to make objective sentencing decisions. They further argue that the discretion denied to judges is shifted to the executive branch, giving prosecutors virtually unchecked power to control sentencing by choosing which charges to file.

Opponents also claim that the reporting requirement is designed to intimidate judges who might otherwise authorize downward departures in the interests of justice. Several judges have either resigned or have openly defied the guidelines because they refuse to pass sentences they deem too harsh. Supporters, however, counter that the legislation removes much-abused grounds for downward departure, such as "diminished capacity," while still allowing judges to depart downward in specific circumstances.

In May 2003 the JUDGES (Judicial Use of Discretion to Guarantee Equity in Sentencing) Act was introduced to repeal provisions of the PROTECT Act that extended beyond child abduction and sexual offenses. As of mid-2004 no progress had been made on the bill.

Pages 88–95 examine the debate.

STATEMENT BEFORE THE U.S. SENATE
Orrin G. Hatch

Republican Senator Orrin G. Hatch is chairman of the Senate Judiciary Committee. He made this speech on April 10, 2003.

YES

Mr. President. I rise in support of the Conference Report to S.151, "Prosecutorial Remedies and Other Tools to End the Exploitation of Children Today [PROTECT] Act of 2003," which truly represents landmark bi-partisan legislation to protect our children. On Tuesday of this week, the House and Senate Conferees met and reached agreement on this important piece of bi-partisan legislation. Earlier this morning, the House of Representatives overwhelmingly passed the legislation by an overwhelming vote of 400–25....

The bill also institutes sentencing reforms so that criminals convicted of crimes against children receive the stiff sentences they deserve. This provision, which was adopted at the Conference, represents a significant compromise from the original House bill containing the so-called Feeney Amendment, which passed the House by a vote of 357–58. Indeed, the overall House bill passed the House by an overwhelming vote of 410–14.

The Feeney Amendment is named for Representative Tom Feeney, the Florida Republican who introduced the legislation. It was signed into law on April 30, 2003.

In response to concerns raised about the Feeney Amendment, I worked with Chairman Sensenbrenner, Senator Graham, and my colleagues to develop a bi-partisan compromise, which was ultimately supported by not only all of the Republican conferees but also by Democratic conferees: Senator Biden, as well as Congressmen Frost, Matheson, and Hinojosa.

A "de novo review" means that in an appeal, the appeal court will substitute its judgment about sentencing matters for that of the trial court. Under the "'clearly erroneous' standard" an appeal court must accept the lower court's findings of fact unless the appeal court is convinced that a legal mistake has been made.

Terms of the compromise proposal

The compromise proposal would: (1) limit—but not prevent—downward departures *only* to enumerated factors for crimes against children and sex offenses; (2) change the standard for review of sentencing matters for appellate courts to a *de novo* review, while factual determinations would continue to be subject to a "clearly erroneous" standard; (3) require courts to give specific and written reasons for any departure from the guidelines; and (4) require judges to report sentencing decisions to the Sentencing Commission.

It is important to note that the compromise restricts downward departures in serious crimes against children and sex crimes and does not broadly apply to other crimes. But because the problem of downward departures is acute across the board, the compromise proposal would direct the Sentencing Commission to conduct a thorough study of these issues, develop concrete measures to prevent this abuse, and report these matters back to Congress.

For those who want to oppose these needed sentencing reforms, I want to remind them that the Sentencing Reform Act of 1984 was designed "to provide *certainty and fairness* in meeting the purposes of sentencing, *avoiding unwarranted sentencing disparities among defendants with similar records who have been found guilty of similar criminal conduct.*" While the United States Sentencing Commission promulgated Sentencing Guidelines to meet this laudable goal, courts unfortunately have strayed further and further from this system of fair and consistent sentencing over the past decade.

A steady increase in downward departures

During the period of 1991 to 2001, the number of downward departures, excluding those requested by the government for substantial assistance and immigration cases along the Southwest border, has steadily climbed. In 1991, the number of downward departures was 1,241, and rose by 2001 *to a staggering total of 4,098*. This chart shows that the rate of downward departures has increased over 100% during this period, and nearly 50% over the past five years alone.

This problem is perhaps most glaring in the area of sexual crimes and kidnapping crimes.

During the last five years, trial courts granted downward departures below the mandated sentence in 19.20% of sexual abuse cases, 21.36% of pornography and prostitution cases, and 12.80% of kidnapping and hostage taking cases. This many departures are simply astounding, considering the magnitude of the suffering by our Nation's youth at the hands of pedophiles, molesters, and pornographers.

Let me give you just one example of the abuse that this sentencing reform will correct.... [A] defendant was charged with possession of 1,300 separate images of child pornography, depicting young children in graphic and violent scenes of sexual exploitation that were sickening and horrible. For example, one of the images included a young girl wearing a dog collar while engaging in sexual intercourse with an adult male. This same defendant was engaging in online sexual communications with a 15-year-old girl.

The Sentencing Guidelines for this defendant mandated a sentence in the range of 33 to 41 months. Yet the trial judge departed downward to a sentence of only 8 MONTHS, citing:

In October 2003 the Sentencing Commission issued a detailed report on downward departures. It found that they had increased most dramatically in "substantial assistance departures," when the defendant agrees to help the government, and also in cases occurring in the Southwest border districts—this was attributed to the rise in the number of immigration cases and the need to dispose of them quickly.

For more on the debate about sex offenders see Volume 9, Criminal Law and the Penal System, Topic 16 Should sex offenders be castrated?

Do you think any of these points justify a downward departure from sentencing guidelines?

(1) the defendant's height—he was just short of 6 feet tall [1.83m] and that would make him vulnerable to abuse in prison; (2) the defendant was naïve; and (3) the defendant's demeanor—he was meek, mild, and compassionate. Now, we all have common sense but this is simply incredible and outrageous. Congress has to act and act now. The compromise sentencing reform provisions contained in the Conference Report are a reasonable and measured response to this problem.

The compromise proposal would simply require judges to sentence these vicious defendants in accordance with the law, and not seek to find new areas or new legal justifications for reducing sentences for these defendants, without specific authorization from the United States Sentencing Commission. Contrary to the oft-repeated claims of its opponents, the compromise proposal is not a mandatory minimum. Judges handling these important criminal cases can still exercise discretion to depart downward—but only when the Sentencing Commission specifies the factors that warrant a downward departure.

For more information about the criticisms of mandatory (compulsory) minimum sentences go to www.famm.org— the Families against Mandatory Minimums (FAMM) website.

De novo review of application of facts to law

The other major reform in the compromise adopted in the Conference Report is consistent with prevailing law: requiring *de novo* review of a trial judge's application of facts to law. Indeed, this is the same standard that applies to appellate review of critical motions to suppress physical or testimonial evidence. There is no reason for appellate judges to give deference to the trial judge on such questions of law. Even after the compromise amendment, the trial judge's factual determinations would still be subject to great deference under a "clearly erroneous" standard. If a discretionary downward departure is justifiable, it is difficult to understand why anyone would be opposed to the appellate courts reviewing them under the same standard that applies to other important areas of law.

Do you think such terms as "epidemic of abuse" help or hinder the force of the author's argument?

Mr. President, I want to take a moment here to remind everyone to focus on the problem that we face—an epidemic of abuse of our children. According to the National Center for Missing and Exploited Children, 3.9 million of the nation's 22.3 million children between the ages of 12 and 17 have been seriously physically assaulted, and one in three girls and one in five boys are sexually abused before the age of 18. Considered in this context, we can have an honest debate about the issues, but we have an epidemic that needs to be addressed and addressed now.

Should Congress be able to limit the power of federal judges to sentence criminals?

In 2003 Congressman Tom Feeney introduced an amendment to the PROTECT Act.
It puts strict limitations on downward departures from federal sentencing guidelines.

We simply have no greater resource than our children. It has been said that the benevolence of a society can be judged on how well it treats its old people and how well it treats its young. Our children represent our Nation's future. I ... urge my colleagues to pass this critical legislation....

I urge my Democratic colleagues to stop the partisan gamesmanship and support this needed legislation. Let's not let our children and communities down. Let's pass this legislation without delay....

> Should the benevolence of a society just be judged on how well it treats its old and its young?

JUDGES ON TRIAL
Adrian Acu

This article first appeared in 2003 in Common Sense, a student/faculty publication of the University of Notre Dame, Indiana.

The USA PATRIOT Act of 2001 made changes to statutes in a number of areas, including online activities and surveillance. It has been criticized by many civil liberties groups.

Do you think that that identical crimes should be given identical sentences? Should personal circumstances also be taken into account?

"Extenuating circumstances" are those that lessen the seriousness of an offense or serve as an excuse for it.

NO

The Justice Department has seen many changes in the past three years, largely due to the massive shock that came with the September 11 attacks. Those changes gave law enforcement personnel and prosecutors enhanced power in the investigation and conviction of suspected criminals. While pieces of legislation such as the Patriot Act may have increased security in the United States, they also have given civil rights activists reason to worry due to their consistent infringement on individual rights.

On July 28, [2003,] [Attorney General] John Ashcroft gave those activists one more reason to worry when he sent out a memo to U.S. attorneys, ordering them to report to him whenever a judge gives a lenient sentence, departing from the mandatory sentencing guidelines even when it is not the result of a plea bargain. John Corallo, spokesman for the Justice Department, has defended the order, saying, "It is an effort to make sure that someone who is convicted of a crime in California is treated no differently than a person who is convicted of the exact same crime in Massachusetts."

Mandatory sentencing guidelines

Now, we are all fans of equality, but we should ask why such a policy is being instituted at this time. In order to answer this question, we need to know more about mandatory sentencing guidelines. Mandatory sentences are established by the U.S. Sentencing Commission for the expressed purpose of regulating sentencing while still allowing for judicial flexibility. The judicial flexibility is allowed for special or rare circumstances, when a judge believes that the mandatory sentencing guidelines are inappropriate. No rigid guideline can truly allow for a just sentencing, for it can never factor in every little nuance in a person's life, their reasons for committing the crime, their remorse after committing it. Why, then, can judges not just choose the lower range of mandatory guidelines for their sentence?

No matter how wide a range a judge is given, there is still the chance that a judge will come upon a case where he or she has a truly remorseful individual, or someone with extenuating circumstances, or someone who is just deserving

Should Congress be able to limit the power of federal judges to sentence criminals?

Attorney General John Ashcroft's memo directed attorneys to report to him judges who impose lenient sentences. Critics argue that this requirement limits judicial independence.

Go to http://www. usatoday.com/news/ washington/2003-08-27-judges-cover_x.htm to read this article, which appeared on August 27, 2003.

of mercy; a situation where the mandatory sentence seems too harsh. One example is cited in a recent *USA Today* article by Richard Willing entitled "Judges go soft on sentences more often." A career criminal was attempting to pawn a shotgun sometime after his release from prison. Because it is illegal for convicted felons to possess firearms, he was arrested. His prior convictions had him facing a mandatory sentence of 30 to 37 months on the possession charge, to which he pled guilty. When it came time for sentencing, however, Judge Paul Cassell gave the criminal 18 months, reasoning that the man was trying to get rid of the gun, and that his previous crimes were non-violent. Upon looking at such circumstances, it seems logical that a lighter sentence than even the low part of the mandatory sentence range, 30 months, was a more just sentence.

Do you think the judge issued a fair sentence in this case?

Placing judges under watch

With John Ashcroft's order, however, a message will be sent which says that a judge will be placed under watch if he or she utilizes their full faculty of reason to establish truly just sentences based not only on a stark and standardized view of the crime and the criminal but on a fuller view of both. In his memo, Ashcroft writes, "The Department of Justice has a solemn obligation to ensure that laws concerning criminal sentencing are faithfully, fairly and consistently enforced." The notion of equalizing punishments, which Ashcroft and Corallo both mention as the motivation for this order, really only makes sense if the Justice Department wants to monitor judges who act too harshly. The Justice Department should watch judges who are overly severe and should punish them for inflicting cruel or unusual punishment on criminals who are undeserving of such treatment. But are there really good grounds for punishing judges for judging with mercy?

Does harsh sentencing act as a deterrent to potential criminals? Are more lenient judges possibly sending out the wrong message?

Reasons for rise in leniency are unclear

Richard Willing also notes in his article that about 18% of cases that have passed through federal circuits in 2001 have had lenient sentences passed without plea bargains. This number is certainly on the rise, as seen when compared to the numbers in 1995, where only 8.4% of sentences were more lenient than the mandatory range. The reasons why judges are giving lesser sentences are still unclear, and some fear that being too lenient means criminals will be out on the streets faster than they should be. But the fact that more and more judges are being lenient seems to suggest that it is not simply a few judges advancing a more liberal agenda. If the

Why might judges be giving more lenient sentences over time? The introduction to this topic and the first article give some possible causes. What other reasons can you think of?

Cassell decision is a good indication of the decision-making that goes into deciding to follow a more lenient course, then there is little to fear that criminals will run rampant, for the seriousness of the crime is taken into account. As stated previously, there are stringent and yet reasonable restrictions to the leeway that judges have, allowing them to be lenient only under special circumstances, meaning that no serious offenders will only get off with a few years in prison unless they have an incredibly good reason. There is essentially no reason, therefore, to limit leniency in judicial decisions.

Enforcing executive control over the judiciary

Ashcroft's order amounts to enforcing executive control over the judicial branch through threat of being monitored, intimidating judges to perhaps act against their better judgment and give unfair decisions. While it is meant to empower prosecutors, giving them some ammunition to make an appeal if a sentence is deemed too light, that power is bought by sacrificing some of the independence of the judiciary. This is too high a cost.

It should be noted that Ashcroft's order comes after the passing of an amendment that piggybacked the "Amber Alert" law passed by President Bush earlier this year, making it more difficult for judges to move away from mandatory sentences. The amendment has faced opposition from the American Bar Association, Chief Justice William Rehnquist, and even the U.S. Sentencing Commission, the ones who have the greatest interest in having their guidelines followed. The reason for their objection is that time is needed to analyze why judges are more frequently giving out more lenient sentences. Perhaps John Ashcroft should also suspend judgment before encouraging judges to be harsher.

Do you think the author is right to argue that there is no reason to limit leniency in judicial decisions? What arguments can you think of to refute this point?

The "Amber Alert" law to which Acu refers became known as the PROTECT Act of 2003. The act provided for the establishment of a national system to assist local and state authorities in finding abducted children—the Amber Alert network.

Summary

The first article is a speech made by Republican Senator Orrin G. Hatch in 2003 in support of the Feeney Amendment. Hatch points out that the courts have moved increasingly further away from a consistent system of sentencing, and the number of downward departures from federal sentencing guidelines has steadily grown. He contends that the problem is greatest in the areas of sexual and kidnapping crimes. He cites an example of a judge giving an eight-month sentence to a sex offender, whereas sentencing guidelines mandate a sentence up to five times as long. Hatch insists that under the amendment judges will still retain discretion to depart downward, but only when the Sentencing Commission specifies factors that allow this. He urges senators to pass the legislation in order to address "an epidemic of abuse of our children."

In the second article Adrian Acu examines the order issued by Attorney General John Ashcroft that U.S. attorneys report to him whenever a federal judge departs downward from federal sentencing guidelines. Acu maintains that mandatory sentences allow for judicial flexibility. He argues that there will always be circumstances in which judges should have the discretion to depart downward from the lowest part of the mandatory sentencing range, and he insists that judges should not be punished for showing mercy in these cases. Acu questions why only lenient sentences are to be monitored and not harsh ones. In his view the order gives the executive branch undue control over the judicial branch. Before encouraging judges to be harsher, he says, it is important to analyze why judges are handing down more lenient sentences.

FURTHER INFORMATION:

Books:

Burbank, Stephen B., and Barry Friedman (eds.), *Judicial Independence at the Crossroads: An Interdisciplinary Approach*. Thousand Oaks, CA: Sage Publications, 2002.

Stith, Kate, and José A. Cabranes, *Fear of Judging: Sentencing Guidelines in the Federal Courts*. Chicago, IL: University of Chicago Press, 1998.

Tonry, Michael, *Sentencing Matters*. New York: Oxford University Press, 1998.

Useful websites:

http://www.americanvoice2004.org/askdave/10askdave.html
Background information on the Feeney Amendment.

http://www.nacld.org/departures
Section of the National Association of Criminal Defense Lawyers site devoted to saving downward departures.

www.ussc.gov
Site of the United States Sentencing Commission, with an explanation of how federal sentencing guidelines work.

The following debates in the Pro/Con series may also be of interest:

In this volume:
Topic 10 Are sentencing decisions affected by minority group status?

In *Criminal Law and the Penal System*:
Topic 13 Do prisons work?

SHOULD CONGRESS BE ABLE TO LIMIT THE POWER OF FEDERAL JUDGES TO SENTENCE CRIMINALS?

YES: Guidelines prevent serious disparities in sentencing: They ensure that offenders receive fair and consistent treatment

YES: In unusual cases judges can depart from guidelines with the authorization of the U.S. Sentencing Commission

SENTENCING GUIDELINES
Are sentencing guidelines necessary?

JUDICIAL DISCRETION
Are judges still permitted to exercise discretion?

NO: A judge must consider the individual circumstances of each case in order to set a fair sentence

NO: The Feeney Amendment severely curtails federal judges' discretion in sentencing. Sacrificing judicial independence is too high a price to pay.

SHOULD CONGRESS BE ABLE TO LIMIT THE POWER OF FEDERAL JUDGES TO SENTENCE CRIMINALS?

KEY POINTS

YES: Far too many pedophiles and child abductors are getting away with light sentences handed down by liberal judges

YES: The reporting requirement is the only way to be sure that judges apply the law equally across all jurisdictions

DOWNWARD DEPARTURES
Are there too many downward departures?

REPORTING REQUIREMENT
Should judges be reported for downward departures?

NO: The number of downward departures simply reflects a careful, enlightened approach to judicial decision-making

NO: The reporting requirement is a means of intimidating federal judges into making decisions against their better judgment

PART 2

THE STATE COURTS

INTRODUCTION

The courts of the 50 U.S. states are courts of general jurisdiction. Whereas the Constitution creates the federal courts and describes and limits their power, the state courts are under no equivalent constitutional limitation. Most cases that can be brought in federal court can also be brought in state court (for example, civil rights or employment cases), and the state courts have jurisdiction over many cases that cannot be brought in federal court (for example, divorce or personal injury suits).

The U.S. system of concurrent jurisdiction shared between federal and state courts is unusual. It reflects a compromise between those Framers of the Constitution who believed that state courts could best protect the interests of citizens and should not be subjected to federal intrusion (the Jeffersonian position), and those who argued the need for federal oversight to protect national interests from undue localism (the Madisonian position). The state courts are therefore meant to act as a check against undue federal power and to ensure adequate protection of state and local interests. They must do so within the bounds of the Supremacy Clause (Article VI), which provides that all judges are bound by the federal Constitution and laws. The division of power between the state and federal courts generates substantial litigation and controversy.

State court systems generally consist of a trial court, an intermediate appellate court, and a state supreme court. The trial court, either through the judge or a jury, is the initial finder of fact, and its verdict is entitled to substantial deference from higher courts. The appellate and supreme courts do not conduct trials but confine themselves mainly to correcting mistakes in the trial court's application of facts to law. States can also have specialized courts to hear administrative or other matters. Since the state courts are meant to protect the autonomy of states, it is not surprising that procedures vary from state to state.

Selection

While a federal judge's term in office (life tenure during good behavior) is specified by the Constitution, state judges are selected according to the rules of the particular state. The question of how state court judges should be selected reflects many of the tensions inherent in the state court system. Each state is permitted to establish its own system of choosing judges, and this arguably promotes the state autonomy the Framers valued. It also permits experimentation and allows us to learn from the success or failure of various methods of judicial selection. On a less positive note, states seem generally reluctant to rethink their judicial selection systems based on their own past experience or that of other states. Nevertheless, the debate rages on. It centers on two related issues. The first, discussed in Topic 8, is whether judges should be appointed or elected. Some argue that appointed judges tend to be better qualified, as well as better protected from the demands of politics. Others contend that judges should not

adds an important dimension to the bench. Female judges, for example, might bring different sorts of life experience and different values to the act of judging. Others are skeptical of these arguments, either because they believe that judging impartially is an act that transcends one's race or gender, or because they resist the idea that gender or race translates into a particular kind

---

"The execution of the laws is more important than the making of them...."
—THOMAS JEFFERSON, LETTER (1789)

---

be protected from politics—that election keeps judges honest and sensitive to the needs of the citizenry. Within the broad debate about election versus appointment are many subissues about how the election system might work, who should do the appointing and by what criteria, and how long terms should last.

Topic 9 examines the second issue. Several of the criticisms of judicial election center on the problem of money. Some critics argue that judicial candidates compromise both their dignity and perhaps more importantly their impartiality, or at least the appearance of impartiality, as well. Topic 9 considers whether public funding of judicial campaigns is a viable solution to this problem.

Minority status
An additional important aspect of the judicial selection controversy is the question of diversity on the bench. Some argue that a judiciary that includes women and people of color

of decision-making. Most would agree that the old barriers, which kept women and people of color off the bench, needed to fall. The more difficult question is whether diversity should be a value that factors into the choice of judges.

This issue leads to another contentious and difficult topic: The role played by race in the justice system. Minority group status can factor into the justice system in many ways. In the criminal justice system in particular the U.S. system finds itself trying, convicting, incarcerating, and even executing black men at a rate far out of proportion to their numbers in the general population. Is this because black men commit crimes at a greater rate? Or does the fault lie in the way the criminal justice system treats black men? Topic 10 raises some of these issues, including the question of whether a more diverse judiciary would help alleviate the problem. It also looks at issues relating to death-penalty sentencing in the United States.

Topic 8

SHOULD STATE COURT JUDGES BE APPOINTED RATHER THAN ELECTED?

YES

"IT'S OBVIOUS: APPOINT"
LAS VEGAS REVIEW-JOURNAL, DECEMBER 12, 2002
STEVE SEBELIUS

NO

FROM "JUDGES: SHOULD THEY BE ELECTED OR APPOINTED?"
WWW.WALLBUILDERS.COM
DAVID BARTON

INTRODUCTION

Unlike the appointment process for federal judges, which is provided for in the Constitution, the process for choosing state court judges is left to the discretion of the states. The basic split is between those states that elect their judges and those that appoint them. But there are many variations within these two categories, and many states use a combination of methods. Experts have long debated whether an appointment system is preferable to an election system. Their arguments reflect the difficulty of balancing the need for judicial independence against the need for judicial accountability.

About 39 states employ some sort of judicial elections. This group includes states that elect lower court judges but appoint judges of the highest court (for example, New York) and also states that elect all their judges (for example, Illinois). Elections can be of two types—partisan and nonpartisan. In partisan elections (as, for example,

in Texas and Illinois) judicial candidates are affiliated with a political party; in nonpartisan elections all candidates run, at least in theory, as independents. However, even in nonpartisan elections judicial candidates may be nominated through political parties (as, for example, in Michigan and Ohio).

The appointment process also varies widely from state to state. Usually the process consists of some form of merit selection by which the governor appoints judges after receiving evaluations of their qualifications from a nominating commission constituted to be either nonpartisan or at least fairly balanced. Once the governor makes his or her choice from the list of nominees, the choice may be subject to legislative approval (as in New York). Variations include the California system, in which the governor submits names to an appointed commission rather than vice versa. The term of appointment, like the term of election, may also vary widely from state to state. In states that employ a full-scale merit selection system (the so-called Missouri Plan), judges are required to run for uncontested retention elections after they have served for a particular period.

> *"If the State has a problem with judicial impartiality, it is largely one the State brought upon itself...."*
> —JUSTICE SANDRA DAY O'CONNOR, *REPUBLICAN PARTY OF MINNESOTA V. WHITE* (2002)

Opponents of elections express concern that they compromise judicial independence. Candidates who are required to run for election are likely to need the backing of a political party: This may apply to nonpartisan as well as partisan elections. Candidates may need to court favor with party regulars to get nominated, and they may display an allegiance to the party once they are on the bench. Critics claim that such politicking is undignified and casts doubt on candidates' ability to decide cases impartially. They further argue that even if judges withstand political pressure, the public perception is that they are beholden.

Critics also maintain that judicial independence remains under threat as long as judges have to run for reelection simply because they may shy away from controversial rulings that damage their chances of being retained. Another disadvantage of judicial

elections is the expense. Candidates in a contested election usually have to campaign, and this requires raising substantial funds. Prospective judges may receive contributions from lawyers or parties who later appear before them in court, and they may therefore feel indebted. Even if judges do not favor contributors once they are elected, critics claim that public confidence in the judiciary is undermined by the suspicion that decisions are driven by a desire to repay campaign donors.

Finally, advocates of an appointment system argue that elections are simply a bad way to choose judges because voters do not have enough information to make a reasoned decision. Even when bar associations take the time to evaluate judges, most voters are either unaware of the evaluations or do not pay attention to them. For example, in Illinois sitting judges who are rated unqualified are almost always retained.

However, supporters of judicial elections emphasize that they keep judges accountable to the citizenry. They argue that the flip side of judicial independence is arrogance, and that judges who have to run for election and reelection are constrained from overstepping their role. Advocates also contend that politics will be part of judicial selection under any model, and therefore it is better to give the populace a direct voice in choosing judges. They point out that there is a high risk of political cronyism if a governor alone has the responsibility of selecting judges. Under this type of system judges tend to be reappointed. While some people claim that this provides stability in the judiciary, others counter that it hands state judges life tenure with no accountability.

Pages 102–109 examine the debate.

IT'S OBVIOUS: APPOINT
Steve Sebelius

Steve Sebelius writes about local and national politics for the Las Vegas Review-Journal, where this article first appeared in December 2002.

The Center for Democratic Culture is a nonpartisan research organization at the University of Nevada, Las Vegas.

Nevadans elect their judges in nonpartisan elections. See http://www.ajs.org/js/NV.htm for an overview of judicial selection in the state.

The author reinforces his argument with a humorous comparison. But do you think this is a fair comparison to make?

YES

✓ If you were to sit down and devise the absolute worst way to put a judge on the bench, you couldn't come up with a method much worse than elections.

The fact that elections seem to be popular with voters, appear to keep judges more in tune with public opinion, and hew to the American preference for democracy are probably the worst arguments for the election of judges, too.

These convictions weren't shaken at the UNLV Center for Democratic Culture's all-day Tuesday forum titled "Judging the Judges: Should We Elect or Appoint Nevada Judges?" If anything, they were affirmed by the stories, opinions, statistics and findings of panelists.

My answer, and, I think, the answer: appointment.

The reasons are myriad, but here's the most important: money. There is simply no way for a judge to solicit money from those who will appear in court and avoid the perception—if not the reality—of bias and favoritism. You simply can't deny it.

Public perception

Election supporters will argue the same perception clouds races from City Council to president, and they're right. You don't have to look far—especially here in Clark County—for politicians who may as well be on the payroll of their contributors.

But while we may cynically know that judges are simply lawyer-politicians draped in black robes, they're not supposed to be that way. We expect senators and assemblymen to be passionate advocates for their ideas. We expect—and we should demand—that judges be objective interpreters of laws, despite their political passions. They are, after all, a check on the power of the legislative and executive branches of government.

But to have judges elected like every other politician is akin to having one team paying the refs in a football game; even if the calls are solid, the perception of bias is there.

As proof, look no further than the District Court race in Department 5, between incumbent Judge Jeff Sobel and attorney (and Judge-elect) Jackie Glass.

COMMENTARY: Women judges

The first female lawyer in the United States was Arabella Mansfield (1846–1911), who passed the Iowa bar examination in 1869. Law schools gradually began admitting women, but often with great reluctance.

Florence Allen

Female judges first appeared on the bench in the 20th century. A notable example was Florence Ellinwood Allen (1884–1966). She became a judge on the Cuyahoga County Court of Common Pleas in Ohio in 1920. In 1922 she was elected the nation's first female state Supreme Court justice. President Franklin D. Roosevelt nominated Allen to the U.S. Court of Appeals for the Sixth Circuit in 1934, and she became the first female federal judge.

When President Jimmy Carter took office in 1977, only six women were sitting on the federal courts. Carter appointed a total of 40 female federal judges, and subsequent administrations have followed his lead. Sandra Day O'Connor (1930–) became the first woman to sit on the U.S. Supreme Court after being appointed by President Ronald Reagan in 1981. Ruth Bader Ginsburg (1933–), an appointee of President Bill Clinton, joined her on the bench in 1993. Today women make up about a quarter of the federal judiciary, and the vast majority of states have at least one woman on their highest court. On being asked if they think women have a distinct approach to judging, Justices O'Connor and Ginsburg both quote former Minnesota Supreme Court justice Jeanne Coyne: "At the end of the day, a wise old man and wise old woman will reach the same decision."

Sobel created headlines when he pointed out to lawyers at the courthouse that he was very aware of who had and had not donated to his campaign. Everyone involved knew he was joking, but underneath the humor was the lingering perception that judges keep track of their contributors.

And Sobel criticized Glass' aggressive fund-raising after he'd heard that Glass' husband and law partner, Steve Wolfson, had told contributors to "get on the winning side." (Wolfson says he made the statement to assuage the fears of donors who worried about offending an incumbent by donating to a challenger.) After Sobel was defeated in a landslide, Glass sent a fund-raising letter to Sobel donors, inviting them to give to her campaign.

How can you avoid the notion that if you don't contribute, you may be on the outs with a judge?

"I think you have to, as a judge, hope that you can do that," says Glass. "You base your decision on the facts, the evidence and the law. And that's exactly what I'm going to do."

Under Nevada law donors who contribute more than $100 to an election campaign have to be identified.

In the same way that Alexander Hamilton (above) claimed that the Framers introduced the practice of impeachment to keep federal judges accountable to the public, some people claim that judicial elections keep state judges accountable to their citizens.

There's no reason to think otherwise of Glass, whose reputation earned her many legal and law-enforcement endorsements. But what about judges who may not be fair to those who have not cut checks? Saying "trust in the system" doesn't cut it.

Advantages of appointment

Appointing judges, by contrast, would remove some of the corrupting influence of money. "Money totally perverts and corrupts the system," says forum participant and unsuccessful judicial candidate John Curtas. "When you hand a dollar to someone, you alter your relationship with that person." And he's absolutely right.

In the federal system, where judges are not only appointed but also earn lifetime tenures, there is less pressure to rule in ways that will appease contributors, or even voters. Nevada Supreme Court Justice Nancy Becker notes that federal judges made hard civil rights decisions that would have been impossible for elected state judges who were subject to the passions of a racist, segregationist public.

It would be hard to argue for lifetime appointments for all judges, however. That's why Missouri invented retention elections, in which only the judge's name appears on the ballot, and voters are asked to keep or reject that person. It's still flawed; a judge targeted for removal would have to raise money to stay in office, and he could still be disrobed for unpopular rulings.

Some say the public is smart enough to elect good judges, but most people have little idea who they're voting for when it comes to the courts. (It's not a secret; both Las Vegas newspapers publish election tabloids with judicial candidate information. The real problem is that, while voters say in surveys they like to elect judges, they really don't care too much when it actually comes to doing it.)

UNLV political science professor Michael Bowers says there's little chance of doing away with judicial elections, but it would be a shame if he were right. The Missouri Plan has its flaws, but it's still marginally better than the system we have in place now. Nevada ought to move in that direction, quickly.

Do you think life tenureship has an effect on the decisions that a judge makes? See Topic 3 Should federal judges be appointed for limited terms?

Use the Internet to find out more about states that use the "Missouri Plan" for judicial selection. What do you think might be the advantages and disadvantages of this system?

Judicial elections usually have a lower turnout than other types of elections, and retention elections have an even lower turnout.

JUDGES: SHOULD THEY BE ELECTED OR APPOINTED?
David Barton

David Barton is the founder and president of WallBuilders, an organization "dedicated to the restoration of the constitutional, moral, and religious foundation on which America was built." This extract is taken from an article on the organization's website (www. wallbuilders.com).

NO

Some states have recently considered proposals that would abolish the election of State judges and replace it with a system of appointed judges who would face periodic retention elections. While supporters of this plan argue that retention elections will keep judges accountable to the voters, it is irrefutable that this plan will give judges a level of insulation from the public they have never before experienced and make them more unaccountable than ever before....

Judicial tyranny

[T]he Founders of our country held succinct opinions on this issue. For example, two centuries ago when the colonists declared themselves independent from Great Britain and had the opportunity to create their own governments, they promptly incorporated into America new and important judicial principles—of which the 1780 Massachusetts Constitution was typical in declaring:

> *All power residing originally in* the people *and being derived from them, the several magistrates and officers of government vested with authority—whether Legislative, Executive, or* Judicial—*are their substitutes and* agents and are at all times accountable to them. *(emphasis added)*

Why do you think the Framers feared judicial tyranny more than legislative or executive tyranny?

The Framers feared tyranny from the judiciary more than from the other two branches, so they placed deliberate limitations on the judiciary. As a result, the Federalist Papers reported that under their plan, "the Judiciary is beyond comparison the *weakest* of the three departments of power … [and] the general liberty of the people can *never* be endangered from that quarter."

This quote is from The Federalist No. 78, written by Alexander Hamilton (1755–1804) in 1788. Go to http://www. constitution.org/ fed/federa78.htm for the full paper.

As part of that plan, the Framers took care to ensure that judges were accountable to the people at *all* times. Although federal judges were appointed and did not face election, the Founders made certain that federal judges would be *easily* removable from office through impeachment, a procedure that today is widely misunderstood and rarely used. While the current belief is that a judge may be removed only for the commission of a criminal offense or the violation of a statutory law, it was not this way at the beginning. As Alexander Hamilton explained, "the practice of impeachments was a bridle"—a way to keep judges accountable to the people....

The author claims that the Framers intended it to be easy to remove a federal judge from office; is this the case? See Topic 4 Is it too difficult to impeach federal judges?

The federal judiciary, because it now enjoys a level of insulation from the people that the Framers never intended and to which they today would vehemently object, is unafraid to reshape American culture and policy to mirror its own political whims and personal values.

Do you agree that the federal judiciary tries to "reshape" U.S. culture? See Topic 1 Is the Supreme Court too activist?

"Judge-made laws"

Judges given increased levels of protection from the public feel freer to advance personal agendas, often manifesting the view expressed by Supreme Court Justice Benjamin Cardozo who declared that:

> *I take* judge-made law *as one of the existing realities of life.*

Benjamin Cardozo (1870–1938) was appointed to the Supreme Court by President Herbert Hoover in 1932.

Americans should not have to fear "judge-made laws" as a reality of life. We elect our legislators to make our laws, and those states that elect judges elect them to apply those laws. If these states reject a system of accountable judges, they undoubtedly will face the same arrogance now so evident on the federal level …

Since the proclivity to reshape culture and values is so frequently displayed by unaccountable judges, why would a state want to adopt such a system? In fact, why would anyone even propose a system to give additional insulation to judges? Because—proponents answer—for judges to campaign to win the votes of citizens makes the judiciary a "political" branch and weakens the so-called "independence" of the judiciary. Yet, as Thomas Jefferson wisely observed:

> *It should be remembered as an axiom of eternal truth in politics that whatever power in any government is independent is absolute also…. Independence can be trusted nowhere but with the people in mass.*

This extract is taken from a letter Thomas Jefferson (1743–1826) wrote to Spencer Roane (1762–1822), a Virginia judge, in 1819.

And is anyone really so naive as to believe that the current appointed "independent" federal judiciary has not become a political branch?…

Contrary to what is asserted by the proponents of appointed judges and retention elections, for judges to campaign and win voter support actually prevents the judiciary from becoming a political branch because citizens can then insist that judges confine themselves to their constitutional roles rather than implement their own political agendas.

Benefit of competition

Another benefit of the direct elections of judges is the competition that occurs between candidates. In contested races, judicial candidates make public the beliefs of their opponents, thus allowing citizens the opportunity to make informed decisions about those whom they want to sit on the bench. On the other hand, if an individual is appointed rather than elected, his personal beliefs might remain unknown to the public until they manifest themselves in harmful judicial decisions. Furthermore, these appointed judges would have at least four uninterrupted, unrestrained years before they would face voters for the first time in a retention election—and even at that time, there would be no opponent to remind voters of egregious decisions.

Do you think unopposed retention elections are a good idea? If not, why?

Those proposing retention elections are not improving State government. Instead, they are violating one of its most sacred principles: they are removing power from the people—something to which Thomas Jefferson strenuously objected:

> *The exemption of the judges from that [from election] is quite dangerous enough. I know no safe depository of the ultimate powers of the society but the people themselves; and if we think them [the people] not enlightened enough to exercise their control with a wholesome discretion, the remedy is not to take it [control] from them, but to inform their discretion by education.*

This extract is taken from a letter Jefferson wrote in 1789. He argues that it is better to have an unaccountable legislature rather than an unaccountable judiciary. What might be the dangers of this?

Jefferson further declared:

> *[I]t is necessary to introduce the people into every department of government.... Were I called upon to decide whether the people had best be omitted in the legislative or judiciary department, I would say it is better to leave them out of the legislative. The execution of the laws is more important than the making of them....*

In addition to these historical lessons, recent experiences demonstrate that in States with an appointed judiciary, judges are quite comfortable in exerting political influence rather than simply upholding and applying State laws.

A case in point: New Jersey

For example, in the 2002 election, the appointed New Jersey Supreme Court reviewed the State law declaring that a candidate's name may be replaced on the ballot only if the "vacancy shall occur not later than the 51st day before the general election" and somehow decided that the 35th day before the election fulfilled the same legal requirements as the 51st day before the election. (Recall that the Democrat candidate was lagging far behind his Republican opponent in the polls; the Democrats convinced the unelected judges to place a more viable candidate on the ballot—in violation of the State law—and Democrats therefore won a U. S. Senate seat they were destined to lose.)

Another case in point: Florida

And who can forget the appointed Florida Supreme Court in the 2000 presidential election? Even though State law declared that all election vote tallies were to be submitted to the Secretary of State's office by 5 P.M. on the 7th day following the election, and that results turned in past that time were to be ignored, those judges ruled that 5 P.M. on the 7th day really meant 5 P.M. on the 19th day, and that the word "ignored" really meant just the opposite—that the Secretary of State must accept *all* results, even those that did not comply with the law.

Judges facing regular elections would not have rendered decisions that ignored such clear legislative language (not to mention basic math or the common meaning of words). Elected judges know that if they make such agenda-driven decisions, they will face a plethora of opponents in their next race who will remind voters of their demonstrated contempt for State law.

The arrogant, elitist proposal that judges should be protected from citizens in this day of rampant judicial political agendas is unthinkable in our free society. History is too instructive on the necessity of direct judicial accountability for its lessons to be ignored today. And while judicial accountability through the use of impeachment on the federal level appears to be a thing of the past, judicial accountability through the direct election of State judges should not be.

> *Democrat Robert Torricelli withdrew his name from the general election ballot for the U.S. Senate after he was rebuked by the Senate Ethics Committee for taking gifts from a donor during the 1996 election campaign. The New Jersey Supreme Court ruled that the Democrats could replace his name on the ballot, saying that it was more important to have a ballot bearing the names of candidates of both major political parties. Republicans appealed the decision, but the U.S. Supreme Court declined to hear the case.*

> *Do you think the author is justified in asserting that elected judges would have rendered different decisions in these cases?*

Summary

In the first article Steven Sebelius argues that elections are the worst possible method of choosing judges. The main problem, he says, is money. He contends that it is impossible for judges to solicit campaign contributions without creating an appearance of bias or favoritism. As an example, he examines a district court election campaign in Nevada. Sebelius argues that a system of appointing judges would avoid "the corrupting influence of money" and would remove pressure on judges to make rulings that appease donors or voters. He favors the Missouri system of retention elections as a replacement for judicial elections in Nevada. Sebelius points out that although the public might claim to want to keep an election system, in reality people do not know enough about the candidates to vote for them, and in any case, they do not show up to vote.

In the second article David Barton argues that appointment of judges gives them an undesirable degree of insulation from the populace. He points to the concern of the Framers that the judiciary would abuse its power. Barton argues that the Framers made it possible to impeach federal judges as a means of keeping judges accountable. He claims that judges routinely misuse their authority by imposing their own political agenda rather than upholding laws. Barton contends that judicial elections give the public the ability to prevent the judiciary becoming a political branch, whereas retention elections destroy this power. He supports his argument with two examples that he claims prove that elected judges have their own agenda—recent rulings from the supreme courts of New Jersey and Florida.

FURTHER INFORMATION:

Books:

Champagne, Anthony, and Judith Haydel (eds.), *Judicial Reform in the States*. Lanham, MD: University Press of America, 1993.

Clegg, Roger, and James D. Miller (eds.), *State Judiciaries and Impartiality*. Washington, D.C.: National Legal Center for the Public Interest, 1996.

Useful websites:

http://www.ajs.org/selection/index.asp
Section of the American Judicature Society site devoted to resources on judicial selection. Provides detailed information on selection methods in each state.
www.fed-soc.org
Site for the Federalist Society. Has detailed reports making cases for both judicial appointments and partisan judicial elections.

www.moderncourts.org
Site "dedicated to improving the administration of justice in New York State." It examines different methods of judicial selection.
http://supct.law.cornell.edu/supct.html/01-521.ZC.html
Text of Justice O'Connor's opinion on the case *Republican Party of Minnesota v. White* (2002).

The following debates in the Pro/Con series may also be of interest:

In this volume:
Topic 9 Should public funds finance judicial election campaigns?

SHOULD STATE COURT JUDGES BE APPOINTED RATHER THAN ELECTED?

YES: Retention elections for appointed judges give the people an opportunity to express their satisfaction or otherwise with a judge's performance

YES: Without having to solicit campaign funds, as elected judges do, appointed judges are free to make decisions without facing accusations of bias and favoritism

ACCOUNTABILITY
Are appointed judges more accountable to the public?

CORRUPTION
Do appointments remove the taint of corruption from the judicial selection process?

NO: Unlike elections, judicial appointments take away power from the people. Judges are sometimes reappointed for several terms without having to answer to the public for the quality of their work.

NO: In systems in which the state governor appoints judges there is a high risk of political cronyism because there are no checks and balances on executive power

SHOULD STATE COURT JUDGES BE APPOINTED RATHER THAN ELECTED?

KEY POINTS

YES: Judicial appointments spare judges the indignity of having to seek nomination with political parties and prevent them feeling obliged to maintain political allegiance once they are on the bench

INDEPENDENCE
Are appointments the best way to maintain judicial independence?

NO: Judicial elections are better because they ensure that judges do not abuse their authority and seek to impose their own political agenda

Topic 9
SHOULD PUBLIC FUNDS FINANCE JUDICIAL ELECTION CAMPAIGNS?

YES
"BRINGING FAIRNESS TO THE BENCH—REFORM JUDICIAL ELECTIONS"
THE MIAMI HERALD, NOVEMBER 17, 2002
J.B. HARRIS

NO
"PUBLIC FUNDING FOR JUDICIAL ELECTIONS: FORGET IT"
WWW.CATO.ORG, AUGUST 13, 2001
ROBERT A. LEVY

INTRODUCTION

Judicial elections exist in some form or another in about 80 percent of U.S. states. Campaigning in these elections has become increasingly expensive during recent years. According to a report titled "The New Politics of Judicial Elections 2002," issued by the Justice at Stake Campaign, 10 high court candidates each raised more than a million dollars for their campaigns in that year. The report also showed that in 20 out of 25 contested races, the candidate who raised the most money won the election.

Many people are concerned that campaign contributions influence the decisions that judges make in the courtroom, and they support reforms in the judicial election process. Some experts have called for spending limits to be placed on election campaigns. However, in its 1976 decision *Buckley v. Valeo* the Supreme Court held that campaign expenditure is a form of speech protected by the First Amendment to the Constitution, and subsequent attempts to impose mandatory caps on campaign spending have failed. Another option would be to offer judicial candidates the option of accepting public funds in exchange for their promise to abide by campaign spending limits. Supporters insist that this plan would guarantee a level playing field for all candidates, but opponents question whether it would be a good use of taxpayers' money.

Commentators often observe that while expensive election contests pose problems generally, they raise particular concerns in the context of judicial races. Whereas legislators, to a degree, are expected to voice certain views, judges are required to remain neutral. Their role is to decide each case that comes before them on the bench on its individual merits, rather than on the basis of their connections to any of the parties involved or their allegiance to particular interest groups.

Studies show that most contributions to judicial election campaigns come from lawyers who belong to a small number of large law firms. A firm will often aggregate its contributions by making a donation from the company itself as well as a number of individual contributions from its lawyers. Other ready sources of contributions are corporations, lobby organizations, or groups whose interests are likely to be adjudicated in court—for example, those with a stake in gun use, tobacco-related illness, medical malpractice, or caps on damages.

> *"Judges across America are trapped in a system that forces them to raise money like regular politicians."*
> —JUDGE JAMES WYNN,
> NORTH CAROLINA COURT
> OF APPEALS (2004)

Critics of judicial elections frequently protest that the necessity to solicit contributions makes judges beholden to donors and may affect the integrity of judicial decisions. They further argue that fundraising reduces respect for jurists and discourages well-qualified candidates—especially those without strong ties to wealthy backers—from seeking office. Some critics advocate restricting or removing private finance from judicial campaigns. This idea has been endorsed by the American Bar Association's Standing Committee on Judicial Independence. In 2002 North Carolina became the first state to implement legislation to establish a voluntary full public financing system for judicial elections. Candidates have to adhere to strict fundraising limits during the primary elections in order to receive full funding for their general election campaigns. Other states are considering similar plans.

Proponents claim that a system of public funding restores trust in an independent judiciary by eliminating any suggestion of impropriety from election campaigns. They also argue that since the funds derive from tax revenues, public finance plans encourage people to vote by giving them a greater stake in election outcomes. Judicial elections traditionally attract a low voter turnout.

Critics oppose public funding for a number of reasons. Some insist that there are sufficient checks already in place on judges' behavior. They point out that the electorate is protected against the threat of judicial impartiality by the requirement that judges issue written opinions to substantiate their decisions, by the appeals process, and also by judicial ethical codes that dictate that judges should recuse themselves from cases in which they may have a conflict of interest.

Other commentators argue that the public financing of judicial elections is simply not feasible since there is no support for it. They point out that each year fewer taxpayers choose to contribute to the Presidential Election Campaign Fund by checking off the appropriate box on their federal tax returns. This reluctance, they claim, reflects a general opposition to public financing among the electorate.

The following articles debate the use of public funding in judicial elections in greater depth.

BRING FAIRNESS TO THE BENCH— REFORM JUDICIAL ELECTIONS
J.B. Harris

J.B. Harris is a trial lawyer. This article first appeared in The Miami Herald in 2002.

Florida's code of judicial conduct prohibits candidates from personally soliciting campaign contributions. However, candidates may establish campaign committees to secure and manage campaign funds and to obtain public statements of support from attorneys. Go to http://www.ajs.org/ js/FL_elections.htm for an explanation of judicial elections and campaigns in Florida.

YES

✓ Anyone who has ever contributed money to a judicial campaign recognizes the effects almost immediately. Judges who once would not give you the time of day say hello to you in passing, shake your hand, smile when they see you and even remember your name when you appear in their chambers for hearings.

This is no coincidence. As the beneficiaries of political largesse, judges sign off on every contribution made to their campaigns, commit to memory their list of contributors and make it a point to thank their supporters in subtle and not so subtle ways.

This occurs even though the law requires the appearance of insularity through the use of "'independent" campaign committees, treasurers, accountants and fundraisers.

It's also no accident that the best firms and most successful attorneys are among regular contributors to judicial campaigns—contested as well as uncontested. By law, monetary contributions are limited to a maximum $500 per campaign. To magnify the impact of giving, however, firms often contribute under the firm name and then encourage or pressure their employees to make individual contributions too. To hedge their bets, some firms even contribute to challengers as well as to incumbents in the same race.

In-kind contributions

Other firms make in-kind contributions for well over $500, by sponsoring expensive cocktail receptions and fundraising activities for judicial candidates. While the value of in-kind contributions remains unrestricted and often goes unreported, such affairs are the primary way in which judicial candidates get to meet their supporters. Most often these supporters are all attorneys.

If anyone doubts the level and frequency of giving in judicial elections, they need only visit the Florida Department of Elections website at election.dos.state.fl.us. Since all contributions are public, the list of contributors to each

The Supreme Court building in Florida. Some commentators have suggested that the only way to maintain an independent judiciary in the state is to use public funds for judicial campaigns.

Do "civilians" have an incentive to contribute to judicial election campaigns?

judicial campaign reads like a Who's Who among the Bar's finest. A rough estimate also suggests that attorney contributions outnumber civilian contributions by a ratio of 50 to 1, perhaps more.

A flawed system

The current system of judicial elections is fundamentally flawed and should be replaced. The system places at odds two democratic ideals that remain irreconcilable in practice: the people's right to freely elect their public officials and the need for an independent judiciary. These competing objectives collide at the intersection of campaign politics, where the odious need for money requires judges to hold out their hands for contributions to be elected—but at the same time the law requires their independence once elected.

Is the author being overly cynical? Does it necessarily follow that a financial supporter would expect some kind of compensation from a judge whom he or she has helped elect?

While this model may work in theory, in practice the necessity of compensating supporters and planning for reelection have infected the judiciary and its decision-making process with the virus of politics not envisioned by the Framers of Florida's constitution.

Because the unseen hand of politics follows a judge into the courtroom like a shadow once elections are over, judges sometimes temper their rulings with an eye toward winning the next election, especially when supporters appear before them. Why offend a supporter with an adverse ruling when a judge will be looking to the same patron for the next election?

Is it ethical for a judge to decide on a case to which he or she has a connection? Do you think this might undermine the idea of an independent judiciary?

This is one reason why judicial sanctions for attorney misconduct are rare and why favoritism seems palpable in some cases and not others.

Serving two masters

Until we replace the current system with one that removes private contributions from judicial campaigns, Floridians will never have a truly independent judiciary.

According to a poll carried out by the Justice at Stake Campaign in 2001, 30 percent of Florida's judges believed campaign contributions had at least some influence on judges' decisions. A generic proposal for public financing of judicial elections found support among 56 percent of judges.

Publicly, judges deny the pressure to yield. Privately, however, they express a grinding frustration at having to serve two masters. Even the fairest judges admit to a subliminal or subconscious effect wrought by the current regime. Whatever the impact, judges should not be forced to choose—by a system that puts them in office—between expediency and fairness.

Forcing judges to make such a choice not only undermines confidence in the judiciary, it also fuels a corrosive cynicism about the ability of the system to render just results. If we continue to keep judges in this political straight-jacket, then let us be honest with ourselves and the public by changing the ubiquitous mantra, which adorns courtrooms throughout the state, from "We who labor here seek only truth," to "We who labor here seek only votes."

In a democracy, we get what we vote for. We also get what we pay for. Two years ago, voters in Florida soundly rejected a ballot initiative endorsed by the Florida Bar that would have replaced the current electoral system with one of judicial appointments. No doubt aware of the political machinations accompanying the appointment of federal judges and fearful of creating a system that would be more political, not less, voters decided to maintain the current system. The status quo, however, merely perpetuates this clash of democratic ideals.

For more about the involvement of politics in the appointment of federal judges see Topic 2 Are politics too influential in the selection of federal judges?

Bring in public funds

To balance these opposing goals, we must remove private money from judicial campaigns and replace it with public funds. In other words, if elections are to remain the people's choice of judicial selection, then the people of Florida must be willing to pay for it in order to achieve and maintain an independent judiciary. Such a plan not only would eliminate or restrict private and in-kind contributions, it would also give the citizens of Florida a greater stake in the outcome of judicial elections—hence a greater opportunity for involvement in the process—than exists under the current regime.

Judicial elections do not usually attract a high voter turnout. Do you think that the use of public funds for judicial campaigns would encourage more people to vote?

The Department of Elections, in turn, would make available to qualified candidates allowances for campaign expenses. Perhaps the number of contestants for any given seat might also be limited. However we fine-tune the new program, its benefits would clearly outweigh its disadvantages.

With big money now needed to buy a seat on the bench, the scales have tipped too far in favor of election politics and private fundraising in judicial campaigns at the expense of judicial independence.

Would the author have a stronger case for claiming that the benefits of a public finance program outweigh the disadvantages if he mentions what the drawbacks are?

The time has come for a change. This change will require removing private contributions from judicial campaigns and replacing them with public funds.

Allowances for campaign expenses not only would level the playing field for all contestants, it would also invest the public with a greater stake in the outcome and remove the pressure on judges to compensate supporters once elections are decided. Until we replace the current regime with one that's more equitable and accessible, the judiciary's independence erodes a little more each day.

PUBLIC FUNDING FOR JUDICIAL ELECTIONS: FORGET IT
Robert A. Levy

Robert A. Levy is senior fellow in constitutional studies at the Cato Institute, a public policy research foundation. This article was published on the institute's website in 2001.

The American Bar Association (www.abanet.org) is the world's largest voluntary professional association. It provides law school accreditation, information about the law, and programs to assist lawyers and judges in their work.

Why do you think voters are generally reluctant to replace judicial elections with an appointment system?

NO

At its meeting in Chicago this month, the American Bar Association unveiled the recommendations of its Commission on Public Financing of Judicial Campaigns. The Commission, allegedly concerned about "inappropriate politicization of the judiciary," has urged that contested elections for state supreme court justices and some appellate judges be publicly funded. Ironically, that proposal will be embraced by the same association of 400,000 lawyers and judges most responsible for politicizing the profession it purports to represent. The ABA officially promotes a liberal agenda on issues ranging from federal gun control to affirmative action to universal health care.

The real goal of the new financing scheme isn't as lofty as the Commission contends. Instead, we are witnessing the opening salvo in a crusade to publicly fund federal and state elections for all three branches of government.

A cure that's worse than the disease

There may be good arguments for merit selection of judges followed by periodic, unopposed retention elections. But contested elections raise serious questions. They've become inordinately expensive, create a perception of impropriety, and may produce judges beholden to deep-pocketed donors with recurring business before the court. While politicians are expected to fight for their constituents, judges are supposed to have an allegiance to the rule of law, not to individual or corporate interests. Still, voters in many states have resisted attempts to replace judicial elections with executive appointments. That's the problem the ABA Commission claims to address. Lamentably, the proposed cure is worse than the disease.

Public funding favors current office-holders by denying to challengers the financial resources needed to overcome the advantages of incumbency. Public funding is opposed by taxpayers; just look at the small percentage who have opted to check off tax dollars for presidential campaigns. Ordinarily, public funding is tied to prior vote counts or fundraising, thereby penalizing new candidates. Without those ties, however, public funding diverts resources to fringe candidates. The Commission blithely wishes away that problem by asserting that only "serious" candidates will receive money. Yet our experience with presidential elections isn't encouraging. Big bucks have fattened the campaign coffers of luminaries like ultra-leftist Lenora Fulani and convicted felon Lyndon LaRouche.

Coerced speech

Naturally, there's the issue of cost, about which the Commission professes no insight and offers no solution. And finally, of paramount importance, there's the moral and constitutional concern over coerced speech. "To compel a man to furnish contributions of money for the propagation of opinions which he disbelieves and abhors," said Thomas Jefferson, "is sinful and tyrannical." Yes it is. But coerced speech is what sustains publicly funded elections. When government tells us what we must say—abridging core rights guaranteed by the First Amendment—it must have a compelling interest in doing so, and it must adopt the least restrictive means available. To fund judicial elections with tax dollars satisfies neither criterion.

Presumably, the compelling state interest is the same for judges as for legislators—to avoid actual or apparent corruption. Then again, the community is much better protected from venal judges than from shady lawmakers. Judges deal with concrete cases in which the interests of the attorneys and the litigants are unmistakable, thus ripe for public scrutiny. Similarly, the judge's link to the outcome of the case is unambiguous. Judges are usually subject to appellate review. Judges decide matters of law, not value-laden policy questions. Judges must substantiate their legal conclusions by issuing a written opinion. And judges in all 50 states are governed by an ethical code, in writing, with prescribed remedies and enforcement procedures.

Among their ethical prohibitions, judges may not hear cases in which they have a personal bias toward a party or a financial interest in a party or in the subject matter. Moreover, the ABA Model Code of Judicial Conduct, adopted in substance by 47 states, permits fundraising only by "committees of responsible persons" acting on behalf of the nominee. Candidates may not directly solicit or accept campaign contributions. In August 1999, the ABA went considerably further. It modified the Model Code to command that judges disqualify themselves from any

Levy uses the word "luminaries" ironically to describe two controversial politicians. Liberal activist Lenora Fulani (1950–) ran for the presidency as a candidate for the New Alliance Party in 1988 and 1992; Lyndon LaRouche (1922–) has run for the presidency on eight consecutive occasions. He began his political career as a Marxist but is now often associated with right-wing views— although he describes himself as a Democrat in the vein of Franklin D. Roosevelt.

Do you agree that the public has less to fear from those who interpret the law than those who make it?

Go to http://www. abanet.org/cpr/mcjc/ mcjc_home.html to view the ABA Model Code of Judicial Conduct, last revised in 2003.

Critics argue that public funding of judicial elections amounts to compelling "a man to furnish contributions of money for the propagation of opinions which he disbelieves and abhors"— a phrase used by Thomas Jefferson in the 1786 Virginia Statute for Religious Freedom.

case in which a party or attorney has donated more than a specified amount (to be determined by each state). That anti-corruption provision is buttressed by comprehensive disclosure obligations.

Unquestionably, the requirement that judges recuse themselves in appropriate cases is less restrictive medicine than compelled speech. Indeed, even the ABA's disclosure mandate can be avoided if parties and attorneys simply declare under penalty of perjury that they have not violated established contribution limits. That way, both political coercion and influence peddling are minimized. At the same time, voters will be free to advance their particular judicial philosophies by contributing to the campaign of their choice.

Contested judicial elections may be a bad idea, but without free speech they are immeasurably worse.

Go to the ABA website to find out the maximum punishment for committing perjury. Is this enough of a check on the conduct of judges?

Summary

In the first article J.B. Harris maintains that the current system of judicial elections in Florida is deeply flawed and needs to be replaced. He argues that despite the rules governing contribution limits, campaign politics threaten judicial independence. Harris asserts that judges temper their rulings with an eye toward pleasing supporters and winning the next election. He suggests that the public loses confidence in the judiciary when it sees judges accepting large donations. His proposed solution is to remove private money from judicial campaigns and replace it with public funds. He argues that this plan would give citizens a greater stake in elections. It would also, he says, level the playing field for all candidates, remove the pressure on judges to compensate supporters, and increase public respect for the judicial role.

Robert A. Levy opposes public funding for judicial contests on several grounds. He is concerned that it would be the beginning of a trend toward public funding for all elections. Nevertheless, he agrees that fundraising for judicial elections causes problems, although he believes many of the problems are offset by safeguards like judicial ethics codes. He suggests that the appropriate solution to these problems would be to move to a system of appointing judges. Under the current system, however, he does not see public funding as a viable solution to the problems of fundraising. First, he fears that public funding favors incumbents since it generally is available only to those with a prior track record of either fundraising or vote-getting. Second, public funding drains money from public coffers. Finally, requiring taxpayers to contribute to these campaigns is, in his eyes, a form of coerced speech.

FURTHER INFORMATION:

Books:

McFadden, Patrick M., *Electing Justice: The Law and Ethics of Judicial Election Campaigns.* Chicago, IL: American Judicature Society, 1990.

Articles:

Wohl, Alexander, "Justice for Rent." *The American Prospect*, vol. 11, no. 13, May 22, 2000.

Useful websites:

http://www.abanet.org/judind/jud_campaign.html
Report on public financing of judicial campaigns, American Bar Association Standing Committee on Judicial Independence.
http://faircourts.org/files/NewPoliticsReport2002.pdf
"The New Politics of Judicial Elections 2002," report issued by the Justice at Stake Campaign.

http://www.wi-citizenaction.org/
Information on campaign finance reform in various states.

The following debates in the Pro/Con series may also be of interest:

In this volume:
Topic 8 Should state court judges be appointed rather than elected?

In *Government*:
Topic 11 Can the wealthy buy their way into political office?

SHOULD PUBLIC FUNDS FINANCE JUDICIAL ELECTION CAMPAIGNS?

YES: Polls indicate that judges feel enormous pressure to raise money and that many favor the idea of public funding

YES: Public funding promotes an equitable system for those candidates who do not have access to big money to buy a seat on the judiciary

POPULARITY
Would public funding of judicial election campaigns be a popular move?

LEVEL-PLAYING FIELD
Does public funding guarantee a level-playing field for all judicial candidates?

NO: The low number of people who choose to contribute to the Presidential Election Campaign Fund proves that public financing of elections does not have broad support among the electorate

NO: Public funding is biased in favor of current office holders, and privately funded candidates are still able to run in elections

SHOULD PUBLIC FUNDS FINANCE JUDICIAL ELECTION CAMPAIGNS?

KEY POINTS

YES: The necessity to solicit campaign contributions makes judges beholden to donors and may affect their objective decision-making

YES: The need to raise funds often discourages well-qualified candidates from running for election

REFORM
Does the judicial election system require reform?

NO: There are sufficient checks in place—such as the appeals process—to prevent judicial partiality

NO: Ethical codes prevent judges from deciding cases in which they have a conflict of interest

STRESS MANAGEMENT

"For fast-acting relief
try slowing down."

—LILY TOMLIN, U.S. COMEDIAN (1939–)

Stress is an almost routine part of 21st-century life. While some people thrive under pressure, most do not. People react in different ways to stressful situations such as problems with loved ones, meeting a tight deadline, or taking an exam. Too much stress can be difficult to cope with and may cause health problems like headaches and stomach cramps. By recognizing the signs of stress, it is possible to control its effects. While it is normal to feel anxious, confused, or even depressed at times, it is essential to talk to someone—a family member, a friend, or a teacher—if these feelings get out of control, persist, or become difficult to deal with. The following article looks at ways to cope with stress.

Coping with stress

If you are going to survive in a modern world, it is essential to learn how to cope with stress. Here are a few tips:

1. Causes and solutions:
- People: A lot of stress is caused by people you know or see on a regular basis. Stop seeing people who make you feel anxious or negative about yourself. If you need help, ask a teacher, counselor, or doctor.
- Unnecessary obligations: It is quite often hard to say no to friends or family. Try to cut back on your extracurricular activities.
- Noise: Make your work and home environment as quiet-friendly as possible. Unnecessary noises can aggravate existing stresses.
- Exposure to the real world: We live in a world full of conflict. If reading the paper or watching TV makes you more anxious, cut them out of your life.
- Bad time management: Do not put things off. Try to get the balance right between study and leisure time. Do not overcommit. Get enough sleep.
- Cramming: Try to avoid last-minute cramming. Set aside adequate time to finish assignments or to study for exams.
- Studying alone: Organize a study group if you find it difficult to study by yourself.

2. It is all about attitude
- Perspective: If you find things too overwhelming, try to put matters in perspective. It is usually not events themselves that are stressful but the importance you attach to them.
- Be positive: Focus on what is good in your life and about yourself. Do not be too self-critical, and avoid being with people who put you down.

3. Take care of yourself
- Put yourself first: Be selfish. Saying no is sometimes necessary.
- Make sure you sleep properly: Disrupted sleep can cause problems later.
- Friends and family: Surround yourself with people who give you support or who make you feel good about yourself.
- Take regular breaks: Even a walk around your room is better than nothing.
- Eat properly: Do not cut meals. Make sure you eat fresh foods. Cut down on caffeine and chocolate.
- Pamper yourself: Do things for yourself that make you feel good.
- Exercise: Play a favorite sport or try to do a relaxation exercise daily.
- Laugh: This is one of the best destressers.

Relaxation techniques: helping with stress

The following tips may help you relax. Get medical advice if your symptoms persist.
- Breathing: Try breathing deeply. Clear your mind of everything, and concentrate on taking deep breaths. This will help lessen tension.
- Body awareness: Be aware of your tension spots. Flex muscles by alternately tensing them and relaxing them.
- Meditation: Meditation can be as simple as mentally focusing on breathing or on a particular word or image. Deep relaxation through meditation is more restful for the body than sleep. It is something you can do by yourself, with friends, or in a class.
- Visualization: Imagine scenes that are relaxing and peaceful. That will help you relax. Get in a comfortable position, close your eyes, and imagine yourself in a setting—real or imagined—that has good connotations.
- Guided relaxation: Listen to relaxation tapes, watch DVDs, or go to classes.

SYMPTOMS TO WATCH OUT FOR:

Early signs:
- Feeling as if you are going to burst into tears all the time.
- Finding it difficult to concentrate and make decisions.
- Being irritable and bad tempered.
- Incredible tiredness.
- Insomnia or disrupted sleep patterns.
- Feeling as if you cannot cope.
- Eating more than usual.
- Feeling of failure.

Extreme symptoms:
- Headaches and migraines.
- Tension, especially around the back, neck, and shoulders.
- Being more susceptible to colds and viruses.
- Extraheavy periods.
- Breathing problems.
- Stomach problems.
- High blood pressure.
- Panic attacks.
- Depression.

Topic 10
ARE SENTENCING DECISIONS AFFECTED BY MINORITY GROUP STATUS?

YES

FROM "JUSTICE MAY BE BLACK AND WHITE"
YORK DAILY RECORD, DECEMBER 27, 2002
SHARON SMITH

NO

"JLARC STUDY FINDS NO RACIAL BIAS IN VIRGINIA DEATH PENALTY SENTENCING"
UNIVERSITY OF VIRGINIA SCHOOL OF LAW, NEWS AND EVENTS
M. MARSHALL

INTRODUCTION

Once a jury has returned a guilty verdict in a criminal case, it remains for the court to pass sentence. In most situations it is the trial judge who decides on the punishment, although in cases in which the death penalty is an option, the responsibility usually rests with the jury. Yet there is debate over whether the courts treat all sectors of the population equally when it comes to sentencing, or whether sentencing decisions are affected by the minority group status of not only the defendant but the jury, the attorneys, and the judges as well.

Many civil rights advocates argue that minority groups receive much harsher sentences. According to a November 2003 study guide prepared by the American Civil Liberties Union (ACLU) in conjunction with a plaintiff group in Cincinnati, "Nationally, an African American male born in 1991 has a 29 percent chance of spending time in prison while his White counterpart has only a 4 percent chance of doing so."

Critics of this view claim that judges are required to follow guidelines when setting sentences. Such rules were introduced to eliminate the handing down of widely varying penalties by ensuring that offenders who committed similar crimes and had similar criminal histories were punished in comparable ways. Federal guidelines, for example, went into effect on November 1, 1987. These guidelines place each crime in one of 43 "offense levels." Judges use a chart to locate a point where the offense level and the offender's criminal history intersect and impose a sentence within that range. Some legal scholars have criticized sentencing guidelines. They argue that while the guidelines may have prevented biased judges from meting out harsh sentences, they have opened the door for biased prosecutors to operate instead. Since prosecutors largely decide what the charge against a person will be, they can seek a conviction on a more serious charge, knowing the judge has no choice but to pass the prescribed sentence. Similar criticism has been raised against the mandatory minimum sentences, which were introduced at the federal level in 1986—and also by the states, although many now have been rolled back—in particular to combat drug crime. According to a 2003 Drug Policy Alliance article, "the average federal drug sentence [in 1986] for African Americans was 11 percent higher than for whites. Four years later … [it] was 49 percent higher."

> *"Equal and*
> *exact justice*
> *to all men…."*
> —THOMAS JEFFERSON,
> THIRD PRESIDENT (1801–1809)

Various reports have been published on fairness in sentencing. The Heritage Foundation—an independent research institute—analyzed more than 53,000 criminal case sentences in Pennsylvania for 1998 to ascertain whether race and gender affected the penalties handed down. It concluded that sentences for Hispanic defendants were about 1.5 months longer than for whites, but that sentences for black defendants were an average of two weeks shorter than for whites. The study also showed that black judges were 8.9 percent more likely to send defendants to prison than were white judges, although it pointed out that black judges tended to work in high-crime areas and, as a minority

themselves, might also feel scrutinized by their peers—both of which factors might influence them to be tougher.

A report presented in Rhode Island in 2002, however, helped highlight another aspect of the sentencing debate. The first part concerned the results of a study, carried out on behalf of the Rhode Island Supreme Court, which demonstrated that the sentences handed down by the state's Superior Court were related to the seriousness of the crime and not to the race or gender of the defendants. However, the second part of the study featured the results of a subsequent survey, which revealed that defendants from some minority groups perceived there was a sentencing bias, whatever the reality.

Commentators believe that nowhere is the subject of alleged sentencing bias more controversial than in cases involving the death penalty, in particular when the victim is white. According to the ACLU, "as of October 2002, 12 people have been executed where the defendant was white and the murder victim black, compared with 178 black defendants executed for murders with white victims." This, critics argue, shows the extreme bias in sentencing decisions.

In September 2000 a Justice Department report called into question the impartiality of sentencing in federal capital cases. It found that more than 70 percent of federal death sentence recommendations between 1995 and 2000 concerned people from minority groups. In June 2001 a new study denied that racial bias was to blame for this figure, citing as cause variations in state laws, prosecutors' decisions, and geographical factors.

The following articles examine this issue in more detail.

JUSTICE MAY BE BLACK AND WHITE
Sharon Smith

Sharon Smith is a journalist for the York Daily Record. This article appeared in the December 27, 2002, edition.

The Honorable John H. Chronister is presiding judge of the Court of Common Pleas in the courts of York County, PA.

The Heritage Foundation is a U.S.-based think tank and an educational and research institution. Go to www. heritage.org to find out more.

Bullet points are a good way to break up statistics and make them clear and easy to understand for your audience.

YES

Just before 9:30 a.m. on a recent Tuesday, a flood of defendants filed through the doors of Courtroom No. 7 in the York County Courthouse.

The defendants appearing before President Judge John H. Chronister that day were white, black and Hispanic, men and women. Their charges ranged from drunken driving to robbery. Chronister sent an older white man, facing his second drunken driving charge, to York County Prison for 15 days. He placed a black woman, holding a child, on probation for two years for writing bad checks.

A black man who stole from Kmart received probation. A white man who tried to trick a store into a refund went to jail. From behind his bench, Chronister was cordial, at times even fatherly. If race and gender factored into any of his decisions, it wasn't obvious. But an analysis performed by The Heritage Foundation, a Washington, D.C.-based research institute, found that race and gender were factors when York County judges handed down sentences in 1998.

In York County, blacks and Hispanics received harsher sentences than whites. On average, judges sentenced blacks to an additional 1.1 months behind bars. They sentenced Hispanics to an average of 2.3 months more than whites.

Heritage Foundation analyst David B. Muhlhausen based his analysis on data kept by the Pennsylvania Sentencing Commission as well as original data collected by the *York Daily Record* on the age, gender, race, ethnicity and experience for Pennsylvania judges who sat on the bench in the Court of Common Pleas during 1998.

The study also found:

- Statewide, Hispanic defendants received longer sentences, about 1.5 months longer, than whites.
- Hispanics in York County were 11.4 percent more likely to receive a sentence to county or state prison than white defendants. Across the state, the probability of incarceration increased 5.8 percent for Hispanic offenders.
- Pennsylvania's black judges tended to deliver sentences that were 2.3 months longer than those given by white judges. York County has never had a black judge.

- Statewide, black defendants received sentences that were two weeks shorter on average than whites.
- In Lancaster County, where every judge was a white male, blacks received sentences that were 1.9 months longer than whites. Hispanic defendants received sentences that were longer by 1.4 months.
- In Dauphin County, where one black judge sat on the bench, blacks received sentences that were 1.6 months longer than whites. There were not enough Hispanic defendants to show a statistical difference in how they were sentenced.
- In York County, female judges were more lenient by a month. Statewide, women handed down sentences that were 1.1 months shorter than those handed down by their male counterparts. Across the state, the probability of being sent to state or county prison decreased 13.2 percent for female offenders.
- In York County, women received sentences that were an average of 2.8 months less than those given to men.
- In York County, those who entered negotiated guilty pleas received sentences that were 3.2 months shorter than those who went to trial. Statewide, a defendant who agreed to such a negotiated plea received a sentence that was shorter by an average of 1.5 months.

Why might women judges be more lenient in sentencing decisions? Do you think women may be more willing to take background and societal factors, for example, into account when sentencing?

Do you think this is fair? Should men and women receive equal sentences for committing the same crime?

Judges deny bias

"As far as I'm concerned, in York County, we don't look at race when imposing sentences," Chronister said. "My goal is to look at each case individually and decide what's appropriate."

Mandatory sentences that apply in certain crimes may be to blame for the disparity found in the study, Chronister said. The study also does not take into account social and economic factors, such as who commits certain offenses and why. "That's out of the judge's control," he said.

Lancaster President Judge Michael A. Georgelis also said that race and ethnicity are not considered when sentences are meted out. "When I sentence, I wear a blindfold," he said. "I think there's no predisposition here."

… To decide a person's sentence, Lancaster judges look at a variety of factors, Georgelis said. Those factors would include a person's education, mental history, any substance abuse issues, and statements of support from friends or family. The burden to present those factors to the judge is on the defendant's lawyer, Georgelis said.…

The Heritage Foundation's study could not analyze the quality of representation that blacks, whites and Hispanics

Do you think the poor and minority groups suffer from bad or inadequate legal representation?

receive because the Pennsylvania Sentencing Commission does not collect that data. The quality of a defendant's legal representation could affect sentencing, Muhlhausen said.

Mark Bergstrom, executive director of the sentencing commission, said it would be inappropriate to assume someone's representation would be of a lower quality because a public defender is involved....

The decision-makers

Diversity on the bench and at the prosecutor's table might also play a role in how people are sentenced. For example, in 1998, blacks in Dauphin County received slightly longer sentences, according to the study.

Dauphin County District Attorney Ed Marsico was surprised by the study's findings in regard to the sentences blacks received in Dauphin County in 1998. "My experience has always been the judges sentence based on a person's crime and record without any regard to race," he said.

At the time those sentences were handed down, Dauphin County had a black president judge, Clarence C. Morrison, who has since retired from the bench. Dauphin County's panel of judges is currently all white.

Morrison's presence on the bench was helpful to all in the system, Marsico said.

"I've been working here for 14 years, and I have found race has not played a role in prosecutorial decisions and sentencing," he said.

Dauphin County President Judge Joseph Kleinfelter was skeptical of the study's findings. "As far as I am concerned, sentencing is color-blind in our Dauphin County Court," he said.

Beyond the bench, Dauphin County has quite a few black attorneys, Marsico said. Marsico has two black attorneys on staff. He said there are far fewer Hispanic than black attorneys in Dauphin County, though.

That appears to be the case statewide.

Despite an explosion in Pennsylvania's Hispanic population during the last decade, the state has fewer than 200 Latino attorneys, said Pedro J. Rivera, president of the Hispanic Bar Association of Pennsylvania. The first Hispanic attorney was admitted to the Pennsylvania bar in 1965, he said.

York County has no Hispanic criminal defense attorneys. Hispanics, though, make up 3 percent of the county's population. The lack of diversity in the judicial system could account for some of the disparity in the sentences Hispanics are receiving.

Some bar associations, including Florida's, are now awarding grants to new law graduates so that they are able to afford to work with low-income groups.

Do you think that the backlash against affirmative action admission policies in universities and colleges may have adversely affected the numbers of lawyers from ethnic minorities? Go to www.google.com, and look up recent affirmative action law cases.

Even in Philadelphia, where about half the population is black or Hispanic, few Hispanic judges sit on the bench, Rivera said. Racial and ethnic bias is a factor, he said. But language and cultural differences might also account for the disparity in sentences....

Why might language and culture be factored into sentencing decisions?

Validation

The Heritage Foundation's findings on how the offender's ethnicity affects his or her sentence are similar to the results the Pennsylvania Sentencing Commission came up with when it recently did its own research for previous years. The commission also found that Hispanics received slightly longer sentences than whites, Bergstrom said. However, the commission found blacks received longer sentences as well, while The Heritage Foundation's study showed blacks to have slightly shorter sentences on average.

The commission does not factor in race and gender when developing sentencing guidelines for the state....

Do you think that greater investment in education would help reduce this problem?

"If a judge is sticking to our guidelines, we would expect sentencing to be race- and gender-neutral," Bergstrom said.

The results of the Heritage Foundation study, for some, validate the perceived disparity in the way minorities are treated when they go to court.

"That doesn't surprise me at all," said Leo Cooper, former head of the York chapter of the NAACP. Cooper pointed to studies looking at the race and ethnicity of Pennsylvania's prison population. For example, blacks make up 35.9 percent of York County Prison's population. They only account for 3.5 percent of York County's population overall....

JLARC STUDY FINDS NO RACIAL BIAS IN VIRGINIA DEATH PENALTY SENTENCING
M. Marshall

M. Marshall published this article on the University of Virginia School of Law website.

Why should location matter? Do you think people in urban areas are more likely to live in ethnically mixed communities and be less likely to discriminate on this basis?

Richard J. Bonnie is John S. Battle professor of law and director of the University of Virginia Institute of Law, Psychiatry, and Public Policy.

This is a large disparity. Do you think nonurban courts use the death penalty as a deterrent? Is this fair?

NO

The race of convicted killers is not a factor in death penalty sentences in Virginia, according to a study by the Joint Legislative Audit and Review Commission, the General Assembly's independent investigative and research arm. But the location of the trial is significant. Urban juries are much less likely to impose capital punishment than suburban and rural ones. The study's findings were discussed at a February 4th panel discussion on the death penalty featuring local defense attorneys Steven Rosenfield and Rhonda Quagliana; Albemarle County Commonwealth's Attorney James Camblos; Rob Lee, director of the Virginia Capital Representation Resource Center; and Law School Professor Richard Bonnie, an expert on the death penalty who has also represented persons facing it. Professor Earl Dudley moderated.

The JLARC report

Calling the study "scientific" and "methodologically sound," Bonnie summarized the key elements in the JLARC report. "It's really a very good study. It tries to ascertain the facts rather than use them in support of an opinion."

"The main [JLARC] finding is a locational effect," he said. "Holding everything else constant, there is a higher percentage of life-sentence cases in urban areas. In suburban and rural areas, there are more death penalties imposed.

"This effect has received little attention. Is the morally relevant community the state? If so, then there is an unequal application across the state. But maybe the morally relevant community is the local community, as in obscenity cases. Why shouldn't that be a legitimate grounding? This is what the General Assembly should be thinking about. Prosecutors are judging whether the jury in their area will impose a death sentence. Among capitally-eligible cases across the state, 30 percent get the death penalty, but in urban areas it's only 16 percent."

An equally significant conclusion was drawn from race data, he said. "There is no race-of-defendant effect here. That is very important for supporters of the death penalty. Furthermore, there appears to be no race-of-victim effect. Based on studies in other states, that was the real question. The report says no. But there is a red flag in the report statistics that seems to show that a case involving a white victim is three times more likely to result in a death sentence than one with a black victim, controlling for all other factors," Bonnie said. "But the data in the sample—200 cases—is not large enough to establish significance. The report says this is probably a result of 'instability' in the capital sentencing numbers. So maybe it's a pink flag."

Bonnie described the Virginia Supreme Court's appellate review of capital punishment cases as "thin," "as passive as any state in the country—meaning that no state is more passive," "highly deferential to trial courts," and "reluctant to interfere." More "comparison reviews" should be made, he said, to ensure that a death sentence in one case is comparable to other cases where it was imposed. He faulted current reviews for using a narrow comparison sample (the court doesn't look at an adequate sample of cases in which a life sentence was imposed) and urged that reviews include any case in which a capital sentencing hearing was held.

Furthermore, Virginia "applies the most rigid rules of procedural forfeiture," Bonnie said. "There is a substantial likelihood that claims not raised by lawyers at trial will not be reached in post-conviction review." Bonnie has represented four capital defendants, three of whom were ultimately executed and the fourth had his sentence commuted to life by then Gov. Wilder.

In 11 years as Commonwealth's Attorney, Camblos has prosecuted three cases in which the defendant was eligible for the death penalty but in no case has he asked for it. "I've never tried one all the way through. But I'm the only person here who has to answer to the families of the victims of murder. That is a whole different picture. That is down in the trenches."

He suggested that the rural/urban discrepancy in capital sentences reflected desensitization to violence in cities, whereas suburban and rural communities retain a greater sense of outrage over murders. "Albemarle is a liberal community. Not as liberal as Arlington [County], more liberal than Nelson [County]. I wouldn't proceed with a death penalty recommendation in a case unless I thought it would fly with the jury. I've never asked for the death penalty, but if I have to I will. It would be under very very limited circumstances. Some circumstances of some cases are

Are people from suburban and rural communities as likely to become desensitized to violence through the Internet, TV, and movies?

Actor Denzel Washington plays champion boxer Rubin "Hurricane" Carter in the 1999 film The Hurricane. *Carter was wrongly imprisoned for triple murder. His conviction was finally overturned, but only after he had spent many years in prison.*

so despicable, so far beyond what we think humans could possibly do."

He said capital cases are so serious that he "gives the defending attorney anything and everything I've got. I don't do that with other cases." Given his experience as a defense lawyer, especially recalling one case in which a client was wrongly convicted on false testimony (though ultimately justice was done), Camblos said he would not consider asking for the death penalty on the basis of witness testimony for which there was no corroborating physical evidence.

Rosenfield argued that capital defendants often get less competent representation and faulted the JLARC report for not assessing that factor. "One percent of Virginia attorneys are publicly disciplined in any year. But for those appointed to represent capital case the figure is 6 percent. One in 10 capital defendants have lawyers who subsequently lose their license to practice. Judges don't choose the legal stars in their communities to handle such cases."

Camblos rejected that claim. "Most judges do choose the stars," he asserted.

"Our system [for handling capital cases] is broken in Virginia," Rosenfield contended. "Trial lawyers defending cases have no right to an investigator. Counties have the police or sheriff. We have no right to know who will come against our client as a witness. In one-third of U.S. capital cases a jailhouse snitch is used in the prosecution's case. We have no right to know that's coming in Virginia. The deck is stacked against criminal defendants here."

Legal assistance to defendants "drops off dramatically" after their conviction, VCRRC director Lee said. "The Habeas process is the quality review process. Many problems with the administration of the death penalty are the result of uneven quality of representation in cases. But all lawyers are not the same."

> Do you think attorneys should give 100 percent to each case whether it is a capital case or not?

> If this is true, why should the defendants in capital cases get such poor representation? Does this go against the "equal and exact justice to all men" that Thomas Jefferson commented on?

Summary

In the first article journalist Sharon Smith reports on research conducted by the Heritage Foundation, an independent research group, which found that race and gender were factors when York County judges in Pennsylvania imposed sentences in 1998. According to the Heritage Foundation report, black and Hispanic defendants were more likely to receive longer sentences than white defendants. Black judges tended to give tougher sentences, although women judges were slightly more lenient. The report suggested that a lack of diversity among judges and lawyers might also play a role in disparities in sentencing. The Heritage Foundation report concludes that the justice system is failing people but mainly people of color.

The second article, by law reporter M. Marshall, focuses on a study by the Joint Legislative Audit and Review Commission (JLARC). It concluded that race was not a factor in death penalty sentences in Virginia. The study found that urban juries were less likely to impose death sentences than those in suburban and rural areas. Such a discrepancy might indicate a "desensitization to violence in cities," Marshall notes. The JLARC study also determined that there was no race-of-victim effect despite statistics suggesting that a case involving a white victim is three times more likely to result in a death sentence than one with a black victim. A panel of defense attorneys who discussed the study's findings and described it as "sound," said that this might not be significant since the sample (200 cases) may not have been a sufficiently large group. Marshall draws attention to claims that capital defendants get less competent legal representation. Defense lawyers reject such accusations, arguing that the deck is stacked against capital defendants for other reasons.

FURTHER INFORMATION:

Books:

Dray, Philip, *At the Hands of Persons Unknown: The Lynching of Black America*. New York: Random House, 2002.

Kressel, Neil J., and Dorit F. Kressel, *Stack and Sway: The New Science of Jury Consulting*. Boulder, CO: Westview Press, 2002.

Useful websites:

http://www.aclu.org/CriminalJustice/Criminal Justicelist.cfm?c=49

American Civil Liberties Union paper on racial bias and the justice system.

http://www.uncp.edu/home/vanderhoof/dp-news/njsct-dp.html

Article examines death penalty sentencing in New Jersey.

The following debates in the Pro/Con series may also be of interest:

In this volume:

Topic 12 Is the jury-selection process fair?

In *Criminal Law and the Penal System*:

Topic 2 Should juries have mandatory representation of people of all races?

ARE SENTENCING DECISIONS AFFECTED BY MINORITY GROUP STATUS?

YES: Independent and reliable research shows that the majority of prison and death-row inmates are from ethnic minorities

YES: Current sentencing guidelines limit judicial discretion and lead to "sentencing by numbers"

RACIAL BIAS
Does the race of the defendant play a role in sentencing decisions?

CONTROLS
Are sentencing guidelines unfair?

NO: Research indicates that in reality sentences are related to the crime and not to the defendant's race or gender—although the public and defendants think the opposite is true

NO: Guidelines set up by the U.S. Sentencing Commission were devised to make sentencing more equitable for minority defendants

ARE SENTENCING DECISIONS AFFECTED BY MINORITY GROUP STATUS?

KEY POINTS

YES: Research has shown that defendants, particularly those facing the death penalty, do not always receive the best counsel and often cannot afford to hire lawyers when going to trial

YES: Studies show that black judges, working in high-crime, city areas, hand out much tougher sentences

LEGAL REPRESENTATION
Do minority defendants receive less than competent representation?

LOCATION
Does the location of crime affect sentencing decisions?

NO: It is unfair to suggest that attorneys who represent the poor are inadequate: Many defense attorneys insist that they provide fair and adequate representation.

NO: Sentencing guidelines are applied statewide in the same way regardless of whether in the town or country

PART 3
SELECTED PROBLEMS IN THE U.S. SYSTEM OF JUSTICE

INTRODUCTION

The U.S. judicial system is massive and complex. The vast majority of the business of the judiciary takes place in state courts, which are courts of general jurisdiction. Particularly since the 1960s, when the Supreme Court held that almost all the guarantees of the Constitution apply in state as well as federal court, most of the courts' procedures are limited and guided by constitutional requirements. The courts are faced with the daunting task of dispensing fairness, due process, and equal justice to a large and diverse population drawn from a wide array of social, economic, racial, religious, and ethnic groups. This section examines some of the problems that arise from this challenging task.

Equal protection?

The Fourteenth Amendment to the Constitution guarantees equal protection under the law. Access to equal justice for minority groups has not been easily attained, however. Many of the early barriers to access were slow to fall. For example, it was not until 1954 that the court prohibited discrimination in juror selection on grounds of ethnicity. Until 1975 women were subject to rules making it easy to exclude them from juries, leading to many all-male juries. Although in theory African Americans had the right to

serve on juries soon after passage of the Fourteenth Amendment, it was common for prosecutors to exclude them from juries through peremptory challenge until the 1986 Batson decision

The problems of access for the poor are particularly intractable. The poor as a class are not a protected group under the Constitution, although unequal treatment of the poor disproportionately affects minorities. Topic 11 considers one aspect of the question of equal treatment for the poor: access to legal services in civil actions. It discusses the history of the Legal Services Corporation and the development of alternative means of access. It considers whether the poor currently have adequate access to the judicial system, and more basically, what level of service the poor are entitled to receive.

The question of equal access is in some respects even more urgent in the criminal context. The poor and minority groups are overrepresented in the criminal courts in relation to their percentage of the general population. The Sixth Amendment has been held to guarantee effective assistance of counsel for criminal defendants regardless of ability to pay. As with civil trials, there is a question of what level of services poor defendants are entitled to. Few would argue that every criminal defendant is entitled to O.J. Simpson's "dream team," yet the perception that he was able to buy justice few can afford troubles many. Unlike civil trials, criminal trials carry the possibility of prison time or even execution.

Capital punishment raises some of the most troubling issues of access to

transferred to the states. In addition to the necessity of unanimous verdicts, the standard that juries consist of 12 people has also been held nonbinding at the state level. Another interpretive issue has been the conflict among provisions. For example, the right to a public trial and the right to a fair trial sometimes conflict. The question of whether there should be cameras in the courtroom, for

> *"The jury, passing on the prisoner's life, may in the sworn twelve have a thief or two guiltier than him they try."*
> —WILLIAM SHAKESPEARE (1564–1616), DRAMATIST AND POET

justice. Some argue that lack of competent counsel is the primary reason some defendants either end up on death row or are executed. In addition, poor defendants, even those facing a possible death sentence, have unequal recourse to experts. Solutions to these problems vary widely from state to state, ranging from fairly well funded public defender systems in states like Illinois to patchwork systems of appointing private counsel, often untrained in criminal work.

Juries

The right to trial by jury in criminal cases is a fundamental one guaranteed by Article III of the Constitution and by the Sixth Amendment, which provides for "a speedy and public trial, by an impartial jury...." These guarantees have been subject to substantial interpretive conflict over the years. Although the right to trial by jury in criminal cases has been held applicable to the states, not all the requirements that exist in federal trials have been

example, involves a difficult balance between the defendant's and public's right to an open trial and the defendant's right to a fair trial. Thus far the Supreme Court has not definitively weighed in on this issue, allowing it to percolate in the lower courts until more evidence is in.

Topics 12 to 14 focus on juries. Topic 12 examines the jury-selection process. It asks if the rules designed to ensure impartial juries are effective, among other things. Topic 13 questions whether jurors should be allowed to play a more active role in trials. Jurors can become bored or confused by the proceedings. But would permitting them to ask questions improve the process? Finally, Topic 14 asks if universally unanimous verdicts would lead to fairer verdicts.

The last two topics in the book focus on expert and child-witness testimony. Topic 15 considers whether experts are given too much importance, and Topic 16 focuses on the reliability of child witness evidence.

Topic 11
DO THE POOR HAVE FAIR ACCESS TO THE U.S. JUDICIAL SYSTEM?

YES
FROM "CIVIL LEGAL AID IN THE UNITED STATES: AN OVERVIEW OF THE PROGRAM IN 2003"
CENTER FOR LAW AND SOCIAL POLICY, SEPTEMBER 2003
ALAN W. HOUSEMAN

NO
"NO MONEY FOR THE VOICELESS"
THE NATIONAL LAW JOURNAL, THE BRENNAN CENTER, PRESS RELEASE
LAURA K. ABEL AND PHILIP G. GALLAGHER

INTRODUCTION

Although some scholars argue that the Sixth and Fourteenth Amendments of the Constitution protect the legal rights of citizens, providing them with, among other things, "equal protection under the law," others believe that the U.S. judicial system favors the wealthy and discriminates against vulnerable groups, such as those with low incomes.

The question of whether the poor have fair access to the judicial system has caused much heated comment. Some people believe that the poor receive substandard representation and advice when they are able to get access to legal services at all. Others believe that more than enough money is directed toward legal aid programs, and that this is in fact a waste of resources that would be better allocated elsewhere. When examining this subject, however, some scholars believe that there are two main issues central to the debate. First of all, commentators should examine whether the poor have

adequate routes to civil legal services, representation by qualified public defenders in criminal cases, and easily accessible advice via helplines and the Internet, for example. It is also important to compare the legal advice and advocacy that the poor receive with that available to middle-income and wealthy Americans.

Historically, the United States has a long-established tradition of supplying civil legal assistance programs to the poor dating back to the 1870s, when the German Immigrant Society (the predecessor of the Legal Aid Society of New York) was established. Over the years legal assistance agencies opened in other cities. In 1911 the National Alliance of Legal Aid Societies was established, but most legal aid agencies continued to work in isolation; they varied from private corporations with paid staff to offshoot bodies of local bar associations whose lawyers donated their time when they could. These early agencies shared certain characteristics—they were greatly underfunded, understaffed, and overstretched: Some estimates state that before the 1960s legal aid reached less than one percent of those in need.

In the 1960s changes in social attitudes—through the efforts of organizations such as the National Association for the Advancement of Colored People (NAACP)—led to greater awareness of the inequalities prevalent in U.S. society based on race, gender, and income. Private charitable foundations, such as the Ford Foundation, began to operate, believing that the provision of legal services was an essential part of the overall fight against poverty. It was, however, President Johnson's War on Poverty that really had an effect on the way in which legal aid programs worked, and under the 1964 Economic Opportunity Act Congress made federal money available for legal aid for the first time.

> "I think legal services is rotten, and it will be destroyed."
> —HOWARD PHILLIPS, CRITIC OF THE WAR ON POVERTY (1973)

By 1970 the basic structure of the legal services program was in place. It was based on the idea that local legal services would serve the client community rather than just dealing with individual problems, and that the same range of legal services would be available to the poor as to the wealthy, among other things. The establishment

of the Legal Services Corporation (LSC) in 1974 further helped facilitate legal services to poor communities. Since then, however, civil legal aid funding has undergone great upheaval largely as a result of growing opposition from the "new right," particularly during the 1980s and 1990s. During Ronald Reagan's presidency, in 1980, Congress drastically reduced funding to the LSC, forcing programs to close offices and lay off staff. After Bill Clinton's election in 1992 there was an initial increase in funding, but federal aid fell from $400 million in 1995 to $278 million in 1996.

Today federal funds (around $329 million) represent less than half of the resources of U.S. civil legal services. The balance of funding now comes from private, state, or local government sources. Although some people argue that the poor suffer unfairly from badly funded programs and inefficient legal representation, some associations are working to redress the balance—the Florida Bar Foundation, for example, awards grants to help law graduates take work in low-income communities.

Others contend that the quality and quantity of legal advice and information available to low-income Americans are greater than ever before. Clients can now seek justice through a number of different channels. They can call one of the increasing number of legal hotlines provided to give advice on issues. The Internet also allows the poor access to advice and information provided by attorneys. Advocates argue that legal assistance is important since it acts as a "check" on the courts and government, allowing poor people the means to challenge decisions that involve them.

The following articles address the debate from a civil judicial perspective.

CIVIL LEGAL AID IN THE UNITED STATES...
Alan W. Houseman

Alan W. Houseman is executive director of the Center for Law and Social Policy (CLASP). He specializes in innovative antipoverty strategies. This is an extract from a 2003 publication.

The holistic approach focuses on analyzing what the client community needs to get ahead—including medical services, counseling, and training—rather than the immediate requests of the client. Do you think this approach will help reduce legal problems in low-income communities? Go to http://www.clasp.org/Projects/Civil_EJN/holistic_advocacy to find out more.

Go to www.google.com, and search for articles on recent legal aid federal funding. Do you think more funds should be spent in this area?

YES

✓ ... How did we get there?

Civil legal assistance for poor people in the United States began in New York City in 1876 with the founding of the predecessor to the Legal Aid Society of New York. In 1965 the federal government first made funds available for legal services through the Office of Economic Opportunity (OEO) and started the "legal services program." The OEO legal services program was designed to mobilize lawyers to address the causes and effects of poverty.

OEO funded full-service local providers, each serving one geographic area, that were to ensure access of all clients and client groups to the legal system. OEO assumed that each legal services program would be a self-sufficient provider— the program would do all advocacy, including major litigation and holistic advocacy, using social workers and others. OEO also developed a unique infrastructure that, through national and state support and training programs and a national clearinghouse, provided leadership and support on substantive poverty law issues, as well as undertook litigation and representation before state and federal legislative and administrative bodies.

In 1974, Congress passed the Legal Services Corporation Act, and in 1975, LSC took over programs started in OEO. The delivery and support structure put in place by OEO was carried over fundamentally unchanged by the Legal Services Corporation when it began to function in 1975. While the LSC Act said that LSC was set up "to continue the vital legal services program," it also explicitly changed the goals of the program. LSC was to ensure "equal access to our system of justice for individuals who seek redress of grievances" and "to provide high quality legal assistance to those who were otherwise unable to afford legal counsel." LSC strengthened existing providers, retained and strengthened the support structure, and expanded the program to reach every county.

Even though there were experiments dealing with delivery of services (e.g., hotlines for the elderly funded primarily through Office of Aging of the Department of Health and Human Services and by AARP), the structure of the federal legal services program remained essentially unchanged until

1996. At that point, Congress reduced overall funding by one-third, entirely defunded the support system, and imposed new and unprecedented restrictions. These included prohibitions on class actions, the seeking attorney's fees, and the representation of some aliens and certain public housing clients. Although there had been some restrictions on what LSC-funded legal services programs could do, particularly with LSC funds, the new restrictions prohibited LSC grantees from using funds available from non-LSC sources to undertake activities that are restricted with the use of LSC funds. No part of a LSC grantee's funds, from whatever source, can be used to undertake activities prohibited by the 1996 restrictions.

In response, a number of LSC providers gave up LSC funds and expanded the non-LSC-funded delivery system. Moreover, many state support entities were eliminated, and, in order to survive, national support entities had to rely on private funding, often from major national foundations. In addition, new intake systems, such as hotlines, developed throughout the country, and use of the Internet expanded to provide information and coordinate advocacy. We also saw new approaches to assist self-represented litigants, often in conjunction with the courts, but including many civil legal aid providers. And most fundamentally, we saw a technology revolution in U.S. civil legal aid.

Now the United States is in the midst of an even larger change. LSC, state Interest on Lawyers Trust Account (IOLTA) entities, the National Legal Aid and Defender Association (NLADA), and the American Bar Association (ABA) are working to create in each state comprehensive, integrated statewide delivery systems, called state justice communities. These state justice communities seek to create a single point of entry for all clients; integrate all institutional and individual providers and partners; allocate resources among providers to ensure that representation can occur in all forums for all low-income persons; and provide access to a range of services for all eligible clients no matter where they live, the language they speak, or the ethnic or cultural group of which they are a member.

The state justice community initiative will result in a fundamental change in how legal aid has been organized in this country.… In short, how the civil legal aid system develops is no longer solely or primarily in the hands of civil legal aid professionals but is now in the hands of a much broader group of people within the justice system.…

> *Organizations such as the Ford Foundation (see http://www.nfg.org/downturn/ford.htm for more information) have been essential to legal aid funding. Do you think the federal government should be responsible for this area?*

> *In 1964 Edward and Jean Kahn published an article called the "War on Poverty: A Civilian Perspective." They argued that local neighborhood law offices and lawyers were a necessary part of the fight against poverty. They believed that these services would provide local residents with a vehicle through which to challenge and influence antipoverty strategies. Do you think this approach would be effective?*

Go to http://www. lri.lsc.gov/abstracts/ abstract.asp?level 1=Technology &level2= Publications& abstractid= 020094&ImageID=5 to read this publication by Julia Gordon.

... The technology revolution

The impact of technology on civil legal aid programs in the U.S. has been substantial. A recent publication—*Equal Justice and the Digital Revolution: Using Technology to Meet the Legal Needs of Low-Income People*—discusses the changes that have occurred. In the past 10 years, our society has experienced a "digital revolution," the implications of which are as stunning as those of the industrial revolution, yet are even more remarkable because these changes are happening in a fraction of the time. Beginning with the affordable personal computer and taking a giant leap forward with the creation of the Internet and the web browser, this revolution has changed how we work, play, communicate, learn, and obtain goods and services.

While new technology is a good and efficient way for people to get to a mass of information in minutes, do you think most low-income people have adequate access to the Internet or know how to use it?

In the mid-1990s, organizations providing civil legal assistance to low-income people were beginning to use new technologies on an increasingly regular basis.... [I]n 2003, almost every legal services advocate has desktop access to the Internet and e-mail and uses those resources daily.... Most full service legal aid programs now have a website, with over 100 sites offering information useful to advocates, clients, or both. Seventy percent of states have a statewide website, most of which also contain information useful both to advocates and clients, and many other states are currently building such sites. Dozens of national sites provide substantive legal information to advocates, and other national sites support delivery, management, and technology functions. Many program, statewide, and national websites are using cutting-edge software and offering extensive functionality.

In addition, more and more states have a central phone number (or several regional phone numbers) clients can call to be referred to the appropriate program or to obtain brief advice about their legal problems. A number of programs are using videoconferencing software either for advocate interaction or to deliver services to clients who cannot come into the office. LSC is at the forefront of promoting advanced technologies....

Some people believe that there is a danger that as demand for these services increases, states may use unskilled or ill-informed people to give out legal information. Do you think there should be federal legislation regarding this?

Legal hotlines

Many legal aid programs and a number of states now operate legal hotlines, which enable low-income persons who believe they have a legal problem to speak by telephone to a skilled attorney or paralegal. Legal hotlines may provide answers to clients' legal questions, analysis of clients' legal problems, and advice on solving those problems so that the case can be resolved with the phone consultation or soon thereafter. Hotlines may also perform brief services when those are likely to solve the problem, and make referrals if further legal assistance is necessary....

Since 1996, there has been a huge growth in legal hotlines. Hotlines are now being used in 165 programs in 48 states, Puerto Rico, and Legal Counsel for the Elderly in the District of Columbia. Some focus on particular client groups, such as the elderly. In 2003, there were 66 senior legal hotlines in 40 states, Puerto Rico, and the District of Columbia....

Are the elderly a largely forgotten group in the United States? Go to the U.S. Administration on Aging (www.aoa.gov) to find out what the main age-related concerns and issues are.

Brief services unit

A new approach that is being tested by AARP/Legal Counsel for the Elderly in Washington, D.C., is the Brief Services Unit, a unit that would be devoted solely to providing brief services to clients that require more than phone contact but do not require the services of an attorney or paralegal for more extensive or systemic representation. This unit would do active intake, including periodic clinics in low-income neighborhoods. Non-attorney volunteers and paralegals would staff the Brief Services Unit with back-up support from attorneys housed in a central office and reachable by the Internet and phones. A wide range of services would be provided using a specially designed website....

Legal aid services are often the only chance that the poor get to receive legal advice. Is it right to staff even low-level offices with nonattorney volunteers?

Self-help litigants and pro se developments

A significant development in civil legal aid in the United States is the rapid expansion of efforts to help people who are attempting to represent themselves in courts. Many U.S. civil legal aid programs are devoting substantial time and resources to efforts to address this issue, and most state court systems are engaged in significant activities because of the large numbers of pro se litigants in their courts....

Conclusion

Civil legal assistance in the United States has, over the last 38 years, developed from a haphazard program with limited, virtually all private funding into a significant $950 million institution. The legal aid program has a long history of effective representation of low-income persons and has achieved a number of significant results for them from the courts, administrative agencies, and legislative bodies....

NO MONEY FOR THE VOICELESS
Laura K. Abel and Philip G. Gallagher

Laura K. Abel is staff writer and Philip G. Gallagher is a Katz Fellow at the Brennan Center for Justice at NYU School of Law, New York. This article was published in 1999.

Do you think the government is constitutionally responsible to provide adequate legal access to the poor? Go the Volume 7, The Constitution.

This article was written during Bill Clinton's administration (1992–2001). Although funding rose initially after Clinton's election, it then fell in 1995–1996.

NO

For 25 Years, lawyers funded by the Legal Services Corp. (LSC) have sought to ensure that at least some of the poor receive fair access to the civil judicial system. Tragically, in a system in which political campaigns are financed by the rich, the poor have almost no voice in either the legislative or executive branch. That leaves the courts as the only branch of the tripartite political system to provide the poor with any opportunity to speak on their behalf, and that access is now sharply curtailed by the paucity of funding for lawyers to represent them.

Carving up the coffers

As the 106th Congress brings its first session to an end, partisans continue to argue over which political party "won" the battle over how to carve up the unexpectedly full budget coffers. But whoever, it was certainly not those who rely on federally funded legal services. Notwithstanding the budget surplus, Congress failed to provide LSC with enough money to fulfill the need of the poor for free civil legal representation.

LSC was allotted just over $300 million, to be distributed nationwide, an amount almost identical to the sum allocated during the Regan and Bush administrations—times of severe budget constraints and executive hostility to LSC's mission. Given inflation, today's allocation is worth less than half the 1981 provision. LSC-funded programs employ more than 3,000 attorneys and are assisted by more than 59,000 private attorneys each year. Even so, in 1997, the American Bar Association estimated that the collective effort of legal services lawyers (including many programs that do not receive LSC funds) meets only about 20 percent of the legal needs of the poor. The situations in which the poor are left underrepresented involve the most pressing of human problems. One in six cases funded by LSC involve domestic violence. Others involve tenants seeking decent living conditions, consumers fighting fraud or extortion, families seeking healthcare or public assistance, employees and others fighting discrimination, and parents fighting for adequate education for their children.

Environmental activist Erin Brockovich is one of several activists who have helped highlight corporate exploitation of poor communities in the United States.

COMMENTARY: Wilma Subra

Ask any member of the public to call to mind an environmental activist, and most people will probably think of a stiletto-clad miniskirted Julia Roberts playing activist Erin Brockovich in the 2000 film of the same name. Wilma Subra, however, is one of the lesser-known heroes of the poor. A grandmother and chemist in her late fifties, Subra has become a champion of many poor communities along the Mississippi River.

Subra: respected activist

For more than 20 years Wilma Subra has directed her professional expertise into helping residents of fenceline communities (people who live very close to industrial plants) fight their battles against big corporations. A well-respected environmental crusader, Subra, who works all over America, has helped more than 800 communities take on or fend off polluters. She has also lectured at Harvard University, testified before Congress, helped draft environmental laws, consulted on cancer clusters and toxic spills, and fought sugar cane growers and landfill operators, among other things. She is respected by both those she helps and those she exposes: "Wilma is a top gun for the environmental movement," says Dan Borne, president of the Louisiana Chemical Association, a business trade group.

Helping the poor help themselves

Subra's main focus has been the 85-mile corridor along the Mississippi from Baton Rouge to New Orleans that environmentalists call "Cancer Alley." Chemical and fertilizer plants and refineries pump out tens of millions of pounds of pollutants—including benzene, toluene, xylene, and dioxine—each year. This has led to thousands of residents in the bayous and along the back roads of the area suffering from complaints ranging from asthma and skin rashes to nerve damage and cancer.

Although she never leads a community's fight, Subra provides people with facts and support. "If you do all the walking and talking," she says, "you're just another hired gun." She knows the questions to ask, what records to request, and how to explain things to often frightened people living in poor conditions. She urges the poor to do their own fact-digging and helps them put together their testimonies, and most of this work she does for free. She has even won around several angry locals who would rather keep their jobs than their health. Community activist Albertha Hasten says, "She makes you feel like you're not illiterate, like you didn't come from the poor side of town. She makes you feel like you're special."

Unfortunately her supporters believe that more people like Subra are needed to make sure that the poor and illiterate are represented properly against big business concerns. They claim that polluters are increasingly targeting poor communities that they feel are unable to fight back.

Each has incredibly high human stakes. For example, the Maryland Legal Aid Bureau recently represented a retired man whose landlord had been attempting to evict him and his wife from a federally subsidized apartment because neighbors complained that his cane made too much noise. Legal Services in North Carolina represented a 10-year-old boy with Down syndrome whose elementary school barred him from after school programs.

But for each client lucky enough to get a lawyer, there are four more with equally compelling problems who can get no help.

Go to Volume 7, The Constitution, Topic 7 Does the Constitution adequately protect the rights of the disabled? *What do you think?*

Keeping the account

Lawyers for the poor also keep courts and government accountable, and enable society's institutions to function more effectively. For example, citing the lack of civil legal assistance, a U.S. district judge recently directed the Social Security Administration to improve the confusing notices routinely sent to SSI beneficiaries. He ruled, "Some of the problems presented by the agency's notices might be alleviated if claimants were represented by legal counsel … [yet] the availability of assistance in dealing with problems raised by SSA's notices is extremely limited." *Ford v. Shalala,* 22 N.Y.L.J. 36 (1999).

In January 2000 Chief Judge Charles Sifton required the SSA to modify its SSI financial eligibility notices so that a "reasonable person" could understand the reason for SSA's actions. Full implementation of this will take several years.

Foes of legal services are powerful and, at times, rabid. Throughout the year, the efforts of LSC supporters have been diverted by the need to repel red herring allegations—among then, that some legal services offices inflated the numbers of clients they served.

The charges were not even relevant. Legal services funding is not tied to the number of eligible people living in the area served by a particular program. Thus, there is no incentive to inflate numbers. Nonetheless, House Republican used the allegations as support for an attempt to slash LSC funding to $141 million. So, instead of working to convince Congress to provide a realistic amount of funding, supporters had to fight a rear-guard action to get even as much as LSC received the year before.

So, who were the winners of the federal budget process? The wine industry received $1 million. Thirty-million dollars went to subsidize the timber industry's construction of roads. And tens of millions of dollars were awarded to oil companies, preserving their privilege of taking oil from public hands at a fraction of the market cost.

Apparently need isn't as important as political connections.

By giving comparative budgetary figures, the authors back up their point that the LSC is underfunded. Quoting reliable figures is a good way to validate a particular argument or undermine an opponent's thesis.

Summary

The first article demonstrates that the poor have access to the judicial system by providing an overview of the routes through which those on low incomes can seek legal advice. Alan W. Houseman concedes that in 1996 Congress reduced funding to the Legal Services Corporation (LSC) and imposed restrictions on the cases and clients that could receive assistance. However, this action served merely to stimulate the expansion of the non-LSC-funded system of legal assistance providers. Civil legal aid is today in the hands of a much broader group who are working to create integrated, statewide systems that make efficient use of resources. Indeed, in Houseman's view access to the judicial system is wider than ever before, given that most people can get on the Internet, where countless websites provide legal information. At the same time, legal hotlines allow those on low incomes, the elderly, and people seeking advice on a specific issue to speak to an attorney or paralegal.

The authors of the second piece are of the view that the U.S. courts are the only branch of the "tripartite political system" that provides the poor with a voice. However, they are seriously concerned that the access those on low incomes have to the judicial system is being curtailed by lack of funds for lawyers employed by legal aid programs. The article refers to decisions made by the 106th Congress in 1999–2000, which failed to provide the LSC with enough money to meet the needs of the poor for free legal representation. The article quotes the American Bar Association (ABA), which in 1997 estimated that the efforts of all legal services (including non-LSC-funded programs) met just 20 percent of the legal needs of people on low incomes.

FURTHER INFORMATION:

Books:

Herivel, Tara, and Paul Wright (eds.), *Prison Nation: The Warehousing of America's Poor*. New York: Routledge, 2003.

Useful websites:

www.clasp.org
Center for Law and Social Policy site. CLASP looks at issues in economic security for low-income families.
http://www.nlada.org/About/About_HistoryCivilI
History of the civil legal aid system in the United States.
http://www.sfbar.org/vlsp/homeless.html
The Homeless Advocacy Project of the San Francisco Bar Association. Focuses on providing free legal and social services to homeless families or families in danger of becoming homeless.

The following debates in the Pro/Con series may also be of interest:

In this volume:

Part 3: Selected problems in the U.S. system of justice

In *Individual and Society*:

Topic 1 Is inequality a problem?

Topic 3 Are women still the second sex?

DO THE POOR HAVE FAIR ACCESS TO THE U.S. JUDICIAL SYSTEM?

YES: This right is enshrined in the Sixth and Fourteenth Amendments to the Constitution

YES: Reductions in federal funding to the LSC have stimulated other funding sources. Technological advances (legal hotlines and the Internet) show that there is enough funding.

CRIMINAL JUSTICE
Do poor criminal defendants have adequate access to effective legal counsel?

FUNDING
Do legal services receive enough funding?

NO: Public defender offices are increasingly underfunded and understaffed—a situation unlikely to attract the best lawyers. Poor communities thus suffer.

DO THE POOR HAVE FAIR ACCESS TO THE U.S. JUDICIAL SYSTEM?

KEY POINTS

NO: Restrictions to and lack of capacity in the modern system of civil legal assistance mean that only one in five low-income people have their needs for legal advice and support met

YES: Legal assistance for the poor has led to a greater level of accountability in institutions, such as government and the courts; legal services benefit society as a whole

EQUAL JUSTICE
Do the poor deserve the same level and quality of legal services as those received by middle- and high-income groups?

YES: All individuals have a right to equal justice before the courts regardless of their circumstances

NO: State provision of legal services takes away the incentive for people to look after themselves; it works against competition and so reduces the quality of legal service

NO: People on low incomes cannot expect comparable legal services since they do not pay toward those services; funding for (and hence level and quality of) legal aid programs will be low priority

Topic 12
IS THE JURY-SELECTION PROCESS FAIR?

YES

"ATTORNEY-CONDUCTED VOIR DIRE,
JURY VOIR DIRE—WHO SHOULD ASK THE QUESTIONS?"
VOIR DIRE, VOL. 1, NO. 2, SUMMER 1995, PAGES 38–39
JUDGE PAT B. BRIAN

NO

FROM "ACLU SEEKS CLEMENCY FOR OHIO DEATH ROW PRISONER WHOSE CASE WAS
TAINTED BY RACIALLY BIASED JURY SELECTION"
WWW.ACLU.ORG, APRIL 18, 2002
AMERICAN CIVIL LIBERTIES UNION

INTRODUCTION

A jury is a panel of between six to twelve people whose task it is to deliver a verdict in a court case. Under the Sixth and Seventh amendments U.S. citizens have the right to trial by jury in most criminal and civil cases, and according to estimates, the United States holds about 95 percent of the world's jury trials. Even so, debate rages over whether the jury-selection process produces the "impartial" juries that the Framers called for in the Bill of Rights: A number of recent cases have highlighted that the selection process might not be as fair as the Framers intended.

Selection for jury service entails a number of stages. First, the court draws up a master list of prospective jurors from rolls such as voter and driver's license records. The court then vets this list and excludes all ineligible people. Potential jurors have to meet certain criteria. To be considered for federal jury service, for example, a person must be a U.S. citizen, have a year's residence in the judicial district in question, be at least 18 years of age, be competent in the use of English, and not have any physical or mental disability that would prevent him or her from serving; also, he or she must not be facing felony charges nor be a convicted felon who has not regained his or her civil rights. In addition, certain categories of people are automatically exempt from jury service, including police officers and some government officials. There are other grounds for exclusion—people over 70 years of age may claim permanent exemption, for example.

From the resulting "qualified list" the court calls a random selection of people to report for jury service. The court may excuse more people at this stage on grounds of "undue hardship or extreme inconvenience." The remainder await their turn to sit on a trial. As trials come up, panels of jurors—of more than the required jury complement—

are sent to a courtroom to undergo the final selection process known as voir dire ("to speak the truth").

This process should produce a fair and representative group of people eligible for jury service. When there is a trial, the judge and lawyers involved need to find out if any of the potential jurors are unsuitable for their specific case. During voir dire the individuals on the panel are questioned—by the trial judge, or the lawyers, or both—to determine whether there are any further grounds for dismissal. For example, if a prospective juror has a personal interest in the case (as in the case of a celebrity such as Martha Stewart or O.J. Simpson), is acquainted with any of the parties or their counsel, or has a prejudice about the parties or subject matter, he or she is deemed unsuitable. The lawyers on either side may request that such jurors be excused "for cause." They may challenge as many candidates as they like on such grounds.

"[T]he accused shall enjoy the right to ... trial, by an impartial jury...."

—SIXTH AMENDMENT,
THE CONSTITUTION

Additionally, the defense and prosecution may make a limited number of exclusions without cause. These "peremptory challenges" may be issued simply on a hunch—no explanation is required. As jurors are excused during the challenge process, others are drawn from the panel to replace them, and the voir dire continues until the required number have been chosen. After that they are sworn in, and the trial proceeds.

Although the aim of this system is to swear in an impartial jury, some critics argue that counsel may make excessive or biased use of their challenges in an attempt to get a jury that is favorable to their point of view. These critics cite cases in which abuse of the peremptory challenge system has led to juries that are skewed—by allowing counsel for one party to exclude jurors on racial grounds, for example.

The system's supporters, however, point to the so-called Batson challenge to prove that the system is fair. Named after the 1986 *Batson v. Kentucky* Supreme Court decision, a Batson challenge enables attorneys to object to any peremptory challenges they believe are issued on grounds of race or gender. Opposing counsel must then give a nonracial or nongender-based explanation of why it issued the challenge. Critics, however, claim that it is not hard for clever lawyers to come up with a nondiscriminatory reason for exclusion—whether true or not. Some argue that peremptory challenges should be eliminated. However, many advocates believe that to do so would dispense with a historic process that has generally led to the swearing of impartial juries. They also claim that peremptory challenges provide essential backup to challenges for cause in that they allow an attorney to exclude a juror whom he or she suspects of being biased without being able to prove it through questioning.

The following articles by Judge Pat B. Brian and the American Civil Liberties Union examine some issues in the jury-selection process.

ATTORNEY-CONDUCTED VOIR DIRE, JURY VOIR DIRE—WHO SHOULD ASK THE QUESTIONS?
Judge Pat B. Brian

Judge Pat B. Brian has sat on Utah's Third District Court since 1987. He was formerly deputy district attorney in California and assistant U.S. attorney in Alaska. This article appeared in 1995 in Voir Dire, the quarterly journal of the American Board of Trial Advocates.

See the introduction to this topic (pages 152–153) for explanations of the terms "voir dire," "for cause," and "peremptory challenge."

YES

Questions continue to arise with the Bar and Bench regarding the jury selection process. The debate is whether the judge should ask jurors questions regarding their "suitability" to serve, whether that task should be performed by trial counsel, or whether questioning the jurors should be the combined function for the judge and the attorneys.

The basic purpose of jury voir dire is to expose any "insurmountable" bias or prejudice harbored by members of the jury pool and excuse for "cause" jurors who will not listen attentively to the evidence, apply the law, and decide the case fairly and impartially. The jury selection process also must provide counsel an informed basis on which to exercise their peremptory challenges. In the final analysis, the object of jury voir dire is to "swear" a fair and impartial jury. No more. No less.

In Utah, jury voir dire is conducted primarily by the judge. The federal courts have used this practice for many years. There does not appear to be any significant trend, either in the state or federal system, to alter this procedure.

A tedious process

For many years I served as a state prosecutor in California. During those years for trial lawyers had the right, in civil and criminal cases, to question the jury. The process was tedious, time consuming, and expensive. It was not uncommon to spend ten to fifteen trial days selecting a jury in a murder case. Also, it consistently took thirty to thirty-five percent of the total trial time to select a jury in routine kidnap, robbery, rape, burglary, theft, and assault cases.

I recall in several "big" cases, defense counsel hiring a "platoon" of psychiatrists, psychologists, astrologists, hypnotists, palm-readers, fortune-tellers, and soothsayers to assist the defense team in selecting a jury. For several days during the jury selection process, I watched with some amusement and amazement the interaction between defense counsel and their "advisors." During each court recess, lawyers and advisors hastily formed their "hallway huddle." Then they boisterously debated, speculated and hypothecated what it meant when prospective jurors smiled, frowned, crossed their legs, scratched their noses, slumped in their chairs, sat erect in their chairs, wore pink shirts, chewed gum, looked at their watches, carried day-planners, wore eye shadow, talked to the bailiff, had unshined shoes, read the *Los Angeles Times*, parted their hair, had no hair, etc., etc., etc. Finally, a jury would be selected and the case would proceed. I doubt that the enormous expenditure of time and money made any appreciable difference in the caliber and quality of the jurors ultimately selected to serve. Interestingly, these same procedures, in varying degrees, are alive and well in many courtrooms today. This process seemed questionable twenty-five years ago. It seems questionable today.

> Here the author employs a form of the device called reductio ad absurdum (reduction to the absurd). That is, his description of counsel, the "platoon" of advisors, and their efforts to select a jury conjures up an image of such comical behavior that it makes the process of counsel-based questioning seem ridiculous.

Toward a shorter process

Contrast the above-described scene with a felony theft case over which I recently presided. The case was called at 9:00 p.m., Thursday morning. Thirty prospective jurors had assembled to serve. Prior to trial, both lawyers submitted written questions to be asked the jurors. After the court completed an initial and thorough examination of the jurors, counsel and the court conferred several times at the bench to discuss further questioning of the jurors. Although the court asked all the questions to the prospective jurors, both counsel took a very active role in the jury selection process. Several jurors were excused for "cause." Finally, counsel passed the remaining jurors for "cause," exercised their peremptory challenges, and a jury was sworn. Jury selection was eminently fair to both parties. The playing field was "level" as it related to the jury. A fair and impartial jury had been selected. This entire process took less than two hours. The case was submitted to the jury approximately then trial hours later.

> In the United States crimes are divided into misdemeanors and felonies. A misdemeanor is an offense usually punishable by a fine or up to one year in a county jail. A felony is a more serious crime or may be a repeat offense of a misdemeanor, and carries a penalty of at least one year in prison.

This case is not unusual in the state district courts, in both civil and criminal matters. Arguably, these jury selection procedures have some meaningful relationship to the fact that Utah has one of the lowest backlogs of cases in the United States. Admittedly, the more complex the case, the more time it will take to select a jury. Nevertheless, there must always be a consistent, responsible, and balanced relationship between the time devoted to selecting the jury and the time spent in "trying the case."

The 2003 feature film Runaway Jury *explored the subject of jury-selection manipulation.*

The general public is undeniably becoming more critical and vocal in expressing what it perceives as the failures of the legal system. This criticism is being laid in the laps of both the Bench and the Bar. Litigation is seen as too spurious, too costly, and too time consuming. Our legal system is perceived as being "totally out of control."

Jury selection must be thorough, fair, expedient, unintrusive, and result in litigants having their disputes resolved affordably, fairly, timely, and impartially. Judges and lawyers must not become distracted or unfocused regarding their respective responsibilities. Our combined objective must always be to establish and implement procedures calculated to select a jury that is fair, impartial, and appropriately screened to do its job, and accomplish this task in the most efficient manner possible. Court-conducted jury voir dire best accomplishes that objective.

> *Would you agree with the author that the U.S. legal system is perceived as being "totally out of control"? Why?*

ACLU SEEKS CLEMENCY ... CASE WAS TAINTED BY RACIALLY BIASED JURY SELECTION
American Civil Liberties Union

The American Civil Liberties Union (ACLU) is a nonprofit and nonpartisan organization that works "daily in courts, legislatures and communities to defend and preserve the individual rights and liberties guaranteed to every person in this country by the Constitution and laws of the United States." This article is dated April 18, 2002.

Alton Coleman and his girlfriend Debra Denise Brown were arrested in July 1984 after an eight-week crime spree across the Midwest that included eight killings, plus rapes, kidnappings, and robberies. Coleman was sentenced to death in three states—Illinois, Indiana, and Ohio, where he was executed by lethal injection on April 26, 2002. Brown faces the death penalty in Indiana but is serving a life sentence in Ohio.

NO

The impending execution of Alton Coleman in Ohio is the result of a conviction reached through a racially biased jury selection process, according to a letter sent to Governor Bob Taft and parole board officials by the American Civil Liberties Union of Ohio and the ACLU's Capital Punishment Project.

ACLU attorneys and a coalition of death penalty reform advocates have urged state officials to grant clemency to Alton Coleman, who is scheduled to be executed on April 26. The letter charged that prosecutors in the Coleman case eliminated 82 percent of potential African American jurors and used nine of its 12 jury strikes to do so. In addition, Coleman's lawyer failed to investigate and present evidence to the jury about his horrific childhood and mental illness.

"Mr. Coleman's death sentence was the product of a trial that was fundamentally unfair," said Diann Rust-Tierney, Director of the ACLU's Capital Punishment Project. "Under the circumstances, we can have little confidence in the system that produced Mr. Coleman's death sentence."

Procedures under scrutiny

With Coleman's case, Ohio joins Texas and Pennsylvania as states in which racially questionable jury selection procedures have come under scrutiny. In February 2002, the U.S. Supreme Court stayed the execution of Thomas Miller-El days before his scheduled Texas execution. In Miller-El's case, prosecutors struck 10 of 11 black prospective jurors.

In 1986, the *Dallas Morning News* published an investigation which determined that from 1980 to 1986, prosecutors in capital cases excluded 90 percent of blacks that qualified for jury selection. According to a 1998 Death Penalty Information Center report on Philadelphia juries, from 1983 to 1993 prosecutors struck 52 percent of all black potential jurors, but only 23 percent of all others.

Critics believe that Alton Coleman was convicted unfairly due to jury selection at his trial.

Convicted prisoners or their lawyers file for a writ of habeas corpus in cases of alleged unlawful imprisonment. The writ enables a prisoner to present his or her case for release in court. In the words of the Supreme Court habeas corpus is "the fundamental instrument for safeguarding individual freedom against arbitrary and lawless state action"—Harris v. Nelson (1969).

Coleman's lawyers have filed a writ of habeas corpus in the Ohio Supreme Court challenging the prosecutor's efforts to racially skew the jury. "Mr. Coleman's claims raise disturbing questions that go to the core of our values of racial equality," said Rust-Tierney.

The Coleman case raises additional questions about a system that is failing nationwide. Last week, the 100th innocent person sentenced to death row was released in Arizona and a long-anticipated Illinois Commission report on the death penalty recommended 85 reforms of the death penalty in that state.

The letter sent to the Ohio State Parole Board ...

April 15, 2002

Ohio State Parole
1050 Freeway Drive
N. Columbus, OH 43229

Re: Alton Coleman

Dear Parole Board Members:

On behalf of the American Civil Liberties Union we ask that you commute the sentence of Alton Coleman to life in prison without the possibility of parole. This relief is warranted because Mr. Coleman's death sentence was the product of a trial that was fundamentally unfair. Prosecutors systematically excluded African Americans from serving as jurors and his lawyer failed to investigate and present mitigating evidence that might well have spared him a death sentence.

Do you believe that lawyers should be able to exclude prospective jurors using peremptory challenges after the candidates have been "deemed eligible by the court" (that is, by the judge or judges)?

During jury selection in Mr. Coleman's trial, the prosecution used nine of its twelve peremptory challenges to exclude otherwise qualified African-American jurors. All of the excused had been passed for cause in the voir dire process and were thus deemed eligible by the court. The Supreme Court has stated repeatedly that racial discrimination in jury selection is an intolerable violation of the Constitution. And when the racial pattern of excluding jurors is as pronounced as in Mr. Coleman's case, the Government must account for its actions. Despite the fact that the prosecution in Mr. Coleman's case eliminated 82% of African-American jurors and used 75% of its peremptory challenges to do so, the Government has yet to provide any explanation for its actions—let alone, demonstrate that racial bias was not a factor. Under the circumstances, we can have little confidence in the system that produced Mr. Coleman's death sentence. In fact, the U.S. Supreme Court recently stayed an execution and agreed to hear the case of a Texas death row inmate where it is alleged that jurors were similarly excluded by the prosecution during the trial because of their race.

Moreover, the failure of Mr. Coleman's lawyer to conduct a basic investigation into his psychiatric history and family background and present this evidence to the jury further undermines our trust in the outcome in his case. Had a basic investigation been conducted, it would have revealed that Mr. Coleman was abandoned in a garbage can by his mother who herself suffered with mental illness; that he was neglected by the grandmother who raised him while she operated a brothel and gambling house in her home. In this environment Mr. Coleman was habitually abused, both physically and psychologically. He was exposed to a number of disturbing experiences including witnessing group sex (sometimes including his mother and grandmother), pedophilia, and bestiality. In addition, he twice suffered head injuries that required hospitalization. Mr. Coleman, now and at the time of his crime, has an IQ far below average and suffers from borderline personality disorder. His mental illness has manifested itself on multiple occasions through extremes of emotion, impulsive behavior, and psychotic episodes. None of this evidence was sought or ever presented as mitigating factors during the sentencing phase of his trial.

The ACLU opposes capital punishment in all cases as a barbarous anachronism and in violation of the Constitution. Mr. Coleman's case particularly merits clemency. Had an unbiased jury been given information about Mr. Coleman's abuse and neglect during his childhood, he likely would not have been sentenced to death. Given the irrevocable consequences of a death sentence, we submit that Ohio should afford Mr. Coleman full consideration for his plea to commute his sentence to life in prison without parole.

Sincerely,

Diann Rust-Tierney
ACLU Capital Punishment Project …

The letter refers to the case of Thomas Miller-El (see page 158). Miller-El was convicted in 1986 of the 1985 shooting of hotel clerk Douglas Walker during a robbery at the Holiday Inn, Irving, Texas. The U.S. Supreme Court granted an indefinite stay of execution on February 15, 2002, six days before Miller-El was to be executed. Visit www. thomasmillerel.com for more information on the case.

Is capital punishment "a barbarous anachronism" (that is, a cruel action that is inappropriate in modern times)? See Volume 1, Individual and Society, pages 174–175, for more information on the death penalty in the United States.

Summary

In the first article Pat B. Brian compares the methods of jury selection in two states of which he has firsthand courtroom experience. In California, where he worked as a state prosecutor and where attorneys could conduct voir dire, he says that in murder cases two to three working weeks could pass in jury selection; he also recalls watching "with some amusement and amazement" as defense counsel and their "platoon" of advisors assessed the suitability of potential jurors for important cases. He contrasts this procedure with a case he tried in Utah, where he is a district judge. In this case he as judge examined the potential jurors, asking questions submitted in advance by the lawyers, who could confer with him during the examination. The lawyers then issued their challenges for cause and their peremptory challenges, and the jury was sworn before lunch on the first day. In Brian's view court-conducted voir dire is the most efficient way to produce a fair jury.

The authors of the second article—the American Civil Liberties Union (ACLU)—highlight the case of Alton Coleman, questioning the motives of some prosecutors when they use peremptory challenges to exclude potential black jurors. In the jury selection process for the trial of Coleman— a black man, since executed—prosecutors eliminated 82 percent of otherwise qualified black jury candidates in this fashion. The authors cite further statistics to back up their argument that juries can be racially skewed. While mainly concerned with opposition to the death penalty, the article implies that the jury-selection process can be manipulated unfairly in an effort to get not justice but the right result for one of the parties.

FURTHER INFORMATION:

Books:

Dwyer, William L., *In the Hands of the People: The Trial Jury's Origins, Triumphs, Troubles, and Future in American Democracy*. New York: Thomas Dunne Books, 2002.

Hans, Valerie P., and Neil Vidmar, *Judging the Jury*. New York: HarperCollins, 2001.

Kressel, Neil J., and Dorit F. Kressel, *Stack and Sway: The New Science of Jury Consulting*. Boulder, CO: Westview Press, 2002.

Useful websites:

www.aclu.org
Site of the American Civil Liberties Union.
http://www.uchastings.edu/plri/spr96tex/juryper.html
"Improving the Jury System: Peremptory Challenges" by Patricia Henley.

The following debates in the Pro/Con series may also be of interest:

In this volume:
Topic 13 Should jurors be allowed to play a more active role in trials?

In *Criminal Law and the Penal System*:
Topic 1 Is the criminal justice system racist?

Topic 2 Should juries have mandatory representation of people of all races?

IS THE JURY-SELECTION PROCESS FAIR?

YES: Court-conducted voir dire prevents lawyers from advocating their case at too early a stage and is more efficient

YES: An attorney may make a Batson challenge if he or she suspects a peremptory challenge based purely on race or gender

VOIR DIRE
Should the questions be asked by judges rather than by lawyers?

LIMITS
Are there safeguards to prevent abuses of peremptory challenges?

NO: Lawyers are better placed to reveal bias than judges. They have a better knowledge of the details of the case and are less intimidating.

NO: It is not hard for a lawyer to come up with a race- or gender-neutral explanation to satisfy the court

IS THE JURY-SELECTION PROCESS FAIR?
KEY POINTS

YES: Peremptory challenges give selection the appearance of fairness and have traditionally produced impartial juries

YES: They form an essential backup to challenges for cause in excluding biased prospective jurors

CHALLENGES
Are peremptory challenges essential to impartial jury selection?

NO: They can be used to stack a jury in favor of a particular party

NO: Such challenges serve little purpose since they are often based on stereotypes

Topic 13

SHOULD JURORS BE ALLOWED TO PLAY A MORE ACTIVE ROLE IN TRIALS?

YES

"KEEPING A JURY INVOLVED DURING A LONG TRIAL"

FORENSIC PSYCHIATRY & MEDICINE: TRIAL CONSULTING AND FORENSIC PSYCHIATRY

HAROLD J. BURSZTAJN, LINDA STOUT SAUNDERS, AND ARCHIE BRODSKY

NO

FROM "THE CURRENT DEBATE ON JUROR QUESTIONS: 'TO ASK

OR NOT TO ASK, THAT IS THE QUESTION': 2. BIASES"

CHICAGO-KENT LAW REVIEW, VOL. 78, NO. 3, 2003

NICOLE L. MOTT

INTRODUCTION

Jury service is a democratic way of giving citizens an opportunity to participate in the administration of justice. More than one million people serve as jurors in state courts each year. The Framers of the Constitution felt that juries, made up of ordinary citizens, were indispensable in acting as a check against the abuse of government officials. Trial by jury was the only right explicitly included in each of the state constitutions passed between 1776 and 1789.

Juries have traditionally been seen as a vital democratic institution because they allow citizens to engage in self-government. As the French social philosopher Alexis de Tocqueville (1805–1859) stated, "The jury is both the most effective way of establishing the people's rule and the most effective way of teaching them how to rule." In recent years, however, juries have been increasingly criticized for reaching

unfair or unpopular decisions. Critics believe that more active jury participation would help prevent such outcomes. They claim that in many cases the court system and officials make it as difficult as possible for jurors to do their jobs. Jurors, they point out, are often treated with contempt, and lawyers and judges use legalese rather than concise, understandable language when explaining difficult concepts. Many judges also prohibit jurors from taking notes during trial; and while some allow jurors to ask questions, others forbid it completely. Other critics argue that increasing juror participation in trials challenges the adversary system and allows jurors to move beyond their objective role as fact finders, thus challenging due process.

The issue of juror questioning lies at the heart of any discussion on jury participation. According to the state rules of procedure, most states have allowed jurors to submit written questions to witnesses during court deliberations. This has expanded in recent years, and many courts now permit jurors to ask questions during, or after, a counsel's presentation of evidence. But legal opinion is divided over whether juror questioning is a positive or negative process.

> *"The hallmark of the American trial system is the pursuit of truth.... [This] is attainable only if counsel successfully communicates evidence to the jury."*
> —OHIO SUPREME COURT (2000)

States usually fall into one of three categories when it comes to the subject of juror questioning. First are the states, like Mississippi, that "condemn" and "forbid" the practice. Second are those where it is not prohibited, but the practice is not usually allowed. Third are those states in which questions are permitted as long as they adhere to certain guidelines. Texas, Georgia, and Minnesota, for example, are among the states that do not allow questioning in criminal cases. Florida, Indiana, and Arizona, however, allow jurors to ask witnesses questions in writing.

Juror questioning is generally more accepted in civil trials than criminal ones, although long, complex cases full of unfamiliar legal terms and expert testimonies may, some scholars argue, benefit from the application of juror questioning. Supporters believe that juror involvement is essential to any fair trial, since misunderstandings can be clarified quickly, jurors are more likely to pay attention to proceedings, and the jury's confidence in reaching a just verdict is enhanced.

Critics, meanwhile, worry that juror questioning affects the constitutional right of the accused to a fair trial. If jurors interrogate witnesses, they begin to take on the role of the advocate, which undermines their neutrality as jurors. Other commentators also argue that questioning delays proceedings, especially when jurors ask confusing or inappropriate questions.

Several cases in which juries have asked questions have had their decisions overturned. In 2000 Judge Ann Marie Tracy authorized jury questioning during a burglary trial. The conviction was overturned by the Ohio First District of Appeals on the grounds that even written appeals from jurors endangered the jurors' neutrality. The Ohio Supreme Court later upheld the right of judges to allow juror questioning, stating that "History has … relegated the jury to a passive role that dictates a one-way communication system. The practice of allowing jurors to question witnesses provides for two-way communication through which jurors can more effectively fulfil their fundamental role as fact finders."

Juror notes have also been a question for debate. Some judges disallow them since they believe that notes distract jurors from testimonies, and that deliberation could be unfairly dominated by jurors with extensive records. But supporters argue that the benefits of giving jurors the means to keep track of key evidence outweighs this objection.

The following articles examine the debate in further detail.

KEEPING A JURY INVOLVED DURING A LONG TRIAL
Harold J. Bursztajn *et al.*

Harold Bursztajn is a psychiatrist and associate clinical professor and codirector of the Program in Psychiatry and the Law at Harvard Medical School. He treats patients and testifies as an expert and trial consultant. Linda Stout Saunders is president of the New Hampshire Trial Lawyers Association. Archie Brodsky is a senior research associate with the Program in Psychiatry and the Law at Harvard.

YES

✓ Presenting complex, unfamiliar evidence to a jury in a long trial in which emotions are running high is a formidable task. When jurors hear a case that stretches over weeks, even months, they often become bored and resentful, making them especially susceptible to falling back on their preconceptions and prejudices. Combine these emotions with a sense of fear and helplessness about going through such an arduous process, and lawyers can foment this mixture into desires for revenge against the defendant, the prosecution, or, as may have happened in the O.J. Simpson case, against law enforcement and social ills such as racism.

Problem of bored jurors

Isolation from loved ones and well-known surroundings results in jurors creating a safe mental environment, especially when exposed to complex evidence that can appear threatening by its very unfamiliarity. Thus, when jurors retreat from the boredom of a long, complex trial by daydreaming or dozing off, they hear the evidence through the filter of their own memories, fantasies, and dreams. For example, psychosis is unfamiliar to most people, so in an insanity defense case, jurors typically re[late to] the familiar experience of being sane, discounting the feasibility of insanity. When complex DNA evidence is introduced in a trial where race is an issue, jurors may fin[d their] own experience of discrimination based on the factor of skin color to be the most salient point [by] which to make their judgments.

"Sequestering juries" means secluding or setting them apart. "Peremptory challenges" are challenges that a lawyer has a right to make.

Of the various reforms proposed, such as not sequestering juries, limiting the use of peremptory challenges, barring television cameras from the courtroom, and shortening the duration of trials, it makes more sense to as[k how] the jury's time can best be used. The most promising reforms are those that would involve the jurors as active responsible participants. One suggestion is to allow juries [to] ask questions of the trial witnesses.

In medicine, the patient's participation in a dialogue with the physician has been recognized as a valuable [part] of the decision-making process. Dialogue is also the [method] of group psychotherapy. A successful medical mode [that] could translate to the courtroom is the group therapy [pro]grams that are used in treating those addicted to self limiting or self-destructive lifestyles. These individual[s are] largely resistant to preaching about the evils of, say, alcohol, but they do benefit from an interactive approach [that] confronts their own preconceptions.

As an example, individuals who have been drinking heavily for years often have atrophied problem-solving skills. In the group therapy session, the group leader elicits each individual's prejudices without endorsing them. If someone says, "Being drunk makes me a better driver," the leader asks how that is so. The person may then explain that without alcohol, he or she becomes so preoccupied by personal problems as to be distracted and over-anxious behind the wheel. The leader then asks, "Is there any other way besides drinking to keep yourself from getting so preoccupied? Does anyone else have any suggestions?" In time, the group members take over more of the work from the leader and build a fund of shared experience that becomes familiar, so that they can draw on it for alternatives to their former beliefs and habits.

> "Atrophied" means wasted away or deteriorated.

Drawing on shared experience

It's likely that juries, too, would deliberate more effectively if they could draw on such shared experience in problem solving. Deliberation is a public interchange—an airing of hypotheses and conclusions in the corrective light of social reality—and not just a silent consultation with one's personal beliefs, feelings, or ideals. But how can jurors engage one another in deliberation if they have been sitting passively for months, as the Simpson jury did?

To set the stage, the jury must be actively involved in the trial itself. The machinery already exists in the practice of allowing jurors to question witnesses through the judge. The Federal Rules of Evidence (Fed. R. Evid. 614(b)) establishes the right of a federal trial judge to question witnesses, and federal and state courts have held that it is within a trial judge's discretion to permit questions from jurors. Judges in at least 30 states are soliciting written questions from jurors and posing them to witnesses after screening them with the lawyers from both sides.

> The 1995 criminal trial of O.J. Simpson for the murder of Nicole Brown Simpson and Ronald Goldman lasted 133 days. Simpson was found not guilty. Go to http://www.law. umkc.edu/faculty/ projects/ ftrials/Simpson/ Jurypage.htm for analysis of the Simpson trial jury.

> The Federal Rules of Evidence govern the introduction of evidence in civil and criminal cases in federal courts.

O.J. Simpson and his defense team in court after his not guilty verdict was announced on October 3, 1995. This high-profile trial has led to proposed reforms in the trial system, including allowing jurors to submit questions in order to clarify issues.

Some legal observers urge that this procedure be more broadly utilized. Studies by the American Judicature Society, the State Justice Institute, and other organizations have shown that allowing jurors to ask questions keeps them alert, focuses their attention on relevant issues, and enhances their sense of participation and responsibility. Judges find these benefits especially clear in complex cases.

Hot to cool decision-making

By encouraging jury involvement, the judge can help the jury move from "hot" to "cool" decision making, a term coined by psychologist Irving Janis. Hot decision making is driven by the passions of the moment; people grasp for instant solutions to relieve emotional pressures and conflicts among themselves. Cool decision making is fostered by openly addressing uncertainty and talking out the issues.

Trial lawyers sometimes seek to stimulate hot decision making, such as when the prosecution plays on the jury's sympathy for crime victims, or, as in the case of O.J. Simpson; when the jury appears to identify with the defendant as a fellow prisoner in the long trial. But when the judge allows jurors to be more than silent observers, and refuses to yield control of the case to the lawyers, the judge can control the heat of the decision making by the tenor of his or her questions to witnesses as well as by guiding the jurors questions. The judge engages jurors in a dialogue, demonstrating by example how they can question not only witnesses, but also each individual juror's personal beliefs and prejudices.

When jurors are invited to ask questions, their concerns and uncertainties can be addressed. Through the leadership of the trial judge, the jurors can explore alternative ways of understanding the grains of truth around which prejudices coalesce. Although trials will never in and of themselves be therapeutic, trials in which jurors participate actively will have the potential for healing rather than exacerbating the divisions in our communities.

Go to http://www.nlrg.com/jrsd/jrupdates/gainedge.html for information about research by the National Legal Research Group into techniques designed to make jurors more involved in the legal process.

Irving Janis (1918–1990) was a research psychologist at Yale University. He is famous for his theory of "groupthink," which described the systematic errors groups make when coming to collective decisions.

Do you think that the author's suggested use of techniques from a therapeutic context is appropriate for a court of law? If not, why not?

THE CURRENT DEBATE ON JUROR QUESTIONS...
Nicole L. Mott

Dr. Nicole L. Mott is a research associate at the National Center for State Courts in Virginia.

NO

X … As stated in an opinion by the Supreme Court of Minnesota, courts are concerned with the effect juror questions may have on due process. In the majority opinion, Chief Justice Blatz stated that "[t]hose who doubt the value of the adversary system or who question its continuance will not object to distortion of the jury's role."

The American Bar Association (ABA) Criminal Justice Standards have guided law policymakers and practitioners since 1968.

Concerns about the drawbacks of jury questioning are suggested by the "cautionary instructions" adopted by many states and identified in the ABA standards. The ABA standards enumerate several points for courts that choose to implement the procedure. For instance, juror questions ought to be used only for important points and to clarify testimony. A concern for how juror questions may transform the juror's role is also apparent. Jurors "are not advocates and must remain neutral fact finders." Further instruction is given to clarify why some questions may not be asked, for instance, due to evidentiary rule objections or interference with litigation strategy.

The juror's role and questioning

In your opinion is the neutrality of jurors jeopardized by their asking questions?

The main concern with implementing this procedure is that through questioning a juror may lose his or her neutrality and become an advocate. But whether a juror's role would change is difficult to ascertain. If a juror's role is similar to that of the judge, what precautions do judges assume when asking questions? A notable difference is that judges are trained in the law and legal procedure. However, any juror question is subjected to scrutiny by the judge as well as both counsel. Critics voice one concern of the potentially negative effect on the jury if an attorney were to raise an objection. Heuer and Penrod's study did not find that counsel was reluctant to raise objections to questions. [T]hey found jurors were not angry or embarrassed when the objections were sustained. In fact, in the Wisconsin trials, jurors typically reported they understood why their questions were not asked.

Larry Heuer and Steven D. Penrod's study "Increasing Juror Participation in Trials through Note Taking and Question Asking" was published in 1996. Go to http://www.cornellcollege.edu/politics/journal/2003/ingrid-spiegel/text.pdf for their 2003 study into why more judges should allow juror questioning.

A common comparison typically used to evaluate the reasonableness of a jury's verdict is whether or not the judge agrees with it. Heuer and Penrod employed this technique to assess any effect on jury verdicts in trials allowing jurors to question witnesses. They concluded that judge and jury agreement rates did not differ between questioning and nonquestioning juries. Agreement rates were determined by comparing the jury's verdict and the judge's hypothetical verdict. Judges were asked to determine what verdict they would have reached in a bench trial. As a further comparison across experimental trials, the verdicts reached by questioning juries did not differ from those that were unable to question witnesses.

How jurors perceive attorneys

Another concern voiced by critics of juror questioning is that jurors will prematurely begin to accept one counsel's hypothesis over another's. This argument suggests that when jurors frame a question they are testing a hypothesis. However, jurors in Heuer and Penrod's study were asked whether they perceived one attorney less favorably than another, which would occur if the jurors had lost sight of their neutrality. In actuality, jurors perceived both attorneys more favorably in the trials that allowed questions than in those without the procedure.

Critics of jury questions also argue that jurors will disproportionately weigh the answers to their own questions. However, when jurors were surveyed, they reported an average of fifteen minutes—or 10% of their deliberations—were spent discussing such answers.

If you were a juror, do you think you would pay more attention to the answers to your questions rather than to those of other jurors?

What attorneys fear

Logistical issues surface among critics of the procedure, primarily among attorneys. Attorneys have expressed concern that jury questioning will alter the strategic plan of how the evidence is presented. However, attorneys who have experienced jury questioning did not encounter these problems. Videotaped testimony creates another logistical concern. For example, jurors would be unable to ask questions of witnesses who testify via videotape. In a Missouri case, the court ruled that jury questions were unfair in trials presenting videotaped testimony.

However, with basic recommendations for implementing jury questions, several concerns are allayed. For instance, the flow of the trial is only disrupted when the questions are not properly managed. Most guidelines suggest that jurors submit their questions in writing after the completion of testimony by a witness. Attorneys have also expressed concern about how a juror is told his or her question will not be asked.

Videotaped testimony is used in court when witnesses are unable to attend because of physical or mental incapacity. Children often testify by this method. Counsel can edit and present videotaped testimony if it will assist the jury in understanding evidence or the relevance of a particular issue.

Domestic diva Martha Stewart, one of America's most successful businesswomen, during her obstruction of justice trial in May 2004. During the trial jurors were allowed to ask questions of Stewart via the judge. Stewart and her codefendant Peter Baconovic were found guilty.

There is no evidence from empirical studies that this is a concern. If the judge instructs jurors that questions may not be asked in open court due to the rules of evidence or an attorney's trial strategy (e.g., the question will be answered at a later time), it is unlikely jurors will misinterpret this ruling as revealed in findings from the Heuer and Penrod study.

"Empirical" means based on observation or experience.

Possible delays

Attorneys, judges, and court managers are concerned that the benefit created by allowing juror questions does not outweigh the burden created as a result of the time delay that would occur. This argument is based on an assumption that jurors will ask numerous, and possibly unreasonable, questions. The study in New Jersey found that the estimated median time added to trials allowing questions was only thirty minutes. Furthermore, the assumption that jurors will be unyielding and unreasonable if provided the opportunity to ask questions is unfounded. A study asking judges in Arizona to rate the reasonableness of juror questions found that judges' ratings were extremely high.

Is 30 minutes an unreasonable amount of time to be added on to the length of a trial if juror questioning is allowed?

Despite this evidence, some courts have been expressly critical of allowing juror questions of witnesses. In one notable case, an Ohio appellate court ruled, "the practice of questioning by jurors is so inherently prejudicial" that there is no need to demonstrate the prejudice specifically. The thrust of this opinion is that the juror's role is transformed once the juror begins interrogating witnesses, so the juror is no longer a neutral decision maker. Among opinions critiquing juror questioning is the oft-cited opinion of Judge Lay proffering that juror questioning promotes a "gross distortion of the adversary system."…

Judge C.J. Lay made this comment during United States v. Johnson in 1989. Despite Lay's criticism of juror questioning, the case failed to establish a rule totally banning juror questioning of witnesses.

Summary

The question of whether jurors should be able to participate more actively in trials has been debated for centuries. In the first article Harold J. Bursztajn, a clinical and forensic psychiatrist, Linda Stout Saunders, president of the New Hampshire Trial Lawyers Association, and Archie Brodsky, a senior research associate at Harvard University, argue that jurors often get bored and restless during long, complicated cases that makes them more susceptible to biases and prejudices. They argue that more active jury participation helps the process by keeping jurors alert and focused. Asking questions, in particular, the authors contend, makes a juror more likely to listen to testimonies and stay focused on the issue at hand. Bursztajn and his co-authors assert that "Through the leadership of the trial judge, the jurors can explore alternative ways of understanding the grains of truth around which prejudices coalesce."

In the second article Nicole L. Mott, a court research associate of the National Center for State Courts, addresses the concerns many commentators have about increased juror participation. Mott quotes Chief Justice Blatz, who stated that "[t]hose who doubt the value of the adversary system or who question its continuance will not object to distortion of the jury's role." Mott points out that the American Bar Association's juror-questioning guidelines are "cautionary" ones, warning that any questions asked must not infringe on juror impartiality, the primary worry about juror-questioning. Another concern is that juror questioning can cause delays if jurors ask numerous, possibly unreasonable questions, and this affects the cost of the trial.

FURTHER INFORMATION:

Books:

Abramson, Jeffrey, *We, the Jury: The Jury System and the Ideal of Democracy*. Cambridge, MA: Harvard University Press, 2000.

Hans, Valerie P., Neil Vidmar, and Hans Zeisel, *Judging the Jury*, New York: HarperCollins, 2001.

Useful websites:

http://www.abanet.org/media/faqjury.html
American Bar Association FAQs about grand jury system.
http://www.juryinstruction.com/article_section/articles/article_archive/article43.htm
2002 article by Thomas Lundy outlining the advantages and disadvantages of juror questioning.
http://www.sconet_state.oh.us/Communications_Office/summaries/2003/0611/020201.asp
Article on the 2003 Supreme Court ruling that juror questioning is within the discretion of a trial court.

The following debates in the Pro/Con series may also be of interest:

In this volume:
  Topic 12 Is the jury-selection process fair?

  Topic 14 Should jury verdicts be unanimous?

In *Criminal Law and the Penal System*:
  Topic 2 Should juries have mandatory representation of people of all races?

SHOULD JURORS BE ALLOWED TO PLAY A MORE ACTIVE ROLE IN TRIALS?

YES: Juror questioning enhances a sense of participation which makes jurors less susceptible to biases and prejudices

YES: If a juror taking notes or asking a witness questions helps justice be served, everything else is irrelevant

IMPARTIALITY
Can jurors remain impartial when allowed to ask questions?

EXPENSE
Is juror participation more important than extra costs if questions cause delays?

NO: Many decisions have been challenged and overturned on the basis that juror questioning is wrong

NO: Jurors may ask irrelevant, confusing, or improper questions which leads to lengthy and expensive trials

SHOULD JURORS BE ALLOWED TO PLAY A MORE ACTIVE ROLE IN TRIALS?
KEY POINTS

YES: It makes jurors more likely to pay attention to difficult or unwieldy testimonies during long trials

YES: It allows jurors a role in the legal process and that assists democracy as the Framers of the Constitution intended

FAIRNESS
Is increased juror participation fair?

NO: Jurors may focus disproportionately on their own questions and on the answers given to their questions

NO: It challenges the right of the accused to a fair trial by endangering the neutrality of jurors. Jurors are not advocates.

Topic 14
SHOULD JURY VERDICTS BE UNANIMOUS?

YES

FROM *"UNITED STATES OF AMERICA V. TIMOTHY JAMES MCVEIGH"*
UNITED STATES COURTHOUSE, DENVER, CO, JUNE 13, 1997, JUDGE RICHARD P. MATSCH
REPORTER'S TRANSCRIPT, TRIAL TO JURY—VOLUME 151
RECORDED BY PAUL A. ZUCKERMAN

NO

"ORANGE COUNTY VOICES: OVERTURN SYSTEM OF UNANIMOUS JURY"
LOS ANGELES TIMES, JUNE 22, 1995
LINDA THRALL WALTERS

INTRODUCTION

"We have a reasonable doubt, and this is a safeguard which has enormous value to our system. No jury can declare a man guilty unless it's SURE. We nine can't understand how you three are still so sure. Maybe you can tell us." This quote, from the 1957 movie classic *12 Angry Men,* sums up for many the crucial role that the jury plays in the U.S. judicial system. Juries exist to make sure that justice is applied fairly, equally, and correctly. Whether unanimous verdicts—that is, when all members of the jury are in agreement—are the best method by which to do this is a matter of debate.

Although many people correctly understand that they have the constitutional right to trial by jury, the Constitution does not actually state that jury verdicts have to be unanimous. The concept of unanimous verdicts dates back to English common law in the 14th century. It applied to

the United States until 1972, when the Supreme Court reevaluated this requirement in *Apodaca v. Oregon.* The court decided that while the Sixth Amendment guarantees the right to a jury trial in criminal cases, it does not require that the jury's verdict be unanimous. The court found that nonunanimous verdicts are permissible in state non-death-penalty trials. However, unanimity of verdicts is still required in federal criminal trials. Despite the Supreme Court's decision, only three states—Louisiana, Oklahoma, and Oregon—allow the use of less than unanimous verdicts in criminal cases. In civil cases some states permit a nonunanimous decision.

Supporters of unanimous verdicts believe that they reduce the chance of a wrongful verdict or of an unreasonable view prevailing. They claim that a group of individuals will be less susceptible to improper influence and political pressure than a single judge. While a judge's decision may reflect his or her biases, the prejudice of any individual juror, advocates believe, will be neutralized in the group of 12 (some states permit juries consisting of fewer members), especially when every member of the jury is committed to reaching a collective decision. Jurors are also likely to have a greater understanding of witnesses who, like themselves, are unaccustomed to the legal process. Of necessity laws are general, and in particular situations they may cause injustice unless specific factors are taken into account. Realizing that circumstances alter cases, the jury provides a necessary element of flexibility. This effect is said to be best achieved if the jurors have to agree among themselves.

"[U]nanimity disempowers narrow and prejudiced arguments that appeal to some groups but not others."

—JEFFREY ABRAMSON, PROFESSOR OF POLITICS (1994)

The jury-selection process is quite rigorous in the United States: A typical jury is made up of people from different social, cultural, and educational backgrounds who have different and sometimes conflicting views and understandings of key issues. The jury may, therefore, simply be incapable of reaching a consensus since some members may have a limited understanding of some of the key issues in the trial. Others may allow factors such as status or wealth to influence how they view the defendant and the evidence. Unanimous decisions therefore—in theory at least—may serve as a check against unfair and improper verdicts being reached due to the bias or irrationality of individual jurors. Some even believe that "hung juries"—when jurors fail to reach a consensus—serve a key purpose since a mistrial has to be declared, and the defendant is then given another chance to have his or her evidence heard by a new jury.

This situation is, however, both time-consuming and expensive, and opponents argue that it best serves neither the defendant nor the justice system itself. Allowing nonunanimous verdicts would, they argue, help reduce costly retrials and free up courtrooms for other deserving trials, preventing some of the logjams that occur currently. Allowing a majority verdict would also lead to more efficient and less time-consuming trials since the jury would spend less time deliberating. However, some legal scholars are also concerned that in such cases the deliberation process may end practically as soon as the required majority is reached to decide the case. Under these circumstances the concerns of any dissenters may not be fully explored or even addressed during deliberations. Advocates of this view believe that unanimous verdicts are more likely to be representative of the community since everyone's opinion, regardless of sex, gender, race, or class, has to be taken into account.

The following two extracts examine the issue in greater depth.

UNITED STATES OF AMERICA V. TIMOTHY JAMES MCVEIGH
Trial to jury

Timothy McVeigh had already been found guilty for his role in the bombing of the Oklahoma City federal building on April 19, 1995, which killed 168 people. These proceedings were to establish his state of mind and any aggravating and mitigating factors.

YES

✓ **THE COURT:** Members of the jury, have you arrived at your special findings and recommendation?

JURORS: Yes.

THE COURT: If the foreman will please hand that to Mr. Manspeaker, who will hand it to me. Members of the jury, you will please listen to the reading of your Special Findings Form A. These findings apply to all 11 counts....

Section I, Intent to cause death:
Question (1) The defendant intentionally killed the victims. *Answer: Yes.*

(2) The defendant intentionally inflicted serious body injury that resulted in the death of the victims. *Answer: Yes.*

(3) The defendant intentionally participated in an act, contemplating that the life of a person would be taken or intending that lethal force would be used against a person, and the victims died as a result of that act. *Answer: Yes.*

(4) The defendant intentionally and specifically engaged in an act of violence, knowing that the act created a grave risk of death to a person, other than a participant in the offense, such that participation in the act constituted a reckless disregard for human life and the victims died as a direct result of the act. *Answer: Yes.*

Section II, Statutory aggravating factors:
(1) The deaths or injuries resulting in death occurred during the commission of an offense under 18 United States Code Section 844(d), transportation of explosives in interstate commerce for certain purposes. *Answer: Yes.*

(2) The defendant, in the commission of the offenses, knowingly created a grave risk of death to one or more persons in addition to the victims of the offense. *Answer: Yes.*

(3) The defendant committed the offenses after substantial planning and premeditation to cause the death of one or more persons and to commit an act of terrorism. *Answer: Yes.*

What reason did McVeigh give for his attack in Oklahoma City? Go to www.cnn.com, and find out.

(4) The defendant committed the offenses against one or more federal law enforcement officers because of such victims' status as federal law enforcement officers. *Answer: Yes.*

Third section, Non-statutory aggravating factors:
(1) The offenses committed by the defendant resulted in the deaths of 168 persons. *Answer: Yes.*
(2) In committing the offenses, the defendant caused serious physical and emotional injury, including maiming, disfigurement, and permanent disability to numerous individuals. *Answer: Yes.*
(3) That by committing the offenses, the defendant caused severe injuries and losses suffered by the victims' families. *Answer: Yes.*

Mitigating factors in Section IV:
(1) Timothy McVeigh believed deeply in the ideals upon which the United States was founded. Number of jurors who so find: Zero.
(2) Timothy McVeigh believed that the ATF and FBI were responsible for the deaths of everyone who lost their lives at Mt. Carmel, near Waco, Texas, between February 28 and April 19, 1993. Number of jurors who so find: 12.…
(3) Timothy McVeigh believed that federal law enforcement agents murdered Sammy Weaver and Vicki Weaver near Ruby Ridge, Idaho, in August, 1992. Number of jurors who so find: 12.
(4) Timothy McVeigh believed that the increasing use of military-style force and tactics by federal law enforcement agencies against American citizens threatened an approaching police state. Number of jurors who so find: 12.
(5) Timothy McVeigh's belief that federal law enforcement agencies failed to take responsibilities for their actions at Ruby Ridge and Waco and failed to punish those persons responsible added to his growing concerns regarding the existence of a police state and a loss of constitutional liberties. Number of jurors who so find: 12.
(6) Timothy McVeigh served honorably and with great distinction in the United States Army from May, 1988, until December, 1991. Number of jurors who so find: 10.
(7) Timothy McVeigh received the Army's Bronze Star for his heroic service in operation Desert Storm in Kuwait and Iraq. Number of jurors who so find: 12.
(8) Timothy McVeigh is a reliable and dependable person in work and in his personal affairs and relations with others. Number of jurors who so find: 2.
(9) Timothy McVeigh is a person who deals honestly

In February 1993 the ATF mounted a raid on a religious cult called the Branch Davidians, who were known to be amassing machine guns and allegedly not paying taxes on them. Ten lives were lost in the raid, four of them ATF agents. A siege that lasted 51 days followed the raid.

What happened at Ruby Ridge? Why was this incident and that at Waco likely to have fueled McVeigh's beliefs about federal law-enforcement agencies and the emergence of a police state?

Two of the jurors found McVeigh to be a reliable and dependable person. Do you think this opinion is at odds with the jury's unanimous verdict that McVeigh should face the death sentence?

with others in interpersonal relations. Number of jurors who so find: 1.

(10) Timothy McVeigh is a patient and effective teacher when he is working in a supervisory role. Number of jurors who so find: 12.

(11) Timothy McVeigh is a good and loyal friend. Number of jurors who so find. Zero.

(12) Over the course of his life, Timothy McVeigh has done good deeds for and helped others, including a number of strangers who needed assistance. Number of jurors who so find: 4.

(13) Timothy McVeigh has no prior criminal record. Number of jurors who so find: 12.

With respect to the provision of extra spaces to write in additional mitigating factors, if any, found by any one or more jurors, the jury has answered none with respect to both of those and stricken them out.

Recommendation, V:

The jury has considered whether the aggravating factors found to exist sufficiently outweigh any mitigating factor or factors found to exist, or in the absence of any mitigating factors, whether the aggravating factors are themselves sufficient to justify a sentence of death. Based upon this consideration, the jury recommends by unanimous vote that the following sentence be imposed: The defendant, Timothy James McVeigh, shall be sentenced to death. The Special Findings appear to be signed by all jurors and dated June 13, 1997.

VI. Certification:

By signing below, each juror certifies that consideration of the race, color, religious beliefs, national origin, or sex of the defendant or the victims was not involved in reaching his or her individual decision and that the individual juror would have made the same recommendation regarding a sentence for the crimes in question no matter what the race, color, religious beliefs, national origin, or sex of the defendant or the victims. Apparently signed by all jurors and also dated June 13, 1997. Mr. Foreman, was this and—were these and are these the jury's special findings and recommendation?

JURY FOREMAN: Yes, they are.

THE COURT: And so say you all?

JURORS: Yes.

Although nonunanimous verdicts are not permissible in federal criminal cases, some states allow such verdicts in criminal cases that do not carry a death sentence.

Juries generally decide criminal sentences only in death penalty cases.

Before people are selected for jury duty, they are questioned by attorneys to find out whether they might be biased or unfair. Opponents of the requirement for unanimity say that defense attorneys often deliberately appoint jurors whom they predict will cause a hung jury. See Topic 12 Is the jury-selection process fair?

THE COURT: I will poll the jury on these recommendations as I did with the verdict. So the juror seated in Chair No. 1: Were these and are these your special findings and recommendation?

JUROR NO. 1: Yes.

[The Court repeats the question, "Were these and are these your special findings and recommendation?" addressing each juror by his or her number. Each juror replies in turn either "Yes" or "Yes, sir."]

THE COURT: Members of the jury, the Court will, as I instructed you in the instructions, sentence in accordance with your recommendation, sentencing the defendant to death. The sentence will be imposed at a hearing at a later time. Mr. McVeigh may be excused from the courtroom....

In July 1997 McVeigh asked for a new trial, citing, among other issues, juror misconduct.

THE COURT: Members of the jury, you have now discharged your duty in this case, having rendered first of all your verdict with respect to the charges and then, of course, these findings and recommendation with respect to the sentence.

Before excusing you from the courtroom, however, there are some things that I want to say to you and do wish to say them publicly.

First of all, I want to thank you on behalf of all of the people of the United States. You have served your country and you have served the system, as we've so often referred to it; but the system is really the democratic system that is our form of government, wherein people are brought together from all walks of life and background and given the responsibility for making the decision. And you have done that.

Now, it may be a matter for you now or at some later time to wonder: Did we do the right thing?

The answer to that question is yes, you did the right thing, not because I believe it one way or the other but because you did it. And that is what we rely upon, 12 people coming together, hearing the evidence, following the law, and reaching the decision.

So therefore, it is done. And you, as the jurors, are the final authority. You are not answerable to anyone for your verdict and your sentencing decision. No one of you can change it or undermine it or impeach it by anything that you may say or do after this. The decision is final.

Now, obviously, this decision will be commented upon, both your verdict and your recommendation. And that, as you well know, is a part of living in a free society....

McVeigh was executed by lethal injection on June 11, 2001.

Studies show that judges and juries agree on the verdict at least 80 percent of the time.

The number of jurors varies by state. What are the arguments for and against reducing the size of juries? Go to www.google.com, and search for articles.

ORANGE COUNTY VOICES: OVERTURN SYSTEM OF UNANIMOUS JURY
Linda Thrall Walters

Journalist Linda Thrall Walters published this article in the Los Angeles Times on June 22, 1995.

NO

X As Orange County desperately searches for cost-cutting measures, there is an avenue to pursue that would greatly contribute to this effort. The California Constitution could be amended to permit less-than-unanimous 10–2 verdicts for conviction or acquittal in all "non-death" penalty cases.

The law enforcement community firmly stands behind this effort, spearheaded by the California District Attorney's Association. This constitutional amendment, if passed by the Legislature, still would require approval of California's electorate.

Verdicts of 10–2 in criminal cases have been lawful in England since 1967.

This appropriate strategy would save Orange County taxpayers millions. This is not a novel idea. England, which serves as our historical point of reference for the jury system, successfully implemented the less-than-unanimous jury vote nearly 30 years ago.

Here the author is referring to the 1972 decision by the Supreme Court that unanimity is not a constitutional requirement. See the introduction to this topic.

On a national level, Louisiana, Oregon, Idaho, Oklahoma and Taxes have all greatly benefited from this approach. The U.S. Supreme Court has expressly approved less-than-unanimous jury verdicts. The law enforcement community strongly believes that the enactment of this reform would enhance our ability to protect the public and reduce the numbers and costs of criminal jury trials without undermining protection of the innocent.

Aims of a jury trial

The purpose of a jury trial is threefold: to search for the truth; to ensure the innocent are protected, and see that the guilty are punished. California law provides that should just one juror disagree with the other eleven, no verdict may be entered. The result is a "hung jury" and mistrial. While the cost of retrying such cases is astronomical, no dollar amount can be placed on the pain and suffering that the victims and their loved ones must once again endure.

Do you agree with the author that the cost of retrials—both financial and emotional—is too much, and therefore nonunanimous verdicts should be made lawful?

As the wife of a police chief and the mother of a police officer, not only do I see the misery inflicted upon victims, but I have firsthand knowledge of the frustrations of law

In the 1957 film 12 Angry Men *Henry Fonda plays a dissenting juror in a murder trial who has reasonable doubt about the defendant's guilt.*

enforcement. Again and again we see ruthless criminals—robbers, rapists, murderers, the dregs of society—walk away or receive reduced charges due to hung juries. This archaic system that protects the guilty and punishes the innocent must be changed.

The author has used a factual and reasoned approach to her argument until this point. Here she makes a more subjective claim—that unanimous verdicts protect the guilty and punish the innocent. Do you think such a claim strengthens her case or not?

Juries are not always impartial and objective

The public perception is that jurors are selected for their impartiality and objectivity. From the perspective of the defense, nothing could be farther from the truth.

Alan M. Dershowitz, nationally recognized criminal defense attorney, blatantly stated in his recent book, *The Abuse Excuse*, that "in most criminal cases a hung jury is a clear victory for the defendant." The defense rarely tries to select 12 impartial, reasonable people. Rather, they search for one or two unreasonable or biased individuals to obstruct a unanimous verdict.

Some commentators argue that rather than being a "clear victory for the defendant," a hung jury is a "dress rehearsal" for the prosecution.

The cost of hung juries

The horrendous fiscal and human cost of a hung jury can be seen in Orange County's Scott Rembert case. In 1992, Rembert and two others were charged with kidnapping student Joseph Kondrath. He was robbed of $1 and shot in the head as he pleaded for his life. The two others charged with Rembert were convicted. Rembert, due to two hung juries, is being tried a third time. The total cost to date is $1.4 million.

It now costs nearly $10,000 a day to run a Superior Court jury trial in Orange County. Norman M. Garland, a law professor at Southwestern University in Los Angeles, states:

> *If you analyze the way cases are selected for prosecution, we can find ... cases that are intentionally not pursued because of budgetary problems. If every defendant decided to push the system to the limit, such as the O.J. Simpson trial ... the system couldn't continue to function.*

In criminal cases the right to a trial by jury—but not a unanimous verdict—is enshrined in the Constitution. The Sixth Amendment guarantees the right to a "speedy and public trial by an impartial jury."

Will the less-than-unanimous jury amendment take away a precious constitutional right? Absolutely not! There is no right to a unanimous jury in the U.S. Constitution.

There is nothing mysterious about unanimity. Almost all decisions of governmental bodies are made without unanimous agreement. Indeed, the U.S. Supreme Court can affirm a death sentence by a vote of 5 to 4 and the California Supreme Court can do so by a vote of 4 to 3.

I hope those of the liberal persuasion will see the merit of this amendment. Precious tax dollars could be redirected to programs supporting education and prevention.

Hopefully, these individuals will join forces with those who dedicate, and many times sacrifice, their lives in an effort to safeguard the civil rights of all.

Society has many demands upon its resources. A constitutional amendment permitting "non-unanimous" verdicts would be a giant step toward providing a more fair, efficient and fiscally manageable criminal justice system in Orange County. Such an amendment would also provide a positive approach to stretching our hard-earned tax dollars, while allowing our justice system to function as it was originally intended.

Which of the author's arguments against the requirement for unanimous verdicts is likely to be the most persuasive to Orange County taxpayers? What do you think the response of attorneys and defendants will be?

Summary

The first article is a verbatim account of the various special findings and recommendation of the jury in the trial of Timothy McVeigh. The defendant had already been found guilty of the Oklahoma bombings—the purposes of this part of the proceedings were to examine McVeigh's state of mind and to decide whether there were any mitigating circumstances. Some of the points are put to the jury as questions; they receive "yes" or "no" answers. The remaining points are statements followed by a record of the number of jurors who agreed with them. As in all federal criminal cases, unanimity was required in the verdict, and only those points on which the jury was unanimous were taken into consideration by the court. The jury decided unanimously that McVeigh should be sentenced to death.

In the second article *Los Angeles Times* journalist Linda Thrall Walters expresses her opposition to the present system of criminal justice in California. According to the California system, every time a jury fails to reach a unanimous verdict, a mistrial must be declared, and the judicial process starts over. The author begins by suggesting that the introduction of majority verdicts would save the state millions of dollars in attorneys' fees, as well as shielding victims and their families from more pain and suffering. More than that, however, it would actually help improve the administration of justice because it would make it more difficult for defense attorneys to go all out for a hung jury, as they are alleged to do at present. Thrall Walters argues that majority verdicts are not unconstitutional, citing as evidence the fact that such decisions are acceptable in the U.S. Supreme Court.

FURTHER INFORMATION:

Books:

Abramson, Jeffrey, *We, the Jury: The Jury System and the Ideal of Democracy*. Cambridge, MA: Harvard University Press, 2000.

Useful websites:

http://www.calbar.ca.gov/calbar/2cbj/97mar/opin02.htm
California Bar Journal article in favor of nonunanimous verdicts in state criminal proceedings.
http://www.law.fsu.edu/journal/lawreview/downloads/243/glasser.pdf
Overview and history of the jury system, with a conclusion in favor of nonunanimous verdicts.
http://www.uchastings.edu/plri/spr96tex/juryuna.html
Public Law Research Institute article outlining the points for and against nonunanimous verdicts.

The following debates in the Pro/Con series may also be of interest:

In this volume:
Topic 7 Should Congress be able to limit the power of federal judges to sentence criminals?

Topic 12 Is the jury-selection process fair?

Topic 13 Should jurors be allowed to play a more active role in trials?

SHOULD JURY VERDICTS
BE UNANIMOUS?

YES: As the jury deliberates, wise counsels will prevail

YES: Individual views have to be debated and cannot simply be outvoted or ignored

CORRECT VERDICTS
If everyone agrees on a verdict, is it likely to be the right one?

DEMOCRACY
Are unanimous verdicts a cornerstone of democracy?

NO: One rogue juror can hijack the other members of the jury, who may agree with a dissident view against their own better judgment

NO: Unanimous verdicts are not enshrined in the Constitution, and the Supreme Court allows majority verdicts

SHOULD JURY VERDICTS BE UNANIMOUS?
KEY POINTS

YES: It is better that a hundred guilty people go free—or are retried—than that a single innocent person be wrongly convicted

YES: Majority decisions imply that the jury was uncertain and cast doubt on the reliability of any verdict thus reached

EXPENSE
Is it worth the cost of hung juries and retrials?

NO: It would be more cost-effective to overturn convictions on appeal than to call a mistrial every time a jury failed to agree

NO: The judiciary must act to prevent defense attorneys intentionally seeking hung juries

Topic 15

IS EXPERT TESTIMONY GIVEN TOO MUCH WEIGHT?

YES

FROM "WHO IS ANDREA YATES? A SHORT STORY ABOUT INSANITY"
FROM "PART III. PARK DIETZ'S EXPERTISE AND PSYCHIATRIC PHILOSOPHY"
10 *DUKE JOURNAL OF GENDER LAW & POLICY* 1 (2003)
DEBORAH W. DENNO

NO

"SUMMARY: THE USE OF EXPERT WITNESSES IN CHILD SEXUAL ABUSE CASES"
BASED ON AN ARTICLE BY SYLVIA LYNN GILLOTTE FOR
CHILD SEXUAL ABUSE INVESTIGATIONS: MULTIDISCIPLINARY COLLABORATIONS
SUMMARY COMPILED BY CURTIS HOLMES AND SHARON MCGEE

INTRODUCTION

"Expert testimony" is evidence given in court by a person with special training, experience, and knowledge in a particular subject. There are expert witnesses covering every type of human activity—such as engineers, accountants, scientists, mechanics, nurses, and physicians.

Many experts are reluctant to testify in court. The forum for resolving differences within their own field of expertise is often far removed from that of a courtroom, where the goal is to reach a definitive decision. Some experts, however, feel that they have a duty to provide evidence for legal questions for both the good of society and the courts. Psychiatrists, psychologists, and physicians are routinely consulted in cases involving child abuse, murder, paternity, and child custody. Judges have the discretion to decide whether expert testimony is reliable (and relevant) enough to the case to be admissible in court. The juries then decide whether to take notice of it when reaching a decision.

Some people argue that too much weight is given to expert testimony in courtrooms today. The use of such testimony can be problematic for a number of reasons. There is a common perception of expert witnesses as "hired guns" who are sought by the prosecution or defense solely to strengthen their own arguments. Experts are paid, sometimes quite handsomely, for their services. Dr. Park Dietz, a high-profile forensic psychiatrist, is said to be paid $300 per hour for his time. Dietz has testified in famous murder trials, including those of O.J. Simpson and Jeffrey Dahmer. Fees are paid according to the expert's level of expertise and experience, and the difficulty of the task they have to perform. Some critics suggest that the payment of high fees weakens the integrity of expert witnesses, since it may influence them to slant their testimony misleadingly, depending on who is paying them. Others respond that it is only right that expert witnesses are properly paid for their time and knowledge while testifying. Some argue that fees should be the same for all expert witnesses to avoid such potential conflicts of interest.

> *"The combination of adequate counsel and [juries'] intuition usually ferrets out dishonest, insincere, or incompetent experts."*
> —WILLIAM H. REID, M.D., M.P.H.,
> *PSYCHIATRY AND LAW UPDATES*

Psychiatrists have commonly given evidence on the mental state of a defendant based on interviews with him or her. Behavioral evidence is, however, a new approach in expert testimony and can include visiting a crime scene, inspecting physical evidence, studying autopsies, or even reading books that might have influenced the defendant. Lawyers may seek to build on such an approach by, for example, asking a physician in a child-custody case which parent is better for the child's welfare, even when neither parent is clinically ill. Medical diagnosis has therapeutic aims such as alleviating suffering. This contrasts sharply with a court where the aim is to identify the cause of a

condition so as to hold people or institutions responsible. Critics say this forces questions on physicians that are at odds with their ethical duties as doctors and invites them to speculate beyond the sphere of their expertise.

Another concern about the growing influence of expert witnesses is the worry that their testimony might simply be wrong. This issue has been dramatically highlighted in the United Kingdom. Over a 20-year period hundreds of parents have been convicted of killing their children based on precedents set by evidence originally given by Professor Roy Meadow, an expert in Sudden Infant Death Syndrome. A growing number of those convictions have since been overturned amid allegations that Meadow's evidence was unreliable, as medical understanding of the syndrome continues to develop. Such events, which cast doubt on the value of expert testimony, may make other experts more reluctant to come forward in the future.

Other commentators argue that expert testimony is still essential since it is there to provide expertise that judges and jurors simply do not possess. Codes of practice, such as the Federal Rules of Evidence, govern expert testimony, although some people question whether they are adequate. The qualifications and suitability of experts need to be properly assessed by peers in the experts' field, they claim.

While many believe that expert witnesses are an important part of criminal trials, whether their testimonies are given too much weight continues to be a matter of debate. The following two articles examine this issue further.

... PARK DIETZ'S EXPERTISE AND PSYCHIATRIC PHILOSOPHY
Deborah W. Denno

Deborah W. Denno is professor of law at Fordham University School of Law. This article was published in the Duke Journal of Gender Law & Policy in 2003.

YES

✓ ... Park Dietz is considered one of the most "prominent and provocative" psychiatric expert witnesses in the country. In one professional capacity or another, he has been involved with a long list of famous homicide defendants: John Hinckley, Jr., Jeffrey Dahmer ... O.J. Simpson (in the civil case), and Ted Kaczynski, to name a few. He can now add Andrea Yates to that list. As the prosecution's star witness in the Yates case, he both interviewed and videotaped Andrea, and he subsequently testified in court about his evaluation....

A desire to emphasize "facts"

Media articles about Dietz claim he is known for emphasizing "facts" rather than "theoretical conjecture" when evaluating a case. Indeed, both Dr. Jonas Rappeport, a renowned professor of Dietz's at Johns Hopkins Medical School, as well as Roger Adelman, one of the prosecutors in the Hinckley case, credit Dietz's precision and "focus on the facts" as major contributions Dietz has brought to modernizing the field of forensic psychiatry....

Dietz's apparent stress on facts, combined with what even Rappeport views as a "rigid" approach towards defendants, has prompted criticism. According to an article about Dietz in *Johns Hopkins Magazine*, "[s]ome forensic psychiatrists" have accused him of presenting "mere informed opinion as solid fact, and [complain] that his standard of criminal responsibility is harsh and unforgiving of mentally ill defendants." For example, during his testimony in the Yates case, Dietz indicated that because Andrea claimed that Satan, rather than God, told her to kill her children, she knew her actions were wrong. Andrea also failed to act in a way a loving mother would if she really thought she was saving her children from hell by killing them.... As one legal critic asked in response to Dietz's comments, "Is one to infer that it is somehow more loving to invoke the name of Jesus while you drown your children than to drown them without any religious commentary?"....

Do you think it is reasonable to expect the explanations of mentally ill people to make sense logically? Or would a logical explanation suggest that they were sane?

[I]n media interviews and his testimony in the Yates case, Dietz has made clear that he does not treat patients in a psychiatry practice. This lack of engagement with patients is "rare" among medical expert witnesses. Rather, Dietz opts to concentrate on research and one-time interviews with criminal defendants. Yet, such a view of the psychiatric world is distorted. For example, it is difficult to comprehend how Dietz can evaluate an individual's normality or abnormality if he only engages in short-term interviews with highly abnormal people. By encountering briefly only the most extreme criminal cases, all Dietz sees is pathology. He has no "control group" as a comparison, no in-depth evaluations of individuals from whom he can learn nuances. Such an approach may explain additional criticisms concerning where Dietz draws the line for distinguishing sanity from insanity.…

Do you think a psychiatrist giving expert testimony should always have experience of treating patients? Or is it better to have someone who is familiar with a wide range of case histories from research?

Consistent with this view, in the Yates case Dietz minimized the defense expert witnesses' testimony that Andrea had suffered years of delusions, auditory hallucinations, and visions of violence. Instead, Dietz claimed that Andrea had, at most, experienced "obsessional intrusive thoughts." Yet, contrary to other high profile defendants pleading insanity, Andrea had a substantial and documented history of mental illness before she killed her children. Not only had she twice attempted suicide, she had also been hospitalized and prescribed anti-psychotic drugs after the birth of her fourth and fifth children. The defense could call experts who had actually treated Andrea, some repeatedly, in sharp contrast to Dietz's relatively brief interview. As one scholar on expert testimony emphasizes, "[t]he legal system assumes that the treating doctor is more credible than a nontreating doctor". …

Is better to have testimony from physicians who have treated a defendant since they know the defendant's history? Or is it better to have the view of a different, independent physician, who may be less biased and see the defendant through fresh eyes?

The attractions of certainty

Nonetheless, Dietz's effectiveness as a witness appears to be due to his alleged emphasis on fact. Because jurors received conflicting expert testimony during the Yates trial, minimal statutory guidance, and unclear stories from both the prosecution and defense, they were left with little to rely on other than the supposed "facts." Compounding this dilemma, the multiple defense psychiatrists gave somewhat contradictory analyses of Andrea's mental state, presumably in part because she had been treated or assessed by a number of them during different stages of her illness. Such a multiple-theory defense narrative contrasted with the more uniform "factual" narrative presented by Dietz…

In fields such as psychiatry "facts" are sometimes hard to pin down. Should it be up to expert witnesses themselves to make this clear to juries?

Almost immediately, Dietz's testimony and post-trial commentary about the Yates case sparked notoriety for the views he expressed both inside and outside the courtroom.... Dietz also tried to justify his career-long tendency to appear primarily for the prosecution. According to Dietz, prosecutors, like good forensic psychiatrists, strive "to seek truth and justice" and therefore to make available all the information important in a case. In contrast, defense attorneys attempt to help their clients—a goal that conflicts with a thorough search for data.... Of course, Dietz's statements imply that defense attorneys and their witnesses want to distort information in some way and shield the truth. The irony of Dietz's points, however, were spotlighted a week later by Andrea's attorneys. They discovered a factual error that Dietz had made during cross-examination....

Dietz's remark only refers to cases such as Yates's in which the defendant has admitted doing the act he or she is accused of, and the only question at issue in the trial is the defendant's degree of criminal responsibility for the action.

A mistake in testimony

Dietz is a technical advisor to two television shows: *Law & Order* and *Law & Order Criminal Intent*.... During the Yates trial, Dietz mistakenly testified that, shortly before Andrea killed her children, *Law & Order* aired an episode involving a postpartum depressed mother who successfully won an insanity appeal after drowning her children in a bathtub. The episode never existed. When Dietz learned of his error, he wrote prosecutors Joe Owmby and Kaylynn Williford and informed them that he had confused the insanity episode he testified about with other *Law & Order* episodes and infanticide cases. Dietz's mistake about such a fact, however, may be part of the grounds for Yates's appeal. It is not a stretch to think the jury may have been affected by Dietz's implication that Andrea was somehow influenced by the show....

Do you think it is a legitimate part of an expert witness's task to try to find evidence that will help the side that is paying him or her? Or should experts restrict themselves to answering questions put to them by counsel or the judge?

Dietz also claimed that the defense experts asked "shocking examples of leading questions" of Andrea and provided only partial, and biased, videotapes of their interviews with her.... According to Lucy Puryear, a Houston psychiatrist who testified for Andrea's defense, Dietz did the same. Puryear added that Dietz edited his eight hours of videotaped interviews with Andrea and only "showed the jury portions that supported his testimony."...

If videotaped interviews are used in evidence, do you think juries should see the whole tape so that they can see the whole conversation in context?

Postpartum depression and psychosis

The Yates trial revealed the degree to which Dietz was unfamiliar with patients diagnosed with postpartum depression or postpartum psychosis and his admitted void in treating patients.... [T]his section makes clear that there is still much to be learned about postpartum disorders and how much they can justifiably mitigate criminal culpability, if at all. At the same time, what is known medically about the disorders—especially their neurobiological aspects—should not be ignored. Two postpartum experts highlighted the problem of such informational inadequacy specifically with respect to the prosecution's approach in the Yates case....

Direct and cross examinations in the Yates trial made clear that Dietz has been asked to consult on an "unusually high proportion" of cases concerning mothers who kill their children. Yet ... the last time he [Dietz] ever treated a female patient with postpartum depression was 25 years ago (in 1977).... Dietz's lack of expertise in postpartum depression and postpartum psychosis is striking given the psychiatric community's recognition of postpartum disorders and the acceptance by both sides that Andrea was afflicted with one. The disorders are included in the Diagnostic and Statistical Manual of Mental Disorders (DSM) ... [which] also clearly recognizes the link between postpartum-related mental disorder and infanticide in the context of delusions. Notably, however, postpartum psychosis is not presently treated as an individual diagnostic classification in the DSM.... Rather, the symptoms are categorized according to the established criteria used to diagnose psychosis (for example, major depressive, manic, or mixed episode). The "postpartum onset specifier" applies if symptoms occur within four weeks after childbirth.

Andrea's postpartum risk factors & life stressors
It appears that Dietz never really adequately investigated or acknowledged Andrea's postpartum risk factors—most particularly in the context of the postpartum period's "unique ... degree of neuroendocrine alterations and psychosocial adjustments," which the DSM emphasizes. In other words, the medical literature stresses that the risk factors for postpartum disorders cover a broad scope of biological, psychological, and social influences. These factors include an individual's personal and family history of depression, biochemical imbalances, recent stressful events, marital conflict, and perceived lack of support from the partner, family, or friends.

Andrea experienced all of the postpartum risk factors that the DSM mentions. She was also subject to a host of family and environmental life stressors shown to be linked to postpartum depression and postpartum psychosis. Dietz only occasionally alluded to these stressors if he mentioned them at all in his testimony....

Postpartum (or postnatal) depression is a form of depression that affects about 10 percent of mothers, beginning from about two weeks after their baby's birth and continuing for several months or more. Its causes are thought to include psychological factors and chemical changes that take place as the mother's body adjusts to no longer being pregnant.

Psychosis is a severe form of a mental illness—such as schizophrenia or depression—in which the sufferer's perception of reality is changed. "Hearing voices" is a common symptom of psychosis.

Do you think it damages an expert witness's credibility if he or she is too partisan in backing one side in the case? Would it be better if such witnesses were appointed by the court rather than hired by the defense or prosecution?

... THE USE OF EXPERT WITNESSES IN CHILD SEXUAL ABUSE CASES
Compiled by Curtis Holmes and Sharon McGee

This is a summary of a much longer article by Sylvia Lynne Gillotte, U.S. attorney and child advocate. It was done as part of the Internet project Child Sexual Abuse Investigations (http://childabuse. gactr.uga.edu/both/ gillote/gillotte_ print.phtml).

The authors use the word "probative" frequently in this article. It means "having the nature of proof or evidence." To say something is probative therefore means that it can be used as evidence in court.

The complete Federal Rules of Evidence can be found at http://www.law. cornell.edu/rules/ fre/overview.html (as provided by the Cornell University Law School).

NO

Expert witness testimony is often an essential evidentiary component in establishing child sexual abuse in court. Children who are sexually abused may exhibit a variety of physical, emotional, psychological, and behavioral symptoms as a result of their abuse. Experts in the field of child sexual abuse often rely upon these symptoms in drawing inferences and conclusions regarding a child's allegations of abuse. Assessment of these various symptoms and indicators requires expertise that is ordinarily beyond the knowledge of judges and laymen. Consequently, expert testimony is needed to establish the probative value of such behaviors and symptoms as they relate to the child's victimization. The admissibility of such testimony, in the form of an opinion or otherwise, depends upon whether the information offered is relevant to an issue before the court and will assist the trier of fact in understanding an issue or subject matter that is ordinarily beyond the knowledge and experience of the average juror.

Establishing credentials
In order to qualify as an expert, a witness must demonstrate sufficient knowledge of the subject matter through specialized training or practical experience to be able to render an opinion upon which the court can reasonably rely. Qualification of an expert is within the sound discretion of the court. Once relevancy has been determined and an expert's qualifications have been properly established, subsequent challenges to the expert's techniques and the basis for his or her opinion will ordinarily focus on how much weight the expert's opinion should be given.

Expert witness testimony is governed by special evidentiary rules that have been recently modified under both the Federal Rules of Evidence and Georgia case law. Professionals in the field of child sexual abuse need to be informed regarding these rules so their testimony in court can be presented in a manner which is both probative and admissible.

Both Georgia case law and the Federal Rules of Evidence have significantly eroded traditional rules limiting expert opinion testimony to personal knowledge of the case or facts admitted at trial. An expert may now base his or her opinion on facts and data that are not otherwise admissible as evidence. Under the Federal Rules, as long as the facts and data are of a type reasonably relied upon by experts in the field when formulating inferences and conclusions on the subject matter, the opinion itself is admissible. Similarly, an expert in Georgia may base an opinion on partial hearsay. As long as the probative value of the evidence outweighs its prejudicial effect, the testimony is admissible. Any margin of error or uncertainty in the expert's specific conclusions goes to the weight accorded the testimony, not its admissibility.

> *"Hearsay" is a legal term meaning a statement made orally outside the court by someone who will not or cannot testify him/herself, as reported by someone else. It is not normally admissible as evidence in court.*

Harper review and the CSAAS

In child sexual abuse cases, an expert's opinion should be based upon the reasonable clinical certainty necessary to make diagnostic and treatment decisions. A party may challenge the admissibility of expert testimony that is based upon theories, techniques, or technologies that are unreliable or have not yet reached a scientific stage of verifiable certainty. Under the Federal Rules of Evidence, an expert must be prepared to demonstrate that the testimony offered is the product of reliable principles and methods which have also been reliably applied to the facts of the case. In Georgia, a challenge of this nature must be made at the time such testimony is offered and the testimony may then be subjected to what is known as a Harper review. Under Harper, a trial court may determine whether a theory, procedure, or technique has reached a scientific stage of verifiable certainty by taking judicial notice of other court decisions or reviewing any evidence presented at trial. In child sexual abuse cases, expert medical and behavioral science testimony may be subject to a Harper challenge and review.

> *The Harper review is the legal standard for expert testimony in the state of Georgia. It is named for Harper v. State, a 1982 murder trial in which a psychiatrist presented evidence obtained from the suspect using a "truth serum." Since this method had not been established with "verifiable certainty" in the science community, the testimony was rejected.*

Appellate courts in Georgia have established that testimony based upon the Child Sexual Abuse Accommodation Syndrome (CSAAS) is reliable under Harper. However, CSAAS testimony is not limited to purposes of rehabilitation or rebuttal since Georgia courts do not appear to make a distinction between pure CSAAS testimony and other behavioral science testimony that is otherwise probative of abuse. Given the evolving nature of evidentiary law governing

> *See http://www.ipt-forensics.com/journal/volume10/j10_2.htm for information on the five types of behavior classified under the CSAAS, which can be used to indicate that a child has been sexually abused.*

expert witness testimony, it would be prudent for professionals in the medical and behavioral science fields to present testimony in court that distinguishes between these two forms of evidence.

Behavioral science testimony may be probative of abuse, especially when accompanied by a credible disclosure on the part of a child. The probative value of such testimony is highest when there is a coalescence of symptoms that are strongly associated with sexual abuse, along with nonsexual symptoms that are commonly observed in sexually abused children and medical evidence of sexual abuse. Probative value declines as sexual symptoms and medical evidence decrease in proportion to nonsexual symptoms.

The "ultimate issue"

In general, lay and expert witnesses alike are not permitted to testify regarding the "ultimate issue" before a court of whether or not a child has been sexually abused. While experts in Georgia have, on occasion, been permitted to provide opinion testimony that touches on the "ultimate issue," such testimony has been limited to circumstances where it appears that the inferences and conclusions are clearly beyond the ken of the average layman. Medical, psychological, and behavioral science experts in child sexual abuse cases should relate their opinion testimony in a manner that does not invade the province of the jury. Rather than offering an opinion that a particular child has been sexually abused, these experts should relate that their conclusions and findings are "consistent with" or "inconsistent with" sexual abuse or other trauma. This form of opinion testimony does not violate the "ultimate issue" rule in Georgia. However, under no circumstance should an expert testify regarding the credibility or believability of a particular victim or witness. Such testimony may be grounds for reversal of a verdict and is not subject to the contemporaneous objection rule. Assessment of the credibility of witnesses is not beyond the ken of average jurors, and therefore, is deemed within their sole province to determine.

Sexual abuse may be proved by the testimony and statements of a child victim alone or with the assistance of expert medical, psychological, and behavioral evidence testimony that is probative of abuse. Physicians can provide opinion testimony that is based upon the child's history, statements, and medical examination, even if the physician's examination of the child reveals no concrete physical

---

This means that children's reactions to abuse as defined by CSAAS, such as "secrecy" and "helplessness," are more valuable as evidence if there are other, specifically medical, symptoms of abuse as well. Without medical symptoms these behaviors could have other causes.

Since it is the jury's responsibility to decide guilt or innocence, it is an established legal principle that witnesses (expert or not) are not asked for their opinion on the question (the "ultimate issue"). The role of witnesses is to provide testimony on matters of fact or background information.

Credibility cannot be judged quantifiably. It is a subjective judgment based on a person's manner when he or she answers questions. Since the outcome of a trial often depends on accepting one witness's testimony and rejecting another's, it is solely the jury's job to decide which witnesses are credible.

evidence supportive of the child's allegations. Psychologists, therapists, social workers, and other professionals with expertise in the investigation, assessment, and treatment of child sexual abuse may also provide opinion testimony that includes psychological and behavioral science evidence of a probative nature.

Expert witness testimony may also be used in a non-substantive manner for the purpose of rehabilitating a child witness whose credibility has been impeached. Such testimony may be used to explain behaviors on the part of a child, which, to a lay juror, may appear inconsistent with the child's allegations of abuse. An expert may also be called upon to explain cognitive and developmental differences in children and adults for the purpose of establishing the need for special procedures related to examination of a child in court or to counter arguments that such differences make children, in general, unreliable as witnesses. Inasmuch as the improper use of leading questions may unnecessarily taint children's statements and disclosures regarding sexual abuse, experts may provide opinion testimony in court related to proper and improper interviewing techniques in such cases.

> One of the behaviors outlined in CSAAS is "retraction," in which the child withdraws an allegation of abuse. Expert testimony may help explain why a child might do this even if the original allegation is true.

> A "leading question" is one that supplies its own answer and merely asks a witness to confirm or deny it. It can only be used about a matter that is not disputed between the parties or to oblige the witness to make an explicit denial.

Fitting the "common profile"

Testimony that a child or other party does or does not fit a "common profile" or class of individuals is generally prohibited. Such testimony is viewed as scientifically unreliable and as inappropriate commentary designed to attack or bolster a witness's credibility. Occasionally, however, experts are allowed to testify regarding the common behaviors of a particular class of offenders in general to explain certain evidence or to demonstrate intent, motive, plan, scheme, or bent of mind.

Allegations of sexual abuse by a parent that arise during separation and divorce or in conjunction with contested custody proceedings should be investigated as thoroughly as any other allegation of child sexual abuse. While experts should be cautious for signs of coaching or improper influencing of a child by a parent, there is little evidence to support the notion that the majority of sexual abuse allegations in such cases are fabricated. Expert witnesses who are called upon to assess and evaluate such allegations should currently avoid such theories as "Parental Alienation Syndrome" that have not yet been tested by objective methods, properly peer reviewed, or determined to be scientifically reliable in court....

> Many of the most highly charged sexual abuse cases arise when one parent accuses the other of abusing their children. The accuser presents the allegations as the reason for the breakup of the relationship. The accused presents them as being motivated by a desire for revenge or to gain advantage in a divorce or custody settlement.

Summary

In the first article law professor Deborah W. Denno argues that expert testimony is given too much weight. She bases her argument on Dr. Park Dietz, the main prosecution witness in the Andrea Yates trial. Denno claims that Dietz's standard of criminal responsibility is unforgiving of mentally ill defendants. Dietz said that because Yates said Satan rather than God told her to drown her children, she knew her actions were wrong and was therefore legally sane. Denno contends that Dietz has a "distorted" view of psychiatry because he no longer treats ordinary patients himself, while his work brings him into contact with only the most extreme crimes. She says that the American Psychiatric Association has recognized the link between postpartum disorders and maternal infanticide, and claims that Dietz failed to take Yates's postpartum risk factors into account. Although Dietz has consulted on many maternal infanticide cases, Denno points out that the last time he treated a patient with a postpartum disorder was 25 years ago.

The second article, by Curtis Holmes and Sharon McGee, is taken from the guidelines for professionals who testify in child sexual abuse cases in the state of Georgia. They argue that expert testimony is a crucial component in establishing child sexual abuse because victims display physical, emotional, psychological, and behavioral symptoms that only experts—not judges or jurors—can reliably assess. Once an expert's qualifications are established by a court, any challenges to their methods or opinion should focus on how much weight their opinion should be given. The guidelines warn that an expert should never testify on the credibility of a victim or witness, because that invades the province of the jury.

FURTHER INFORMATION:

Books:

Ceci, Stephen J., and Helene Hembrooke, *Expert Witnesses in Child Abuse Cases: What Can and Should Be Said in Court*. Washington, D.C.: American Psychological Association, 2001.

Malone, David M, and Paul J. Zwier, *Expert Rules: 100 and More Points You Need to Know about Expert Witnesses*, (2nd edition). Notre Dame, IN: National Institute for Trial Advocacy, 2001.

Tindall, Laura Jane, *Ethics Reference Guide for Expert Witnesses*. Loxahatchee, FL.: Dynamic Ingenuity, 2003.

Useful websites:

http://www.facs.org/fellows_info/bulletin/2003/gorney1003.pdf
Paper by Mark Gorney on ethics and expert witnesses.

http://www.lectlaw.com/files/exp21.htm
The 'Lectric Law Library page on expert witnesses.

The following debates in the Pro/Con series may also be of interest:

In this volume:

Andrea Yates: The importance of expert testimony, pages 200–201

Topic 14 Should jury verdicts be unanimous?

IS EXPERT TESTIMONY GIVEN TOO MUCH WEIGHT?

YES: Some experts are paid exorbitant fees, and that can influence their integrity and credibility as witnesses

YES: Experts have provided unreliable evidence and improper testimony in the past in some cases. This has led to a reversal of some verdicts on appeal. Better guidelines and codes of practice for expert testimony are needed.

INTEGRITY OF WITNESSES

Can paying experts high fees affect the search for truth in court?

RELIABILITY

Is expert evidence too relied on in court?

NO: It is only fair that experts are paid compensation for the money they lose in their professional capacity while testifying. Fees are based on their time, experience, expertise, and out-of-pocket expenses such as travel.

YES: Psychiatric witnesses, for example, are expected to provide behavioral evidence, such as visiting a crime scene, that takes them too far away from their usual sphere of expertise

NO: Experts have the knowledge and expertise, especially in child sexual abuse and psychiatric profiling, that judges and jurors simply do not have

YES: There are many "professional" expert witnesses around who do not know enough about a subject key to a trial. Better procedures and guidelines for checking an expert's suitability to testify are needed.

IS EXPERT TESTIMONY GIVEN TOO MUCH WEIGHT?

KEY POINTS

TYPE OF EVIDENCE

Are experts providing evidence outside their expertise?

PROCEDURE

Are the procedures for vetting expert witnesses inadequate?

NO: Behavioral evidence is a relatively new type of evidence, but it is one that respected forensic psychiatrists believe is very useful in their work

NO: It is not in the attorney's interest to use an expert who can be easily discredited. The procedures for vetting experts are more than adequate, and the evidence they give is important.

ANDREA YATES: THE IMPORTANCE OF EXPERT TESTIMONY

"If those of you who are honorable, conscientious, and learned don't show up, then who do you think will…?
—U.S. COURT JUDGE ON EXPERT WITNESSES (2002)

In March 2002 Andrea Yates, a Texas mother of five, was convicted of drowning three of her children. She may yet have to stand trial for the murder of her two other children. During the the trial a number of expert witnesses—in this case psychiatrists—gave evidence. The defense argued that Yates was mentally ill, did not know what she was doing, and was legally insane. The prosecution held that Yates was legally sane despite being mentally ill. According to Texas law, a defendant cannot be considered insane if he or she knows that their conduct was wrong. In spite of the strong expert testimony in the defense's favor, the jury found Yates guilty in less than four hours. The Yates case raised questions about the use of expert witness testimony and the treatment of the insane in the criminal justice system.

Expert witnesses

Expert testimony is the presentation of information by a qualified specialist before a court to give background on some technical issue relevant to the case. Expert witnesses are paid for their time, experience, expertise, and out-of-pocket expenses during a trial. The fees are paid by the attorney or the client. Some experts are, however, reluctant to testify in court: They fear that their findings will be misunderstood or used out of context. Nonetheless, other professionals feel that it is their responsibility to give courtroom testimony: They believe that solid evidence is best provided by the most qualified experts. Critics of expert testimony, however, point out that criminal law moves beyond clinical issues into questions of personal responsibility and morality. Physicians, for example, are sometimes asked to comment on areas—such as the level of criminal intent—that are in reality far removed from their field of clinical diagnosis.

Texas v. Yates

Psychiatric expert witnesses are common in criminal trials involving pleas of insanity. In *Texas v. Yates* (2002) Dr. Phillip Resnick, a psychiatric expert on parents who kill their children, appeared for the defense. Resnick diagnosed that Yates was suffering from schizophrenia and depression, and said that she did not know the difference between right and wrong when she drowned her children. Yates was religiously obsessive and under the delusion that she was a bad mother who could only save her children from her evil influences by killing them. Resnick stated that although Yates knew killing her children was illegal, she felt that she was acting in their best interest.

Other psychiatrists testifying for the defense determined that Yates was in "deep psychosis" at the time of the murders. In a seven-year period Yates had given birth to five children, had a miscarriage, and had suffered from both postpartum depression and postpartum psychosis—both debilitating conditions—since her fourth pregnancy. Although usually prescribed Haldol, an antipsychotic medication that had worked for her in the past, Yates had been given a new "experimental" cocktail of drugs just days before the murders. The medication was made up of drug dosages well above those recommended by Food and Drug Administration guidelines. Some commentators believe that had Yates been prescribed Haldol, the tragedy could have been averted.

Dr. Park Dietz

The prosecution's central expert witness in the Yates trial was Dr. Park Dietz, a forensic psychiatrist. In a *New York Times* interview after Yates was convicted, Dietz revealed his views on forensic psychiatry and the reason why he nearly always appears on behalf of the prosecution: "I believe that the proper role of a forensic psychiatrist is to seek the truth, not to help any party to the case." Dietz admitted he found the Yates case especially troubling and commented: "It would have been the easier course of action to distort the law a little, ignore the evidence a little, and pretend that she didn't know what she did was wrong."

Yates's defense had its own criticisms of Dietz's testimony. At the trial Dietz referred to an episode of the TV show *Law & Order*, for which he acts as technical advisor, in which a woman drowned her children and was later judged insane. No such episode existed, but some commentators believe that the seeds had been sown and the jury believed that Yates could have been influenced by the program. The defense also claimed that Dietz edited his videotaped interviews with Yates to show only the parts that backed up his testimony. Some critics have also alleged that Dietz was an unsuitable expert witness since he had little experience in postpartum depression or psychosis, the mental illnesses from which Yates was suffering.

Insane or evil?

In the end the jury found Yates guilty. Some critics believe that the alleged "expert witness testimony" of Dietz may have unfairly influenced the jury. Yates's case has thrown up all kinds of questions regarding the guidelines for allowing an expert witness to testify and the fact that too much weight is often put on the testimony of a professional who lacks the expertise to testify properly on a subject significant to a trial outcome. In the meantime, however, Yates is serving a life prison sentence, although her lawyers are appealing the verdict.

Topic 16

SHOULD CHILD WITNESS EVIDENCE BE ADMISSIBLE?

YES

FROM "ADJUDICATION OF CHILD SEXUAL ABUSE CASES,"
THE FUTURE OF CHILDREN
JOHN E.B. MYERS

NO

FROM "PART 1: THE SALEM SYNDROME"
INVESTIGATOR 25, JULY 1992
L. EDDIE, WITH THE ASSISTANCE OF A. LANG

INTRODUCTION

Since the 1980s there has been a large increase in the number of children being admitted as witnesses in court. Because of children's vulnerability and inexperience when it comes to participating in what is normally an adult-oriented court—with all its confusing information, convoluted procedures, and unfamiliar language—the law of most countries holds that children should give evidence only in exceptional circumstances. The most commonly cited are cases of alleged child sexual abuse—a crime that by its nature is private and often impossible to prove without the uncorroborated testimony of the child. Indeed, it is the dramatic increase in the reporting of child abuse and neglect since the 1970s that has resulted in the increasing appearance of children at juvenile and criminal proceedings. Therefore, it is in the context of child sexual abuse that the issue of the admissibility of child witness evidence is most often debated.

There are a number of strands to such a debate. First is the issue of testimonial competence—what age must a child be before his or her evidence can be considered seriously by a court? In the words of the first of the two articles that follow, such competence requires "basic cognitive and moral capacities" —a child must be able to observe and remember events, and must understand the difference between the truth and a lie. In the past the minimum age for testimonial competence was considered to be 10 or 12 years of age in the United States, 8 in the United Kingdom and elsewhere.

However, during the 1980s child sex abuse cases increasingly began to hear testimony from children as young as four or five years old. Legislation was also modified to aid the admissibility and accuracy of such testimony. Most U.S. states now have evidentiary codes that permit "leading" a child victim of alleged sexual abuse and shield laws that permit a child witness to testify behind a one-way screen or by video.

Another presumption of many legal experts is that children are basically honest and tell the truth—particularly when talking about abuse of the body and when they demonstrate sexual knowledge they would not otherwise have. However, the 1980s and 1990s saw the collapse of a number of infamous cases in the United States and elsewhere that hinged on child witness evidence.

> *"A blend of credible and non-credible claims by young children often coexist within a single allegation, rendering the task of deciding the truth quite difficult."*
>
> —STEPHEN J. CECI, PSYCHOLOGIST (1995)

In the McMartin preschool case, for example, more than 200 charges of sexual abuse were made against seven adults at a childcare center in the Los Angeles suburb of Manhattan Beach. A series of trials followed over a period of six years, all of which ended in either acquittals or hung juries. Eventually the case was thrown out entirely because many of the children could not be believed—some claimed they witnessed a beheading, others swore they had seen one of the adults fly through the air. The lives and reputations of many individuals were destroyed by the case.

Frequently the blame for such failed prosecutions is laid at the door of the interviewers—the social workers, police, and trial prosecutors. In the McMartin case interrogators were found to be so aggressive that many of the children were soon unable to separate fact from fiction. If children are more susceptible to this form of pressure than adults, critics ask, shouldn't their testimony be considered warily by the courts?

Surveys have found jurors, judges, and attorneys are indeed less likely to believe young children than older witnesses. Nonetheless, after much conflict many experts now conclude that while children are not hypersuggestible, nor are they superresistant to suggestions about their own bodies.

Crime surveys suggest preschoolers are more likely to be abused than older children—and that their testimonies result in fewer criminal convictions because of preconceptions about their lack of credibility. How can justice be secured for such children other than by allowing their uncorroborated evidence in court and by making testifying as stress-free and accurate as possible?

Then again there is the argument that the adversarial nature of the legal processes in the United States are in themselves another form of abuse. Should a child have to testify at all, when doing so is liable to do him or her more harm than good? In France and Sweden, for example, much of the evidence for any case is gathered in a preliminary, pretrial investigation. This fact tends to reduce the necessity of children appearing in court even in cases of sex abuse.

The two articles that follow address some of the key issues of the debate.

... CHILD SEXUAL ABUSE CASES
John E.B. Myers

John E.B. Myers
is a professor
at McGeorge
School of Law
in Sacramento,
California. He is a
leading authority
on child abuse
litigation. This is
part of an article
that appeared in
The Future of
Children, a journal
published by
Princeton
University and
the Brookings
Institution.

YES

Child sexual abuse is a serious crime in all states, and many children testify in criminal trials. Children also testify in several types of civil proceedings. When a parent sexually abuses a child, proceedings may be initiated in juvenile court. The juvenile court has authority to protect the child by placing the youngster in foster care or leaving the child at home under supervision from an appropriate agency. The juvenile court also has authority to order abusive parents to participate in treatment to reduce the likelihood of future abuse.

Finally, sexual abuse allegations can be heard in civil divorce proceedings....

Regardless of the type of litigation—criminal or civil—child sexual abuse is often exceedingly difficult to prove. The U.S. Supreme Court has observed that "[c]hild abuse is one of the most difficult crimes to detect and prosecute, in large part because there often are no witnesses except the victim." In many cases, the child's testimony is the most important evidence. It is ironic that children are victimized because they are weak, and yet children's strength on the witness stand is often their best hope for protection.

Children's competence to testify ...

Before a child may testify in court, the judge must be convinced that the child is competent to testify. Testimonial competence requires basic cognitive and moral capacities. The child must be able to observe and remember events, must understand the difference between truth and falsehood, and must appreciate the duty to tell the truth in court. The vast majority of children as young as three and four possess these capacities. In addition to the cognitive and moral capacity to testify, children must take a religious oath or a secular affirmation to testify truthfully.

There was a time in American law when children below specified ages—typically 10 or 12—were presumed to lack testimonial competence. When a young child was brought to court, the judge asked questions to assess the youngster's cognitive and moral capacities and ability to take an oath. If the child possessed sufficient understanding, the child

A third factor is the ability to tell the difference between fiction and reality—this has proved a crucial question in many cases. Do you think three- or four-year-old children have this ability?

testified. During the era when children were presumed incompetent, most youngsters passed this preliminary test.

As time passed, states abandoned the presumption that children were incompetent to testify, and today the presumption in most states is that children are competent. Although judges still question young children to make sure that they understand the proceedings, most children are allowed to testify.

Do you think, on balance, that it is good that this presumption has changed? What are the main reasons for your view?

Believability of children's testimony

While most children have the cognitive and moral capacity to be competent witnesses, competence is not the same as believability. A witness may be competent to testify but unworthy of belief. Thus the crucial question is, can children be believed?

At the outset, it is worth asking whether children deliberately lie about sexual abuse. By age three, children learn to bend the truth. There is no evidence, however, that children are any more or less prone to lie than adults. Although children—particularly adolescents—sometimes deliberately fabricate allegations of sexual abuse, research reveals that deliberate fabrication is uncommon, particularly among young children. Moreover, young children are not very good at maintaining a lie. Of greater concern than deliberate lying is the possibility that young children who are not abused may be coached or led into believing that they are....

Why would a parent or someone else want children to believe they had been abused, or to coach them in how to answer questions as if they had been?

The possibility that flawed interviewing distorts children's memories is one of the most important issues facing professionals working to protect children....

Interviewing young children is a delicate and difficult task. Done poorly, interviews undermine the ability to protect children and raise the specter of false allegations. Done well, interviews help children reveal their memories....

Closing the courtroom

In criminal cases, the U.S. Constitution guarantees the defendant a public trial. Additionally, the Constitution guarantees the press and public a right to attend criminal trials. Although these constitutional rights are important, they are not absolute, and, in appropriate cases, the judge may close the courtroom to the public and the press. Closing the courtroom is particularly appropriate when children must describe degrading and embarrassing acts. Nevertheless, the need to protect children does not justify closure in every case. Indeed, the U.S. Supreme Court ruled unconstitutional a law that closed courtrooms for all children. In deciding

Can you think of other situations in which you think a courtroom should be closed to the public? Or is it in everyone's best interest to keep it open?

whether to close the courtroom for a particular child, the judge considers the child's age, the nature of the sexual abuse, and the psychological strength and stability of the child.

Face-to-face confrontation with the defendant

In criminal cases, the U.S. Constitution guarantees persons accused of crime the right to face-to-face confrontation with the witnesses against them, including children. For many children, however, facing the defendant is the most difficult aspect of testifying. Moreover, psychological research discloses that face-to-face confrontation undermines some children's ability to testify. Goodman and her colleagues observed children testifying in criminal court and discovered that youngsters who were most frightened of the defendant experienced the greatest difficulty answering questions.

What do you think are the reasons why this right was considered important by the Framers of the Constitution?

Although the defendant's constitutional right to face-to-face confrontation is important, it is not absolute. With its 1990 decision in *Maryland v. Craig*, the U.S. Supreme Court ruled that, in selected cases, children may be spared the ordeal of face-to-face confrontation. Before confrontation may be curtailed, however, the judge must determine that a face-to-face encounter would cause the child serious emotional distress that interferes with the ability to communicate. Mere nervousness or reluctance to testify is not sufficient to curtail the defendant's confrontation right.

The video alternative

During the 1980s, many states enacted laws authorizing video testimony by children in criminal cases. Although video testimony laws vary from state to state, a common scenario allows the child to testify in the judge's chambers rather than the courtroom. The judge, jury, defendant, and spectators remain in court where they watch the child's testimony on a television monitor. The primary goal of video testimony is to reduce children's stress. The Supreme Court's decision in *Maryland v. Craig* cleared away obstacles under the U.S. Constitution to allowing selected children to testify outside the physical presence of the defendant....

Although everyone in court can see the child on the video monitor, the child's monitor only shows the judge and the counsel who is asking questions.

The confrontation right is more limited in civil courts because the charges are considered less serious. Do you agree with this reasoning? Or should both courts use the same rules?

The right to face-to-face confrontation is strongest in criminal trials. A more limited confrontation right applies in juvenile and family court cases, which are civil rather than criminal. When parents are accused in juvenile court of abuse, judges have considerable latitude to spare children the ordeal of face-to-face confrontation. The same is true in family court, where it is common for children to testify in the judge's chambers, away from parents.

Cross-examination

The right in criminal cases to confront witnesses includes the right to cross-examine them. Although cross-examination is important, the Supreme Court has ruled that "judges retain wide latitude … judges have authority to protect children from harassment and intimidation, and this authority applies in criminal and civil litigation.…"

What practical steps do you think a judge could take to prevent a child witness being harassed and intimidated, while preserving the defendant's right to cross-examine the witness?

Reducing children's stress and improving their testimony

Although testifying is difficult for most children, the difficulty should not be exaggerated. Children are strong and resilient, and most of them cope with testifying and move on with their lives. Indeed, with proper preparation and support, some children are empowered by testifying. Runyan and his colleagues found that, for many children, "the opportunity to testify in juvenile court may exert a protective effect on the child."

Because children's testimony in court is so often indispensable to their protection, the wiser course is not to seek ways to keep them off the witness stand, but to help children testify more effectively. The first step toward improving children's testimony and reducing their stress is familiarizing them with the courtroom.…

If a child is being abused by someone close to him or her, convicting that person of the crime, and so removing the child from the abuser's power, is essential to the child's protection. Can you think of other crimes in which conviction is important for the same reason?

A number of communities have "court schools" for children who are scheduled to testify. Children attend "classes" where they learn about court. Role playing is used to allow children to practice testifying about innocuous events unrelated to their abuse. These worthwhile programs reduce the fear of the unknown and boost children's confidence.

One obvious way to reduce children's stress is to allow a parent or other trusted adult to remain in the courtroom while the child testifies. In appropriate cases, the judge allows the support person to sit near the child. In some instances, however, courts will preclude this if the adult is also to be a witness in the case. Research by Goodman and her colleagues reveals that the presence of a supportive adult enhances children's ability to answer questions. Moreover, when a supportive adult is present, children are less likely to give inconsistent answers to questions or to recant. The search for truth is advanced by the simple step of providing emotional support for child witnesses. Providing such support violates none of the defendant's rights.…

Other witnesses are barred from this supporting role because they may have a stake in the outcome of the case (for instance, he or she may be the person who made the accusation in the first place).

PART 1: THE SALEM SYNDROME
L. Eddie, with the assistance of A. Lang

Laurie Eddie is a clinical psychologist from Australia. This article was published in Investigator, a magazine encouraging debate.

See the "Famous American Trials" site at http://www. law.umkc.edu/ faculty/projects/ ftrials/salem/ SALEM.HTM for information and resources on the Salem witch-hunt.

See http://web.utk. edu/~kstclair/221/ ergotism.html for a discussion of the symptoms from a modern medical viewpoint.

NO

In the days when religion was an obsession, and the fear of the devil was enough to produce widespread hysteria, it was common to charge people with witchcraft. Most of those alleged to have been witches were harmless old women, who, living alone, and with few friends, were easy targets for persecution.

One of the worst examples of this hysteria took place in the Massachusetts Bay colony of Salem Village, in 1692. A number of adolescent females frequented the kitchen of the local minister, Rev. Samuel Parris, listening to the stories told by an old Negro slave of the household, Tituba. Soon, several of them started to display strange behaviour in the presence of their family and friends; screaming uncontrollably, convulsing on the floor, running on their hands and knees, growling and barking like animals. Their behaviour soon spread and other children were soon behaving in a similar fashion.

This type of behaviour, hysterical in its origins, was diagnosed by the superstitious citizens of Salem as something sinister; and the local doctor confirmed their suspicion when he pronounced that the children had been bewitched. The local clergymen agreed that these attacks were due to Satanic persecution. But they went further; they declared that the Devil was acting through human intermediaries, to attack the children. Asked to name their tormentors, the children named three local women, Tituba, Sarah Good and Sarah Osburne.

Accusations out of control

At a preliminary hearing, to resolve the problem, the children gave a remarkable demonstration, rolling around, apparently in agony, screaming that they were being attacked by invisible creatures which were touching them and pinching them. They were, they claimed, being taunted by imps which sat on the rafters then flew down to peck at them.

Sarah Good and Sarah Osburne were too scared to speak, but Tituba freely admitted her knowledge of the satanic creatures of the invisible world, and the rituals which were used to harness these creatures. She convinced the audience that the infestation of evil was far worse than they suspected and she implicated Sarah Good and Sarah Osburne, and many others, whom she claimed were involved in a conspiracy with Satan against the inhabitants of Massachusetts Bay.

Instead of settling events, the hearing had the opposite effect, it unleashed a wave of mass-hysteria.

To make matters worse, the girls took on the role of oracles and mediums, for they alone were able to point out to authorities the "witches" responsible for the terrible evil sweeping the countryside. The girls responded willingly to this role, identifying anyone they held a grudge against. Then, in turn, anyone who spoke in defence of any accused, were themselves arrested on suspicion of being in the service of the devil. One, Martha Corey, was denounced simply because she expressed her disbelief at the claims being made by these children.

In the end, twenty-two people were executed. Had they continued naming the powerless members of the community there is little doubt that the persecution would have continued for a long time. However, when the girls named several clerics renowned for their piety, including Samuel Willard, the President of Harvard College, the magistrates flatly told them they were mistaken. And from that point "common sense" prevailed, as it was realized that people were being condemned on the testimony of a few excited girls. As doubts increased, the hysteria died away, and no further people were named.

This phenomenon is often seen when a person is accused of something (such as being a witch) that cannot be proved or disproved. His or her only hope of pardon is to deflect the charge by making the same accusation against someone else.

Do you think the magistrates were responsible for allowing the accusations to get out of control in the first place? Could the trials have been prevented if they had shown the same skepticism toward the earlier accusations?

A case of repressed sexuality?

While the Salem children never directly mentioned "sex" or any related connotations of sexual abuse, in the delicate language of that time, the females were said to have been "tormented by invisible hands." Yet it is obvious from their statements that many of the symptoms described in their hysterical attacks were related to their severely repressed sexual emotions. It is for instance very significant that in all the evidence presented there are no records of young males being molested by these "evil spirits."

It is important that there is a recognition of the fact that sexual energy exists, and is quite strong, in many young children. Unfortunately, there is a tendency to either overlook the latent sexuality in children, or to deny the sexual behaviour in children. As was demonstrated in several recent examples, this type of behaviour, which is entirely normal, is

The author seems to be saying that girls are more likely to experience repressed sexual emotions than boys. Do you agree?

In previous centuries the onset of puberty roughly coincided with the age when children entered the adult world. Today improved nutrition means children reach physical maturity more quickly and so sometimes begin to experience sexual feelings a few years before they legally become adults or attain the emotional maturity needed to conduct sexual relationships.

What do you think are the reasons that sometimes lead authorities to take this attitude? Why do you think certain issues, such as witchcraft or child abuse, are more likely to provoke this attitude?

See http://www. religioustolerance. org/ra_roch.htm for further background on the Rochdale affair.

often present but is rarely noted. However, when "therapists" advise parents of "abnormal" behaviour to look for, as evidence of sexual abuse of their children, the parents tend to note "abnormal" behaviour which has in fact always been present.

There is also a concerted movement by certain individuals to "believe the children," to assume that whenever a child makes allegations of sexual assault, that the child must be speaking the truth, otherwise, how could they know about "these things." This belief often overlooks the fact that, in most of these types of instances, due to their poor questioning techniques, it was the therapists who planted the ideas in the children's minds in the first place.

After Salem, legislators, realizing the danger of accepting such unsubstantiated evidence from young children, incorporated into legislation certain legal safeguards, in order to prevent a repetition of such persecutions. Interestingly enough, while the law included such precautions, it has been clearly demonstrated in recent times that child welfare authorities, police and prosecutors have frequently ignored such essential precautions, and virtually taken the law into their own hands and assumed that the offenders were guilty.

A procedural travesty

Thus, in June 1990, when allegations were made that children were being sexually abused in devil-worship rituals, it triggered a major reaction by social workers in Rochdale (UK). In a series of dawn raids, twenty children from a local housing estate were seized by social workers and taken into the "care" of the local Social Welfare Department.

Before any determination of the facts could be made, the children were rushed before the court, and the SWD had them made wards of the court (an order which in effect did not really place them under the control of the courts, but rather under the direct control of the SWD).

Despite the protests of parents, and attempts by solicitors representing the parents, the children were held incommunicado, totally isolated from their families and friends, forbidden even to receive letters, birthday or Christmas cards since the SWD claimed that cult members could use secret codes, or signs in the mail to intimidate the children.

After eleven months in the "care" of the SWD, during which time the SWD sought to have some of the children adopted, the matter finally reached a court hearing.

After a hearing which lasted forty-seven days, Justice Douglas Brown dismissed all charges against parents and threw the entire matter out of court. He delivered a stinging rebuke to the SWD for serious errors of judgement for the manner in which they had handled the affair.

As was later shown, this shameful episode was triggered by a six-year-old dyslexic boy, who had spoken to his teacher about ghosts. As evidence was to show, he was a very impressionable child, and had watched the horror video, *The Evil Dead*, twice the night before he spoke to his teacher.

When he spoke with the teacher he had been confusing events from the video with reality. As a result, what he told the teacher, stories of satanic rituals where children had been sexually abused, related to the video, but had been confabulated into his perception of reality. The teacher, concerned at what she was told, quite correctly contacted the police. However, it was at that point that things went horribly wrong. The police failed to exercise the most basic precautions. Instead of checking the truth of these claims, they accepted them as factual. So, when the child named other friends, claiming that they too had been victims of ritual abuse, the authorities assumed the worst and set in motion procedures which led to these children being seized in the pre-dawn raids on their homes.

Young children are sometimes unsure of the distinction between fiction and reality, so may assume that something they see in, say, a movie has happened in real life. The age when children understand this distinction varies according to the mental development of the child.

Should the police automatically believe child accusers just because they are children? Or should they treat children in the same way they treat adults?

Fundamental errors

The judge severely attacked the SWD for failing to elicit the truth before rushing headlong into action and seizing the children. He claimed that the social workers involved were so obsessed with the persecution that rather than bothering to determine the facts they had simply accepted what they wanted to hear, and refused to listen to anyone who questioned the veracity of the allegations of this child.

He particularly castigated the senior social worker responsible for the conduct of the prosecution, for his failure to read the Butler-Sloss Report which examined a previous case of alleged child sex abuse and clearly set out a number of recommendations for interviewing children in such matters. (Rochdale's director of social services later resigned following this criticism.)

In his judgement Justice Brown stated that it was a disgrace that this prosecution had been brought on the flimsiest of evidence and he dismissed all claims that any of the families had been involved in any form of devil-worship, or sexual abuse of their children....

Dame Elizabeth Butler-Sloss chaired a commission looking into an outbreak of unfounded abuse allegations in Cleveland, northern England, in 1987.

Summary

In the first of the preceding articles the debate on child witnesses is illustrated by looking at the example of sexual abuse cases. Here the victim (the child) is often the only witness to a serious crime, so if the abuser is to be convicted, it is crucial that the child's evidence should be admissible in court. While the courts require witnesses to have "basic cognitive and moral capacities," most states now presume such competence in children. Even very young children are able to observe and remember, and they know the difference between the truth and a lie. The article also points out that research has found that children are unlikely to lie about sexual abuse. Meanwhile, most states leave the judge discretion to decide how far the constitutional rights of the defendant (to cross-examine the witness, say) may be curtailed in the interests of protecting the child.

The second article also looks at cases of alleged child sexual abuse but argues they show that children's evidence should be treated with caution. In Salem in 1692 hysteria unleashed by the "repressed sexual emotions" of a group of teenage girls led to the deaths of 22 innocent people. The precautions that legislators took from then on with regard to child witness evidence are, however, ignored in many modern child abuse cases. In Rochdale, Yorkshire, in 1990 the inability of a six-year-old boy to distinguish between fantasy and reality caused 20 children to be taken into care unnecessarily. In the authors' view the latent sexuality of children is often denied. This combines with poor interviewing techniques by social workers and police, which plant ideas in children's minds and fail to secure the truth.

FURTHER INFORMATION:

Books:

Ceci, Stephen J., and Maggie Bruck, *Jeopardy in the Courtroom: A Scientific Analysis of Children's Testimony*. Washington, D.C.: American Psychological Association, 2000.

McGough, Lucy S., *Child Witnesses: Fragile Voices in the American Legal System*. New Haven, CT: Yale University Press, 1994.

Poole, Debra A., and Michael E. Lamb, *Investigative Interviews of Children: A Guide for Helping Professionals*. Washington, D.C.: American Psychological Association, 2003.

Useful websites:

http://nccanch.acf.hhs.gov/pubs/usermanuals/courts/witness.cfm
Administration for Children and Families' resource page

on child witness issues.

http://www.pbs.org/wgbh/pages/frontline/shows/innocence/readings/childwitnesses.html
Stephen Ceci and Eduardus de Bruyn's article "Child Witnesses in Court: A Growing Dilemma."

The following debates in the Pro/Con series may also be of interest:

In this volume:

Topic 11 Do the poor have fair access to the U.S. judicial system?

SHOULD CHILD WITNESS EVIDENCE BE ADMISSIBLE?

YES: Children are unlikely to lie about sexual abuse. Often in such cases young witnesses are found to have sexual knowledge they would not otherwise have.

YES: Research has found children to be remarkably resistant to false suggestions, particularly to those that regard their own bodies

SEXUAL KNOWLEDGE

Can children always be relied on to tell the truth about sexual abuse?

SUGGESTIBILITY

Is it true that children are no more suggestible than adults?

NO: Even young children have a latent sexuality—a fact that many interviewers deny or choose to overlook—so their motives may not always be innocent

NO: Surveys have found that even trained interviewers often have their own hypothesis about the truth before speaking to a child

SHOULD CHILD WITNESS EVIDENCE BE ADMISSIBLE?

KEY POINTS

YES: Children would not undergo the trauma of a trial unnecessarily. They would only accuse someone of abuse if they had good reason to do so.

YES: Children may be the only witnesses to a crime—especially if they are its victim—so their testimony cannot always be replaced by other forms of evidence

MALICIOUS INTENT?

Should accusations made by children against adults always be believed?

ESSENTIAL TESTIMONY

Is it essential to use children's testimony?

NO: Children can easily make up accusations out of spite without understanding the consequences either for themselves or for the accused

NO: The difficulties of relying on children's testimony are so great that physical evidence or adult witnesses should be used instead

GLOSSARY

acquittal finding a criminal defendant not guilty of the charge against him or her.

adjudication a judgment or decision by a court or jury regarding a case.

admissability a decision on whether evidence is legally and properly introduced.

adversarial system a judicial system that allows arguments between opposing parties before a judge or a judge and jury.

affidavit a voluntary statement or declaration confirmed under oath.

affirm ruling of a higher court that the judgment of a lower court should stand. See also appellate jurisdiction.

affirmative action steps taken to remedy past discrimination, for example, by a firm favoring recruitment of minority groups.

amendment (1) an additional provision of the Constitution; (2) an addition or change to an existing document or plan. See also constitution.

appeal a request made after a trial asking a higher court to decide whether the trial was conducted properly.

appellate jurisdiction the legal authority of a court to hear appeals from a lower court.

arraignment a court proceeding in which the accused is told the charges and asked to plead guilty or not guilty.

bail the temporary release of a prisoner pending trial, usually on surety of money.

bailiff courtroom assistant to the judge.

bench conference discussion of courtroom procedure either on or off the record between judge, counsel, and sometimes defendant, out of hearing of the jury.

bench trial trial before a judge without a jury.

bill the draft of a proposed law being considered by a legislature.

Bill of Rights the first 10 amendments to the Constitution, passed by Congress in 1791, that guarantee citizens certain rights.

brief a legal document prepared by an attorney in support of his or her client.

capital offense a crime punishable by death.

case any proceeding, action, cause, or lawsuit initiated through the court system.

checks and balances the power of each branch of government (legislative, judicial, executive) to limit that of the others.

circuit court jurisdiction composed of one or more counties or states.

civil law law dealing with the private rights of individuals, groups, or businesses. See also criminal law.

clause a section of a legal document.

closing statement lawyer's summary of the evidence at the end of a trial.

code a collection of laws promulgated by a legislative authority, such as that of a city.

common law law based on precedent rather than statute. See also precedent.

constitution laws that define the way a state is organized and governed.

crime an act or failure to act that violates a law for which a penalty is set by the state.

criminal law branch of law dealing with crime and punishment. See also civil law.

cross-examination the questioning of the opposing side's witnesses.

direct examination the questioning of a witness by the party calling him or her to the stand. See also cross-examination.

discrimination the unfair treatment of people on the basis of race, color, creed, sex, or other characteristics rather than on individual merit; the denial of equal protection in law.

dissenting opinion in a trial or appeal the written opinion of a minority of judges who disagree with the decision of the majority. See also judge.

district attorney a state prosecuting attorney.

evidence information presented in testimony or in documents that is used to persuade the judge or jury to decide the case in favor of one side over another. See also admissability.

executive branch the branch of government that enforces the law. The U.S. executive is headed by the president and comprises executive offices and agencies.

federal district court the court of original jurisdiction in most federal cases. The only federal court that holds trials in which juries and witnesses are used.

felony a grave crime for which the penalty in federal law may be death or more than one year's imprisonment.

guided discretion the freedom of juries in capital cases to decide whether to impose life sentences or death sentences under standards dictated by the court.

habeas corpus the right of every person not to be detained without trial.

hearing a formal proceeding in which the accused is given notice of charges against him or her and may present a defense.

higher law the superiority of one set of laws over another.

impeachment the constitutional process whereby the House of Representatives can "impeach" (accuse of misconduct) federal government officers for trial in the Senate.

independent counsel an attorney hired to be impartial, representing neither side.

indictment formal charge issued by a grand jury stating that there is enough evidence to justify a trial; used primarily for felonies.

instruction a direction given by a judge to the jury regarding the law in a case.

Jim Crow laws laws supporting the segregation of races. In 1896 the Supreme Court upheld such laws under the "separate but equal" doctrine.

judge a public official with authority to hear and decide cases in a court of law.

judicial branch the area of the government that interprets laws and resolves legal questions. See also executive branch.

judicial review the process by which courts decide whether laws passed by Congress or state legislatures are constitutional.

jurisdiction the legal authority of a court; or the exercise of judicial power within certain geographic boundaries.

jurisprudence the study of legal philosophy.

jury a body of men and women selected to reach a decision (verdict) in a trial.

legal defense a legally recognized excuse for a defendant's actions.

legislative branch the branch of government that passes the laws. The Senate and House of Representatives are the legislative branch of the federal government.

legislative supremacy a system of government in which the legislative branch has the most power.

libel something false written about a person that damages his or her reputation.

lobbying influencing or persuading legislators to introduce a bill or vote a certain way on a proposed law.

objection a statement by an attorney opposing testimony or admission of evidence.

peremptory challenge part of pretrial jury selection that allows each side to dismiss a certain number of possible jurors without giving any reason. See also voir dire.

perjury deliberately giving false, misleading, or incomplete testimony under oath.

precedent past decisions that guide current court cases.

ratify to sanction formally—for example, when the president negotiates a treaty, the Senate must ratify it for it to become law.

unenumerated rights rights recognized by the courts but not specifically listed in the Constitution or Bill of Rights.

verdict a final trial decision by a jury read before court and accepted by a judge.

voir dire the process by which opposing lawyers question prospective jurors to get as favorable or as fair a jury as possible.

writ of certiorari Supreme Court order directing lower courts to transmit records for cases it will hear on appeal.

Acknowledgments

Topic 1 Is the Supreme Court Too Activist?

Yes: From "A Hand in the Matter" by Cass R. Sunstein, originally published in the March/April 2003 issue of *Legal Affairs* magazine. Copyright © 2003, *Legal Affairs*, Inc. www.legalaffairs.org. Reprinted by permission.

No: From "Upholding the Law" by Orin S.Kerr, originally published in the March/April 2003 issue of *Legal Affairs* magazine. Copyright © 2003, *Legal Affairs*, Inc. www.legalaffairs.org. Reprinted by permission.

Topic 2 Are Politics Too Influential in the Selection of Federal Judges?

Yes: From "Selecting Federal Judges: The New, Less Partisan California Plan" by John Dean, www.findlaw.com, June 8, 2001. Used by permission.

No: From "Rejection Sustained" by Randall Kennedy, *The Atlantic Monthly*, September 2002. Used by permission.

Topic 3 Should Federal Judges Be Appointed for Limited Terms?

Yes: From "Should U.S. Supreme Court Justices Be Term-Limited?: A Dialogue" by Akhil Reed Amar and Vikram David Amar, www.findlaw.com, August 23, 2002. Used by permission.

No: "Statement of Chief Justice Walter L. Murphy of the Superior Court before the House Subcommittee on Judicial Selection and Retention," October 4, 2001. Used by permission.

Topic 4 Is It Too Difficult to Impeach Federal Judges?

Yes: "We Hold These Truths: The Case for Impeaching Rogue Judges" by Dennis Shea, *Policy Review: The Journal of American Citizenship*, May-June, 1997, Number 83. Used by permission.

No: "The Senate's Epic Hypocrisy" by Geoff Metcalf, www.WorldNetDaily.com, January 11, 1999. Used by permission.

Topic 5 Should Supreme Court Candidates Be Asked Their Views on Legal Issues during Confirmation Proceedings?

Yes: "The Right to Ask" by Marcia Greenberger, *NCJW Journal: The Fight for Choice*, Spring 2002. National Women's Law Center Copyright © 2002. Used by permission.

No: "Why Litmus Tests Threaten the Integrity of Our Courts" by Brennan Center for Justice, October 1999. Used by permission.

Topic 6 Should Federal Judicial Applicants Have to Meet a Formal Set of Requirements?

Yes: "Bush Ends American Bar Association's Prescreening of Judicial Nominees" by John Andrews, World Socialist Website, April 6, 2001. Used by permission.

No: From "Remarks by the President on Judicial Independence and the Judicial Confirmation Process" by George W. Bush, Office of the Press Secretary, The White House, In Focus: Judicial Nominations, May 9, 2003. Used by permission.

Topic 7 Should Congress Be Able to Limit the Power of Federal Judges to Sentence Criminals?

Yes "Statement before the U.S. Senate" by Senator Orrin G. Hatch (R-Utah). Statement before the U.S. Senate, April 10, 2003. Public domain.

No: "Judges on Trial" by Adrian Acu, *Common Sense*, October 2002. Used by permission.

Topic 8 Should State Court Judges Be Appointed Rather than Elected?

Yes: "It's Obvious: Appoint" by Steve Sebelius, *Las Vegas Review-Journal*, December 12, 2002. Used by permission.

No: From "Judges: Should They Be Elected or Appointed?" by David Barton, www.wallbuilders.com. This extract is taken from the website. Used by permission.

Topic 9 Should Public Funds Finance Judicial Election Campaigns?

Yes: "Bringing Fairness to the Bench—Reform Judicial Elections" by J.B. Harris. This article first appeared in *The Miami Herald*, November 17, 2002. Used by permission.

No: "Public Funding for Judicial Elections: Forget It" by Robert A. Levy, Cato Institute, August 13, 2001. Used by permission.

Topic 10 Are Sentencing Decisions Affected by Minority Status?

Yes: From "Justice May Be Black and White" by Sharon Smith, *York Daily Record*, Friday, December 27, 2002.

No: "JLARC Study Finds No Racial Bias in Virginia Death Penalty Sentencing" by Michael Marshall, University of Virginia School of Law. Used by permission.

Topic 11 Do the Poor Have Fair Access to the U.S. Judicial System?

Yes: From "Civil Legal Aid in the United States: An Overview of the Program in 2003" by Alan W. Houseman, Center for Law and Social Policy, September 2003. Used by permission.

No: "No Money for the Voiceless" by Laura K. Abel and Philip G. Gallagher, *The National Law Journal*, The Brennan Center. Used by Permission.

Topic 12 Is the Jury-Selection Process Fair?

Yes: "Attorney-Conducted Voir Dire, Jury Voir Dire—Who Should Ask the Questions?" by Judge Pat B. Brian, *Voir Dire*, Volume 1, Number 2, Summer 1995. Used by permission.

No: From "ACLU Seeks Clemency for Ohio Death Row Prisoner Whose Case Was Tainted by Racially Biased Jury Selection" by American Civil Liberties Union, April 18, 2002. Used by permission.

Topic 13 Should Jurors Be Allowed to Play a More Active Role in Trials?

Yes: "Keeping a Jury Involved during a Long Trial" by Harold Bursztajn, Linda Stout Saunders, and Archie Brodsky, *Forensic Psychiatry & Medicine: Trial Consulting and Forensic Psychiatry*. Used by permission.

No: From "The Current Debate on Juror Questions: To Ask or Not to Ask, That Is the Question" by Nicole L. Mott, *Chicago–Kent Law Review*, Volume 78:3. Used by permission.

Topic 14 Should Jury Verdicts Be Unanimous?

Yes : From "*United States of America v. Timothy James McVeigh*" (trial transcript), United States Courthouse, Denver, CO, June 13, 1997. Public domain.

No: "Orange County Voices: Overturn System of Unanimous Jury" by Linda Thrall Walters, June 22, 1995. Used by permission of the author.

Topic 15 Is Expert Testimony Given Too Much Weight?

Yes: "Who Is Andrea Yates? A Short Story About Insanity" From "III. Park Dietz's Expertise and Psychiatric Philosophy" by Deborah W. Denno, 10 *Duke Journal of Gender Law & Policy 1* (2003). Used by permission.

No: "The Use of Expert Witnesses in Child Abuse Cases" by Sylvia Lynn Gillotte, summary by Curtis Holmes and Sharon McGee, *Child Sexual Abuse Investigations: Multidisciplinary Collaborations*, UGA-Center for Continuing Education. Used by permission.

Topic 16 Should Child Witness Evidence Be Admissible?

Yes: From "Adjudication of Child Sexual Abuse Cases," *The Future of Children*, a publication of The Woodrow Wilson School of Public and International Affairs at Princeton University and the Brooking Institute. Used by permission.

No: From "Part 1: The Salem Syndrome" by L. Eddie, with the assistance of A. Lang, *Investigator* 25, July 1992. Used by permission.

The Brown Reference Group plc has made every effort to contact and acknowledge the creators and copyright holders of all extracts reproduced in this volume. We apologize for any omissions. Any person who wishes to be credited in further volumes should contact The Brown Reference Group plc in writing: The Brown Reference Group plc, 8 Chapel Place, Rivington Street, London EC2A 3DQ, U.K.

Picture credits

Cover: Corbis: Joseph Sohm; ChromoSohm, Inc.
Corbis: Bettmann 72/73, 159, Dave G Houser 115, Nancy Kaszerman/Zuma 172, Pacha 147, Jason Reed/Reuters 43;
Corbis Saba: Najlah Feanny 91; **Corbis Sygma:** 200/201; **Kobal Collection:** Beacon/Universal/ George Kraychyk 134, United Artists 183; **Library of Congress:** 104, 120; **PhotoDisc:** Hisham F Ibrahim 6/7; **Photos.com:** 124/125; Photos12.com: Collection Cinéma 156; **Rex Features:** Peter Heimsath 69, Greg Mathieson 55, Ron Sachs 93, Sipa Press 168

SET INDEX